A POLICY OF FREE EXCHANGE

Large Print Edition published 2014 by Skyler J. Collins.
Visit: www.skylerjcollins.com

Originally published in 1894.

ISBN-13: 978-1495474798
ISBN-10: 1495474798

A POLICY

OF

FREE EXCHANGE

ESSAYS BY VARIOUS WRITERS

ON THE

ECONOMICAL AND SOCIAL ASPECTS OF FREE EXCHANGE

AND KINDRED SUBJECTS

EDITED

By THOMAS MACKAY

EDITOR OF 'A PLEA FOR LIBERTY'

NEW YORK

D. APPLETON AND CO.

1, 3 AND 5 BOND STREET

1894

'LET not the people—I mean the masses—think lightly of those great principles upon which their strength wholly rests. The privileged and usurping few may advocate expediency in lieu of principles, but depend upon it we, reformers, must cling to first principles, and be prepared to carry them out, fearless of consequences. . . . I yield to no man in the world (be he ever so stout an advocate of the Ten Hours Bill) in a hearty good-will towards the great body of the working classes; but my sympathy is not of that morbid kind which would lead me to despond over their future prospects. Nor do I partake of that spurious humanity which would indulge in an unreasoning kind of philanthropy at the expense of the independence of the great bulk of the community. Mine is that masculine species of charity which would lead me to inculcate in the minds of the labouring classes the love of independence, the privilege of self-respect, the disdain of being patronised or petted, the desire to accumulate, and the ambition to rise. I know it has been found easier to please the people by holding out flattering and delusive prospects of cheap benefits to be derived from Parliament rather than by urging them to a course of self-reliance; but, while I will not be the sycophant of the great, I cannot become the parasite of the poor; and I have sufficient confidence in the growing intelligence of the working classes to be induced to believe that they will now be found to contain a great proportion of minds, sufficiently enlightened by experience to concur with me in the opinion that it is to themselves alone individually that they, as well as every other great section of the community, must trust for working out their own regeneration and happiness. Again I say to them *Look not to Parliament, look only to yourselves.*'—*From a Letter of Richard Cobden, dated October* 21, 1836.

ESSAYS AND CONTRIBUTORS.

I. *The Science of Economics and its relation to Free Exchange and Socialism* 1
By HENRY DUNNING MAC LEOD.

II. *The Coming Industrial Struggle* . . . 47
By WILLIAM MAITLAND.

III. *National Workshops* 85
By ST. LOE STRACHEY.

IV. *State Socialism and the Collapse in Australia* . 103
By the HON. J. W. FORTESCUE.

V. *The Influence of State Borrowing on Commercial Crises* 143
By WYNNARD HOOPER.

VI. *The State in Relation to Railways* . . . 163
By W. M. ACWORTH.

VII. *The Interest of the Working Class in Free Exchange* 211
By THOMAS MACKAY.

VIII. *The Principle of Progression in Taxation* . . 249
By BERNARD MALLET.

IX. *The Law of Trade Combinations* . . . 275
By the HON. ALFRED LYTTELTON.

PREFACE.

THE articles contained in this volume have been written by the various authors independently. For the title, the preface, and for such general argument as is to be found in the book as a whole, no responsibility necessarily attaches to the writers, who are answerable each for his own contribution and for that only.

The title suggests that the principle of Free Exchange is capable of inspiring a constructive policy, in which freedom is limited only by a mutual respect for the freedom of all, that is, by the reciprocal responsibility inherent in every voluntary act of Exchange: the articles have been arranged, as far as possible, according to the natural sequence of thought; and for this attempt to give an appearance of unity of design the Editor is alone responsible.

The first paper, from the pen of Mr. H. D. Mac Leod, gives an historical sketch of the course of economic speculation with regard to the doctrine and policy of Free Exchange. He traces the rise of freedom of internal and international trade from the teaching of the French Economists and Adam Smith, and points out how the misconceptions of Ricardo and his followers on the subject of value have led mankind astray, and confused in the most mischievous manner all our ideas on the economic mechanism of society.

Free Trade, he argues, is the first great benefit which just economic reasoning has conferred on this country. The task before this and the next generation must be the clear establishment of the truth that a largely increased production of wealth and its equitable distribution among all classes of the population can be attained only by developing the facility and the multiplicity of exchange—in other words, by Free Exchange; and, further, that this rule is applicable to all forms of value, whether they be labour or credits or material commodities.

Mr. Maitland draws attention to a problem of the immediate future. The adoption of Free Trade by America will produce, without doubt, great industrial changes. If we are to retain our markets, in face of the decreased cost of production which this policy will permit in America, we must cast off from us all unnecessary burdens and all unnecessary restrictions. Mr. Maitland's argument is designed to show that our political leaders are very little alive to the reality of this danger. Changes such as he forecasts can only be met by permitting the principle of Free Exchange to be the distributor both of capital and labour. It is one of the evil consequences of Protection that, even when men become persuaded of its injustice and folly, they cannot return to Free Trade without causing considerable economic disturbance. We are about to encounter an industrial crisis arising from this cause; and it is Mr. Maitland's argument that such redistribution of the industrial markets, as is inevitable, will come on us more gradually and with less suffering, if we accept the principle of Free Exchange in every relation of life. Thus encountered, the process of change need have for us no terror, for it must ultimately lead to an ever-increasing satisfaction of human wants at an ever-decreasing expenditure of human exertion.

Mr. Strachey gives an account of the *Ateliers Nationaux* of Paris in 1848. The attempt was there made to give labour a right to force the community to purchase it for wages. This violation of the principle of Free Exchange rapidly— in three months' time—produced anarchy and revolution.

Mr. Fortescue's paper deals with a somewhat similar attempt in our own Colonies to carry on civilization by that vast system of public works which is most briefly described under the term State Socialism.

Another aspect of the same problem is treated by Mr. Hooper from the purely financial point of view. The pledging of the credit of taxpayers for government borrowing and government trading is a contravention, possibly in many cases a necessary contravention, of the principle of Free Exchange. Mr. Hooper shows how treacherous a basis for the expansion of industry this method affords, and how readily it lends itself to the creation of disastrous financial complications.

Mr. Acworth deals with the vexed question of State-interference in railway management. He shows what a limited amount of truth there is in the allegation that a railway is a monopoly. On the important question of tariff legislation, subject to the necessity of State-interference legislative, judicial, and executive for the purpose of preventing undue preferences and unreasonable discriminations, he is disposed to leave the public and the railways to deal with each other on the principle of Free Exchange. In most other respects he suggests that more advantage will be gained by an enforcement of publicity than from any other form of regulation. Just as in the great Free Trade controversy, the maxim was laid down that a hostile tariff is best combatted by a more thorough free trade, so Mr. Acworth argues that the difficulties arising out of an alleged monopoly, like a railway, are best overcome, not by turning it into a real monopoly in the hands of a government department, but by subjecting it as far as possible to the health-giving influence of publicity and Free Exchange.

Mr. Mackay's paper deals with the principle of Free Exchange in its relation to the property of the working classes in their own labour and in their own savings. The argument seeks to justify the opinion that Free Exchange is capable of becoming to labour what a right of free mintage is to bullion, viz. a certain guarantee of employment and wages; further that, in the vast series of exchanges which constitute the economic mechanism of a free community, the value of labour must unceasingly tend to enhancement. It is, therefore, to the organizing influence of Free Exchange that labour has to look for the realization of its legitimate ambition.

Here the controversial portion of the volume may be said to end. The two papers which follow, though not, strictly speaking, covered by the title, have a relevance which is sufficiently obvious. Mr. Mallet's paper is a theoretical discussion of one aspect of the interesting problem of taxation. The principle of progression or graduation has been already, as he points out, either avowedly or unconsciously adopted in the financial system of most civilized countries, and its extension is to be looked for in the future. Unless the theory be deliberately adopted that taxation is to be used as a lever for redressing the inequalities of fortune between the different classes of a community, there is, he thinks, much exaggeration both in the fears and in the hopes which this proposal evokes. In the distinction, as stated by Jevons, between value and utilities, he finds a defence of a progressive as opposed to a merely proportional rate of taxation; but he shows that at a point, which can only be discovered by actual experiment, the abstraction by the State of the surplus wealth of individuals may become not merely a deduction from the wealth of a country, but a positive bar to its further growth; further, that taxation is just and politic when it aims at equalizing the sacrifice imposed on individuals, but that it is the reverse when it seeks to equalize incomes.

Mr. Lyttelton, in explaining the state of the law with regard to trade combinations, has adhered strictly to the legal aspect of the question. If there is any force in the argument contained elsewhere in the book that, as regards labour as well as all other forms of wealth, Free Exchange, and not coercive combination, should be our rule of guidance, it is obvious that an estimate of the intricacies of the law of trade combinations is an interesting and pertinent addition to the controversy, even though, as in this case, the writer confines himself to a statement of fact, and takes no responsibility for the general argument in which his narrative may serve as an illustration.

THOMAS MACKAY.

SYNOPSIS OF CONTENTS.

I. THE SCIENCE OF ECONOMICS AND ITS RELATION TO FREE EXCHANGE AND SOCIALISM.

Present chaotic condition of economic speculation, its cause, due to neglect of proper definition of the subject-matter of a Science. Adam Smith not the founder of Economics and Free Trade. Political Science due, like medicine, to the sufferings of mankind, its birthplace was France . . . . *Page* 4

Early attention paid to theory of money, but true principle of trade much misunderstood 5

The sect of the 'Economists.' Their opinions, their contention in favour of Free Trade 6

An abstract of their doctrine, establishing Liberty and the right of Property as fundamental principles of civilized society . . . 7–10

Their doctrine concerning commerce; their assertion that exchangeability is the essence of wealth; their denial of the title of wealth to labour and credit, the error of this exclusion demonstrated . 10–15

The service rendered by the Economists in exposing the fallacy of the Balance of Trade doctrine that in every exchange one side was a loser 15

Their opinion that neither side lost or gained; that labour engaged in agriculture was the only productive labour; all other labour sterile and unproductive 15, 16

Such doctrine provocative of reaction. Adam Smith and Condillac show that in commerce both sides gain, the immense importance of this demonstration 17

Adam Smith's further criticism of the Economists shows the error of confining term wealth to material products of the earth; he includes labour and credit in the category of wealth, but later on loses sight of this, and proposes various irreconcileable definitions . . 18–20

The confusion introduced by J. B. Say's adoption and misconstruction of one expression of the Economists; 'Production, Distribution, and Consumption' 21

J. S. Mill the disciple of Say. His definitions of wealth, their inconsistency. In the hands of Say and Mill the science brought to an *impasse* 21–25

Summary of the bearing of doctrine of Economists and Adam Smith on Free Trade; various infringements of Free Trade considered and shown to be robbery. Protection, Slavery, the law of the 'Maximum,' all are forms of Socialism . 25–30

Error of supposing that England

should abandon Free Trade because other nations have not adopted it. 'If one tariff is bad, two are worse' 31

Next, the relation of economic speculation on socialism. This turns mainly on the definition of value 34

The contradictory statements of Adam Smith, the true theory held by Economists and the ancients, error introduced by Locke. Adam Smith's doctrine considered at length, his hopeless attempt to make labour an invariable standard of value, its inadequacy demonstrated 35–40

The same confusion throughout Ricardo, his dogma that labour is the foundation of all value, its obvious untruth 40, 41

McCulloch and Carey take the same view 42

The importance of this doctrine consists in the fact that it is made the foundation of socialism 42

The doctrine that working men are the creators of all wealth and value tested by ten examples . . . 43

Credit, its nature, and the obvious absurdity of saying that working men have given it its value . 44

Credit is a mass of exchangeable property, in the creation of which manual labour has had absolutely nothing to do 45

The alleged equity of socialism based on the Ricardian doctrine of value is thus disproved 46

Labour has value, as being exchangeable, and there is no reason to withdraw it from the operation of the principle of Free Exchange, which is at once equitable and beneficent 46

Conclusion that the basis of value is exchangeability, and that the chaotic state of Economics is due to the neglect of this principle 46

II. THE COMING INDUSTRIAL STRUGGLE.

The inaugural address of President Cleveland suggests that the Manchester school, if dead in England, has come to life again in the United States 49

America the only really protectionist state. The policy has failed, and a new era is beginning . . . 50

In England, on the contrary, we are retracing our steps and returning to protection 51

The object of this paper to forecast the result of this policy in the two countries 52

The view of President Cleveland contrasted with that of English politicians: quotations from his inaugural address and from speeches by Sir William Harcourt, Mr. Arnold Morley, Sir John Gorst, Mr. Campbell Bannerman, Mr. John Burns 52–57

President Cleveland's policy the beginning of the end of protection. Opinion that this will enable us to compete successfully with American manufacturers entirely erroneous. The reduction of cost of production in America will, for the first time, make their competition formidable to us 58

Some of the conditions of English and American manufacture considered 59

American high wages, under present conditions, exaggerated. Probability that with free trade they will rise and take from us our skilled labour 62

The change of policy in America to

be regarded with equanimity if we were adhering to free trade . 64
Still we are in possession—only our own criminal folly can rob us of it 65
Looking at home, there is much to disquiet us—politicians doling out protection to secure votes. Policy of Mr. Bright and Lord Shaftesbury compared 67
Mr. Chamberlain reintroduces protection under the alias of constructive legislation. Mr. Burns on 'reproductive' work . . . 69
Scepticism of Socialists or Protectionists as to progress, as illustrated by State pension proposals . . 71
American protection an object lesson: a corrupt policy of Give, give, with burden falling ultimately on agricultural class, and in the end general exasperation and collapse . 72
In England the burden is to be put on the capitalist class, with the result that capital will be destroyed or forced to emigrate. . . . 74
Mr. Chamberlain fears the competition of a free trade Ireland, but not of a free trade America 74
American labour troubles, protests against artificial or protective monopoly 75

Mr. John Burns' admission of the hopelessness of labour protection 75
Impossibility of walling-in a country or a trade without ruin to its best interests 76
Expectation that wages will advance in a free market justified by experience 76
Necessity of a policy of retrenchment: burden of war preparations and foreign policy; the enviable position of America 78
Position of the Colonies . . . 80
The problem before a nation dependent like England on foreign trade —necessity for economical public administration. 81
A market set free from the dread of labour troubles and the burden of vexatious taxation would retain capital buried in hopeless enterprises in Argentina, Africa, and elsewhere 82
President Cleveland and Sir William Harcourt typical of the views of their countrymen. Summary of the situation 83
Hope expressed that we may be warned in time by the obviousness of the danger 84

III. NATIONAL WORKSHOPS.

I. Socialistic theories of nationalization and municipalization to be tested by facts 87
The national workshops of 1848 an experiment in this direction . 88
Hence their importance and relevancy in any consideration of socialistic principles . . . 88
II. The national workshops a deliberate and bona fide attempt to put socialistic principles in practice. 89
As proved by the text of the Decree 89

III. Louis Blanc, a convinced Socialist, at the head of the experiment; the superintendence entrusted to Émile Thomas, a practical man of business, though not a Socialist 90
Louis Blanc armed with practically absolute powers 90
IV. Text of Decrees formulating the *droit du travail* and the *Ateliers Nationaux*. 91
V. The organization described . 92
VI. The evidence of the correspondent of the *Economist* . . . 93

Mr. Nassau Senior describes the work as an exact counterpart of the 'parish farm' 94
Evidence of Victor Hugo and of M. Émile Thomas 94
The result—insurrection, street-fighting, and 12,000 men shot in the streets 95
VII. M. Thiers on another experiment in collectivism . . . 96
Report of surveyor on work of unemployed at Millbank . . . 97
VIII. English experience of parish farms and under old poor law very similar 98
IX. Two solutions offered—that of the Socialists and that of the advocates of Free Exchange . . . 99
X. A plain summary of the case against Socialism 101

IV. State Socialism and the Collapse in Australia.

Dr. Pearson's *National Character*, due to the inspiration of Australia . 105
His account of Australian State Socialism 105, 106
Its alleged success in Australia, the assumption that it is inevitable elsewhere 106, 107
The religion of the State as outlined by Dr. Pearson—it promises great good, *but demands proportional sacrifices*; it is omnipotent, it is never inexorable ; it bestows benefits freely ; its use of statistics as an advertisement and a liturgy . . 108-114
The turn of the tide—imaginary surpluses detected. Statistical statement of the course of collapse 114, 115
Judged by the test of finance, State Socialism in Australia a failure 116
The time has now come to 'demand proportional sacrifices' . . . 117
Will the 'demand' be answered. The earlier example of New Zealand 118
The exodus of the taxpayer; the absentee debtor. The prayer of the State religion has two clauses— 'Give us our daily bread, *and forgive us our debts*' 119
The case of those who must remain considered : the salaried official, the first victims of retrenchments ; the public service discouraged 120
The people on the land, being unorganized, their share of pillage has been less than that of the town dwellers, and their burden from protective tariffs more oppressive— on them the bill for 'proportional sacrifices' now falls . . 121, 122
An awkward and disagreeable awakening for the agricultural class, the true workers of the colony ; their natural resentment at garbled accounts, delusive assertions as to reproductive public works; labourers diverted from agricultural industry by artificial work in the towns by means of borrowed money . . . 123, 124
The State in its perplexity has recourse to various doubtful financial expedients 124
Conclusion that, financially, State Socialism has failed, benefits have been squandered, and the obligations of the taxpayer strained to the verge of repudiation, new oppressive and arbitrary taxation has been imposed on the industrious, gambling has been encouraged, and a low tone of commercial morality has grown up 125-128
The ethics of public life too have suffered. The adventures of Sir G. Dibbs 129
The decay of parental authority under the educational policy of the State 130

State Socialism has corrupted the national character—a fact all the more lamentable in view of the nobler early traditions of the country, and of the necessity of basing recuperation on national character 132

The prospects of State Socialism elsewhere. In Australia it has been carried out at the expense of the British capitalist. In Europe it must be based on the taxation of the successful 134

Can the system endure? it can make beggars, but not one millionaire, and must end in bankruptcy; then comes a revulsion of feeling, when it is too late 137

Yet it seems inevitable that State Socialism will come and be the death-cry of our civilization . 139

V. THE INFLUENCE OF STATE BORROWING ON COMMERCIAL CRISES.

Commercial crisis, a general definition 145

Certain well-marked characteristics to be further described . . . 145

Inflation and collapse, followed by long period of inactivity and liquidation 146

The peculiar position of the banker, who (unlike other traders) is always a debtor, on balance; his need for careful choice of 'securities' 147

The Buenos Ayres waterworks and the Barings. The collapse due to the rash engagements of the firm and the refusal of the investing public to support it 149

The Baring and Overend catastrophes compared. Popular belief in the ability of foreign governments to create 'productive works,' the cause of much ill-considered lending 150

There will always be speculation; the security of a well-planned industrial undertaking better than the security based on excessive taxation. Abuse of State guarantee 151

The tendency of politicians to find excuse for extending the sphere of State action. From 1820 to 1870 the country was freeing itself from many mischievous forms of State-interference. The present reaction not yet gone very far . . . 152

The present inquiry confined to the financial consequences of this policy. Method of raising capital in London market 153

The case of a foreign or colonial government raising a loan for 'productive public work;' the inflation of trade, the demand artificially created ceases. The illustration of Argentina 154

Natural that Great Britain should advance capital to new countries; objection to this being done through Government loans 155

Greater safety of a more gradual development through the application of capital by private enterprise 156

Argument that instruments of production should be in hands of government involves a mistaken view of functions of government. Young countries may try experiments, but the fact of their youth will not prevent failure . . . 157

The capitalists of Great Britain the principal creditors of the world. A breakdown in any one country therefore alarms and paralyzes credit all over the world . . 158

Summary of reasons why government borrowings are more likely to draw countries into difficulty than private borrowings: (1) Government borrows more than necessary; (2) the money does not go so far; (3) its credit, depending on the taxation of its subjects, being greater, its power to throw good money after bad much less limited, hence chance of larger collapse . . 159

Too ready belief of borrowers of their ability to pay, and carelessness of issuing finance houses, combine to make a certain danger; the promise of a government not always a good guarantee 159

Economic objection to loans at home to enable government to carry on public works, one or two instances mentioned 160

Conclusion, that the present tendency to increase the interference of government in matters relating to trade and commerce ought to be diminished 161

VI. THE STATE IN RELATION TO RAILWAYS.

The relation of the State to railways may take one of five forms . 165

Two forms may at once be excluded 165

A third, viz. State ownership of railways which are let out to be worked by private enterprise, now out of fashion in this country, though favoured at one time by Sir Rowland Hill, adopted in Italy, in Holland, and in a sense in France 166

In England there are left two possible methods—State ownership and private ownership under State control 166

Wide ramifications of the subject 167

Objections alleged against our present system considered and answered—waste of competition, bloated dividends a tax on trade, unwillingness to make concessions, granting of undue preference, occasional effete or incompetent management 168–171

Arguments in favour of State ownership considered and appreciated; State should own monopolies; economy in rate of interest on capital due to superior credit of State, also due to unification of management; State would work railways for the benefit of community . 171–173

Would-be reformers unable to agree as to principle on which rates are to be based 173

The matter not to be decided by *a priori* arguments but by observation of practical experiment. Some of the State-managed railways of the continent the worst in the world. Railways of Baden, Belgium, Prussia, Australia 174–179

The result summed up: (1) State management does not reduce the price of services; (2) Management more costly; (3) and danger of political corruption great 179

State management of Post Office criticized 180–185

Admitting that State railways are undesirable, the limits and occasions of State control have next to be considered, under two heads—(1) as affecting public safety, (2) as regulating tariffs 186

The first of these turns on the interpretation, in each case, of the old maxim, *Sic utere tuo ut alienum non laedas*. Construction of new lines, compulsory dispossession of owners, promoters to show that they have sufficient prospect of financial support, publicity of accounts. Level crossings, signalling, interlocking, &c. 186–190

The crucial point, however, is tariff regulation, necessary within certain limits 191
Justification of State control considered, on the ground that a railway is a monopoly; that it has acquired property by compulsory powers; that the authorizing Act of Parliament secured, by way of bargain, certain advantages to the public 192-195
Hence maximum rates, their futility as a means of securing free contract and equality of charges. Difficulty of applying the principle . . 195
The controversy as to what constitutes undue preference considered 196
'Personal discriminations' unknown in England. Discriminations favouring special classes of goods and special localities frequent 197

The difficulties to be overcome by any tribunal for the regulation of rates 198-203
Conclusion that the authority of the Executive cannot beneficially undertake much more than purveying information.—Mr. Justice Wills, on the danger of ill-considered innovations 203
Experience in this country and in the United States confirm these views 204
Satisfactory result of 'publicity' in Massachusetts 205
Summary of results. State ownership undesirable. State control unavoidable. General conclusion in favour of the present system. With publicity 'the eventual supremacy of an enlightened public opinion' is matter of certainty—on this we must rely 207-210

VII. THE INTEREST OF THE WORKING CLASS IN FREE EXCHANGE.

The property of a man in his own person the origin and foundation of all other property . . . 213
As necessary corollary from this follows the right of the free exchange of labour and of the wages of labour 213
No need to discuss questions of prehistoric title. Modern title to property rests on legal acts of exchange 214
The influence of Free Exchange in the economic organization of society limited, but still operative; civilization means the extension of that influence 215
The purpose of the paper to consider the influence of Free Exchange as it affects the property which the labourer has (1) in his own labour, (2) in his own savings . . . 217

1. Labour the poor man's most important possession . . . 217
General functions of a market. The labour market contrasted with the gold market. The appreciation of gold doubtful; the appreciation of labour obvious and certain. Free mintage means a continuous demand for gold. Free Exchange has a similar function to perform for labour 218
The Malthusian fallacy that subsistence is limited, is analogous to the trade unionist fallacy that opportunities for labour are limited 219
How far at present is Free Exchange acting as a free mintage for labour? 219
The mobility of labour considered—some comfort to be found in progress already made 220

The wages of domestic service considered—argument that Free Exchange and the bargain in detail have been beneficial and a cause of rising wages 222
The modern trade unionist blind to the advantages of Free Exchange 223
His objections considered—argument that better conditions of labour must come from an increase of exchangeable supply, i.e. *the increased production of the proper things in their proper quantities and places* 224
This economical distribution of effort (i.e. labour and capital) to be effected only by Free Exchange 225
Injustice and inexpediency of a compulsory minimum wage, the cause of the congestion of labour, known as the Unemployed problem . 226
Doubt expressed whether this coercive policy is conducive to the main object of trade unionism . . 227
Other forms of restriction on Free Exchange. Municipal trading. Larger forms of enterprise claimed as the monopoly of Government; consequent congestion of capital and labour in the smaller industries 227
The terms 'employable' and 'competent' considered. Free Exchange the necessary condition of the growth of these characteristics 228
The art of capitalization, a form of exchange, the coping-stone of industrial competence. . . . 230
Savings a cause of firmness in the labour market, contrasted with poor law relief, which has an opposite effect 231
2. The property of the poor man in his benefit society and savings bank considered 232
Argument that saving is a process of exchange. 232
Illogical nature of the Socialist's dissent from a particular form of exchange. 233
The savings of the working class a practical refutation of collectivism 235
Question of savings banks; comparison instituted between Government savings banks, commercial banks on the Scotch system, and co-operative banks in Germany and elsewhere 236
A sound system of credit developed by banks compared to the fertilizing waters of the Nile 237
Argument that these advantages can be secured to the labourer by co-operative banking. . . 238, 239
Improvement in working class insurance under free competition 241
Controversy in the co-operative movement between advocates of dividend-on-purchase and dividend-on-wages 243
A neglected element in the co-operative theory. The most satisfactory co-operation is the subdivision and distribution of capital and labour in a free market 245
M. Rostand's comparison of the sterile antagonism of Lassalle to the constructive beneficence of the life-work of one of our English co-operative worthies . . . 248

VIII. The Principle of Progression in Taxation.

Two theories stated as to the legitimate purposes of taxation . . 251
(1) For the sake of revenue necessary for economical administration of public services . . 251
(2) For bringing about an equalization of incomes 252
Desire for economy now less powerful than before, hence new schemes for raising revenue. Among others

progressive or graduated taxation 252
A preliminary question—What are the legitimate purposes of taxation? 253
If theory (1) as above prevails, there will be no burdensome taxation for any class. If theory (2) be to any extent adopted, then progressive taxation may become a formidable weapon 253
This preliminary question not here considered 253
Object of paper to discuss (1) the abstract principle of progression, (2) its practical value as a method of taxation 253
Taxation to be levied (1) in proportion to benefits enjoyed, or (2) according to ability to pay 254
This last the view of Mill. Equality of sacrifice not realized when necessities of life were taxed, hence taxation of luxuries. A tax levied on property and income to some extent a recognition of the principle of graduation 254, 255
Its indirect recognition in this country; its popularity with the democracy 255
The question therefore presses and deserves attention 256
Mill argues that the 'same percentage' does not insure equality of sacrifice, recommends exemption of smaller incomes, but rejects graduation 256
Mill's conclusions unsatisfactory 257
The subject viewed from the standpoint of Jevons' theory of the distinction between utility and value. Statement of this theory, and a justification of the principle of progression based thereon 257

Admitting the justice of the principle, other considerations to be taken into account: (1) variability of term 'luxuries' as between different classes of men and different times; (2) a satisfaction of a primary want, a step upward in the path of civilization; (3) Free Exchange daily bringing within the reach of the million what were formerly the luxuries of the great 261
These considerations, pointing to the beneficence and levelling influence of wealth accumulating under a system of Free Exchange, suggest the necessity of a limit to the principle of progression . . . 264
Description of the nature of this limit 265
Can an equitable rate of graduation be fixed? 265
Justice of the exemption of the lower incomes 265
Difficulty of fixing the scale of graduation for the higher incomes . 266
Next, is graduation satisfactory in practice? 267
M. Leroy-Beaulieu in favour of a light and uniform tax . . . 267
Mr. Goschen and M. Leroy-Beaulieu quoted to show how large a proportion of the national income of civilized countries is in the hands of small proprietors . . 267, 268
Unproductive nature of progressive taxation—if excessive, it tends to defeat its object; if moderate, little more productive than uniform or proportional taxation . . . 269
Both fears and hopes with regard to this principle of taxation exaggerated. If used for equalizing taxation, and not for equalizing incomes, a useful adjunct to taxation 273

IX. The Law of Trade Combinations.

Growth of combination in modern commerce 277
Large companies and trusts press on the individual trader as Trade Unions do on the individual workman 277
The conflict apt to be oppressive. Necessity of preventing physical violence 278
Early laws against combination, now out of harmony with modern ideas 278
The scope of the article to discuss the question as affected (i) by the Criminal Law, and (ii) by the Civil Law 279
(a) The Criminal Law as laid down in The Conspiracy and Protection of Property Act, 1875; the effect of this statute; sections 3 and 7 quoted; ambiguity of term 'intimidate;' its analogy with the Corrupt Practices Act, 1883; intimidation according to Mr. Justice Cave must include the threat of personal violence. The case of Gibson v. Lawson; of Curran v. Treleaven. Conclusion that the statute of 1875 leaves a very absolute power in the hands of trade combinations
 279–284
(b) The Criminal Law as defined by the Common Law of Conspiracy; its scope and authority considered; possibility of its application in the case of Gibson v. Lawson; the exemption contained in section 3 of the statute of 1875 considered
 285–287
The remedy of the Civil Law. The Mogul Steam Ship Company v. McGregor, Gow & Co. The case of Temperton v. Russell . 287–289
The decisions in these two cases contrasted; suggestion that they are not governed by the same rule; probability that they will either be more clearly distinguished or the decision in one or other reversed 290, 291
Summary 292

I.

ON THE SCIENCE OF ECONOMICS AND ITS RELATION TO FREE EXCHANGE AND SOCIALISM.

HENRY DUNNING MAC LEOD.

I.

ON THE SCIENCE OF ECONOMICS AND ITS RELATION TO FREE EXCHANGE AND SOCIALISM.

ALL persons who are interested in the so-called science of Economics know only too well the melancholy and deplorable state into which it has fallen. It is such a chaos of contradictions that very many persons refuse to believe that there is any such science at all[1].

The cause of this lamentable confusion is that there are fundamental concepts of it, which are wholly irreconcileable with each other, just as there have been in the earlier and imperfect stages of most other sciences, such as astronomy, optics, and many others.

A science is a body of phenomena all relating to a single fundamental general concept. Thus dynamics is the science which treats of the laws governing the phenomena of force; optics is the science of the laws governing the phenomena of

---

[1] In 1870 Stanley Jevons, after having read my works then published, as he has very handsomely acknowledged in his preface, spoke of Political Economy as the 'shattered science'—an expression which has acquired a certain popular vogue. Long previous to this, in 1856, when I had occasion to study the works on Economics then current in their relation to credit and banking, I had pointed out their defects, and said, in the Introduction to Vol. II of my *Theory and Practice of Banking*: 'We have no hesitation in saying that the whole system of Political Economy, as laid down by Ricardo and developed by Mr. John Stuart Mill, is utterly and radically bad'—which gave prodigious offence at the time. I also said: 'The time has come when all Political Economy must be rewritten.' After thirty-eight years people are beginning to find out that this is true.

light; and so on. Economics is often said to be the science of wealth. What, then, is wealth? What is that quality of things which constitutes them wealth? Economics can only be the science of the laws which govern the phenomena relating to that quality which constitutes things wealth.

It was long an assured opinion in this country that Adam Smith was the founder and creator of political economy and free trade. A once prominent politician is reported to have said that political economy and free trade sprang perfect and complete from the brain of Adam Smith, as Minerva did from the head of Jupiter. Such ideas, however, show a complete ignorance of the history of Economics, and are now quite abandoned by all persons who have studied the subject.

In fact, it is contrary to nature that it should be so. Great sciences are not created by a book. They invariably arise from small beginnings, just as the mighty Danube flows from a spring in the garden of a German burgher. Men begin to observe certain phenomena connected with some single general fundamental concept. Then others extend it to a larger number of phenomena based on the same concept: and so at last, by the contributions of an increasing number of observers, it grows into a great science, just as the Danube from a tiny spring is swollen into a mighty river by multitudes of tributary streams.

Every one with a scientific instinct can at once perceive that Adam Smith's work is pervaded by a combative air, that every part of it is evidently written *at* something preceding, and that it was intended to overthrow a prior system.

As a matter of fact, Economics was founded as a science by an illustrious sect of philosophers in France in the middle of the last century, who were the first to perceive and declare that there is a positive and definite science of Economics, based upon demonstrative reasoning, in the same way as the physical sciences.

The science of Economics, like medicine, has arisen out of the calamities and misery of mankind, caused by the violation of true economic principles; and every advance in economic theory has originated in some great pressing practical evil.

The first department of Economics to be reduced to scientific principles was that of money. Charlemagne caused the pound weight of silver to be adopted as the standard of money in all Western Europe; and he divided it into 240 pennies. The mediaeval sovereigns clipped, curtailed and debased their coinages, but declared that the clipped and debased coin should pass at the same value as good coin. Philip le Bel was particularly conspicuous for issuing debased coin, for which he was consigned to the Inferno by Dante. This degradation of the coin produced such intolerable evils and misery to the people that Charles V of France referred the matter to one of his councillors, Nicolas Oresme, who addressed to him a treatise on money, which may be said to stand at the head of modern Economics. In consequence of similar evils in Poland, Sigismund I requested Copernicus to draw up a treatise on the subject. This has recently been discovered and printed in the new edition of his works. These two treatises laid down the true principles of money, which are now accepted by all sound Economists.

For many centuries all governments enacted laws regarding trade without suspecting that there are any fixed principles on the subject. Sometimes they favoured free trade, sometimes protection; sometimes they cockered up one species of industry, sometimes another, according to the whim of the moment. They never seem to have had the faintest idea that the true principle was to leave every industry alone, and allow each one to develop itself according to its natural tendencies.

Every one has heard of the glories of the reign of Louis XIV; but few probably have any idea of the terrible reaction, and the incredible disasters and misery of the end of his reign. These may be learnt from contemporary writers and also from Taine's *History of the Ancient Régime*. Soon after the death of Louis XIV, John Law was allowed to try in France his scheme of paper money, which had been previously rejected by the Scottish Parliament. The result was that disastrous catastrophe known by the name of the Mississippi Scheme. In 1749 Turgot, then a young man of twenty-two, began to reflect upon these terrible calamities, and endeavoured to discover the error of Law's system. Turgot associated with himself Gourlay, an eminent merchant who was a keen advocate of free trade, Quesnay the king's physician, Le Trosne, Mirabeau *père*, the Abbé Baudeau, and many others, who formed themselves into a powerful sect under the name of the 'Economists.' These men were the first to perceive and declare that there is a positive and definite science which may be named Economics.

They found France divided into a number of separate and semi-independent provinces, each of them surrounded with customhouses, which were an intolerable barrier to commercial intercourse; every species of industry was loaded with minute and oppressive regulations; a very large portion of the human race was groaning under the bonds of slavery; in every country persons were relentlessly persecuted for their religious opinions. The Economists held that these commercial, personal and religious oppressions were contrary to the fundamental rights of mankind.

They proclaimed as the indefeasible natural rights of mankind the freedom of person, the freedom of opinion, and the freedom of exchange or of commerce.

Quesnay (who was the real founder of the science) and his followers, reflecting on the intolerable misery they saw around them, struck out the idea that there must be some great natural science, some principles of eternal truth founded on nature itself, with regard to the social relations of mankind, the violation of which was the cause of the hideous misery of their native land. The name Quesnay first gave to it was *natural right*; and his object was to discover and lay down an abstract science of the natural rights of men in all their social relations. This science comprehended their relations towards the government, towards each other, and towards *property*. The term *politique* in French might in a certain way have expressed this science; but the word was so exclusively appropriated to the art of government that they adopted for it the name 'political economy,' or 'economical philosophy'; and hence they were named 'the Economists.' Dupont de Nemours, one of their number, proposed the name of *physiocratie*, or the government of the nature of things; and hence they were often called the physiocrates; but the word, having been appropriated to certain doctrines of the sect which are now shown to be erroneous, and abandoned by all subsequent Economists of note, has fallen into disuse, and the term political economy, or Economics, which is now more commonly used, has survived.

Now it is evident that this wide and extensive scheme comprehends not only a single science, but a whole multitude of sciences; and we shall henceforth confine ourselves strictly to that part of it which relates to commerce or exchanges.

Quesnay's first publication, *Le Droit Naturel*, contains a general inquiry into these natural rights; and he afterwards in another work, called *Maximes Générales du Gouvernment Économique d'un Royaume Agricole*, endeavoured to lay down, in a series of thirty maxims or general principles, the whole basis of the economy of society. The twenty-third of these declares that a nation suffers no loss by trading with foreigners; the twenty-fourth declares the fallacy of the balance of trade; the twenty-fifth says: 'Let entire freedom of commerce be maintained; for the regulation of commerce, both internal and external, the most sure, the most exact, the most profitable to the nation and to the State, consists in entire freedom of competition.' These maxims entirely overthrew the prevailing system of political economy. This was the work of Quesnay and his followers; and, notwithstanding certain errors and shortcomings mentioned below, they are unquestionably entitled to be acknowledged as the founders of political economy and free trade.

We may now give a brief abstract of the doctrine of the Economists, by which they vindicated the principle of liberty and the right of property.

The Creator has placed man upon the earth with the evident intention that the race should prosper; and there are certain physical and moral laws which conduce in the highest degree to ensure its preservation, increase, well-being and improvement. The correlation between these physical and moral laws is so close that if either be misunderstood, through ignorance or passion, the others are also. Physical nature, or matter, bears to mankind very much the relation which the body does to the mind. Hence the perpetual and necessary relation of physical and moral good and evil to each other.

Natural justice is the conformity of human laws and actions to natural order; and this collection of physical and moral laws existed before any positive institutions among men. And while their observance produces the highest degree of prosperity and well-being among men, the non-observance or transgression of them is the cause of the extensive physical evils which afflict mankind.

If such a natural order exists, our intelligence is capable of understanding it; for if not, it would be useless, and the sagacity of the Creator would be at fault. As, therefore, these laws are instituted by the Supreme Being, all men and all states ought to be governed by them. They are immutable and irrefragable, and the best possible laws; they are necessarily the basis of the most perfect government, and the fundamental rule of all positive laws, which are only for the purpose of upholding that natural order which is evidently the most advantageous for the human race.

The evident object of the Creator being the preservation, the increase, the well-being, and the improvement of the race, man necessarily received from his origin not only intelligence, but instincts conformable to that end. Every one feels himself endowed with the triple instincts of well-being, sociability, and justice. He understands that the isolation of the brute is not suitable to his double nature, and that his physical and moral wants urge him to live in the society of his equals in a state of peace, goodwill and concord. He also recognizes that other men, having the same wants as himself, cannot have less rights than himself, and therefore he is bound to respect their right, so that other men may observe a similar obligation towards him.

These three ideas—the necessity of work, the necessity of society, and the necessity of justice—imply three others—

liberty, property and authority—which are the three essential terms of all social order.

How could man understand the necessity of labour or obey the irresistible instinct of self-preservation without perceiving at the same time that the instrument of labour, the physical and intellectual qualities with which he is endowed by nature, belong exclusively to himself, that he is master and the absolute proprietor of his own person, that he is born and should remain free?

But the idea of liberty cannot spring up in the mind without associating with it that of property, in the absence of which the first would only represent an illusory right without an object. The freedom the individual has of acquiring useful things by labour includes necessarily the right of preserving them, of enjoying them, and of disposing of them without reserve, and also of bequeathing them to his family, who prolong his existence indefinitely. Thus liberty conceived in this manner involves and is dependent on the idea of property, which may be conceived in two aspects, as it regards moveable goods, and as it regards the earth, which is the source from which labour ought to draw them.

At first property was principally moveable; but when the cultivation of the earth was necessary for the preservation, increase, and improvement of the race, individual appropriation of the soil became necessary, because no other system is so proper to draw from the earth all the mass of utilities it can produce; and secondly, because collective property would have produced many inconveniences as to the sharing of the fruits, which would not arise from the division of the land, by which the rights of each are fixed in a clear and definite manner. Property in land is, therefore, the necessary and legitimate consequence of the principle of personal and moveable property. Every man has, therefore, centred in him by the laws of Providence certain rights and duties, the right of enjoying himself to the utmost of his capacity, and the duty of respecting similar rights in others. This perfect protection of reciprocal rights and duties conduces to production in the highest degree, as well as to the greatest amount of physical enjoyments. Thus the Economists established freedom and property as the fundamental right of mankind—freedom of person, freedom of opinion, freedom of exchange or commerce; and the violation of these they maintained to be contrary to the laws of Providence, and therefore the cause of all evil to men.

We must now examine what their doctrines were regarding exchanges or commerce.

While they expressly declared that exchanges, or commerce, were one of the departments of economical philosophy, they most unfortunately devised another and alternative name for it, which being misinterpreted by a subsequent very distinguished French writer, has been the cause of all the mischief and confusion of the science in recent times.

They termed the department of economical philosophy relating to exchanges, or commerce, the 'production, distribution and consumption of wealth.' It might not be very apparent to the general reader how in the mind of the Economists these two concepts are identical, and meant exactly the same thing; and we must now explain the interpretation of this latter expression given to it by its authors.

They defined the word wealth to mean the material products of the earth which are brought into commerce and *exchanged*, and those only. The products of the earth, which were consumed by their owners without an exchange, they termed *biens*, but not *richesse*. They steadfastly refused to admit that labour and credit are wealth; because they alleged that this was to allow that wealth can be created out of nothing. They constantly maintained that man can create nothing, and that *ex nihilo nihil fit*.

By production they meant obtaining the rude produce from the earth and bringing it into commerce.

But this rude produce is scarcely ever fit to be used by men. It has to be fashioned and manufactured in a multitude of ways, to be transported from place to place, and perhaps sold and resold more than once before it is ultimately purchased for use and enjoyment.

All these intermediate operations of manufacture, transport

and sale between the original producer and the ultimate purchaser the Economists termed *traffic*, or distribution.

The final purchaser, who bought the product for his own use and enjoyment, and so took it out of commerce, they termed the *acheteur-consommateur*; because he consummated, or completed, the operation.

Consommation, in the language of the Economists and of all French writers before them, meant simply purchase, or demand; it involved no idea of destruction.

The *consommateur*, or consumer, was the person for whose benefit all the preceding operations took place. Production was only for the sake of consumption, or demand; and consumption, or demand, was the measure of reproduction; because products which remain without consumption, or demand, degenerate into superfluities without value.

The complete passage of a product from the original producer to the ultimate consumer, or purchaser, through all its intermediate stages, the Economists termed commerce, or an exchange; and as any man who wished to consume, or purchase any product, must have some product of his own to give in exchange for it, he was also a producer in his turn. Hence, in an exchange, things are produced, and consumed or purchased, on each side. An exchange has only two essential terms—a producer, or seller, and a consumer, or purchaser. These are the only two persons necessary to commerce; and they often exchange directly between themselves, without any intermediate agents.

Hence the 'production, distribution and consumption of wealth,' as defined by the Economists, meant simply the commerce, or the exchange, of the material products of the earth, and of these only.

But distribution was often used as synonymous with consumption. Hence 'production, distribution and consumption,' 'production and distribution,' and 'production and consumption' all meant exactly the same thing—the commerce or exchange of the material products of the earth.

It must be carefully observed that these expressions were one and indivisible; and they must not be separated into their component terms. They all meant simply supply and demand.

The Economists, by restricting the term wealth to the material products of the earth, made materiality and labour the accessories or accidents of wealth; but they did not make them the *principle*, or essence, of wealth. The *essence*, or *principle*, of wealth they held to consist in *exchangeability*; because they expressly excluded the material products of the earth which were not brought into commerce and exchanged from the term wealth.

Now, considering that the Economists admitted and declared that there is a positive and definite science of exchanges or commerce, how is it possible to restrict it to the commerce or exchanges of material products only? It must evidently and necessarily comprehend *all* exchanges, or all commerce in its widest extent and in all its various forms.

There is a gigantic commerce in labour; there is a colossal commerce in rights and rights of action, credits, or debts. How is it possible to exclude the commerce in labour and the commerce in rights and rights of action from the general science of exchanges, or commerce?

The basis of the science of Economics is the meaning or definition of the term WEALTH. The Economists admitted that exchangeability is the real essence of wealth; but they clogged it with the limitation that it only applied to material products, and denied it to labour and credit, which equally possess the quality of exchangeability. But this is contrary to the fundamental principles of natural philosophy. Bacon long ago pointed out that when the quality or the concept which is at the basis of a science is once determined, all quantities whatsoever which possess that quality, however diverse in form they may be, must be included among the elements or constituents of the science. This is what Plato calls the one in the many, i.e. the same quality appearing in many different forms. It would be just as rational to restrict the term force to the force of men and animals, and to exclude gravitation from the term force.

Ancient writers for 1,300 years unanimously held that

exchangeability pure and simple is the sole essence and principle of wealth; that everything which can be bought and sold, or exchanged, is wealth, whatever its nature or its form may be.

Aristotle defined wealth to be *all* things whose value can be measured in money. Here we have a fundamental concept, of the widest generality, and fitted to form the basis of a great science. Out of this single sentence of Aristotle the whole Science of Economics is to be evolved, just as the great oak is developed out of a tiny acorn.

In an ancient anonymous dialogue Socrates is made to show that money is only wealth where and when it can be exchanged, or purchase other things; where it cannot be exchanged, or purchase other things, it is not wealth. He shows that anything which can be exchanged for, or purchase other things like money, is wealth, for just the same reason. He says that persons gain their living by giving instruction in the sciences. Therefore, he says, the sciences are wealth—αἱ ἐπίστημαι χρήματα οὖσαι; and that those who possess them are wealthier—πλουσιώτεροί εἰσι. This is the first recognition, of which I am aware, that labour is wealth.

Demosthenes showed that personal credit is wealth; because a merchant can purchase goods with his credit equally as with money.

The Roman jurists showed that rights and rights of action, such as credits or debts, are wealth, because they can be bought and sold.

Thus, after 800 years from the time of Aristotle, the Roman jurists completed the science, because they completed the number of its constituent elements. There is nothing which can be bought and sold or exchanged, or whose value can be measured in money, which is not of one of these three forms, or orders of quantities: (1) material products; (2) personal qualities, i.e. labour which can be exchanged for wages, and character which may entitle to credit; and (3) abstract rights.

There is no trace in ancient writers of any such doctrine as that labour and materiality are necessary to wealth and value. Thus they answered, 2,100 years ago, the doctrine of the Economists that labour is necessary to wealth, because they declared that personal qualities and abstract rights are wealth, and they recognized three orders of economic quantities. These can be exchanged against one another in six different ways; and these six different kinds of exchange constitute commerce in its widest extent and in all its forms and varieties.

The relation of these quantities to each other is termed their value; and the laws of natural philosophy show that there can be only one general law of value, or a single general equation of Economics.

We have thus a definite body of phenomena, all based upon a single general concept; separate and distinct from all other phenomena, and circumscribed by a definition, which constitutes a science, and may be designated as pure, or analytical, Economics.

Thus, if any one had conceived the idea of describing the mechanism of these exchanges, or of commerce, Economics might have been the eldest born of all the sciences; but there was no science in existence in those days to serve as a model for the creation of a science of Economics; and a long and dreary interval had to elapse before the moderns reached the perfection of the ancients, all to redound to the immortal glory of Bacon, who was the first to point out that the physical sciences must first be created to serve as models before it is possible to create the sciences of society.

For many centuries it was held that money alone is wealth; and we must briefly state some of the consequences which flowed from this doctrine, which produced innumerable wars and other calamities.

A strange consequence flowed from the doctrine that only money is wealth. It was held for many centuries that in an exchange what one side gained the other lost. What the persons who maintained this doctrine would have said to an exchange of products it would be difficult to imagine. They quite forgot that when persons bought things with money they obtained a satisfaction for their money. Nevertheless, for centuries, the wisest statesmen and philosophers maintained that in commerce what one side gained the other lost. They held that foreign commerce which did not produce an importation of money was a loss to the nation. Accordingly, in every country, laws were made to encourage the importation of money and to prohibit its export. This doctrine was the cause of innumerable wars. J. B. Say, writing in the first quarter of this century, says that during the last three hundred years fifty had been spent in wars directly arising out of the dogma that money alone is wealth. About the end of the seventeenth century it began to be perceived that it was absurd to maintain that money alone is wealth; and the term was enlarged to include all the material products of the earth which conduce to man's subsistence and enjoyment. But still they held to the doctrine of the balance of trade, which was based on the assumption that, in every transaction of commerce, what one side gained the other lost.

The first merit of the Economists was that they entirely overthrew the doctrine of the balance of trade; and they made a considerable advance in Economics by maintaining that in commerce neither side gains or loses.

The Economists maintained that labour engaged in agriculture is the only form of productive labour; because, they alleged, it is the only one in which the value of the produce exceeds the cost of production. The excess of the value of the produce over that of the cost of production they called the *produit net*; and they maintained that, as this is the only increase of wealth to a country, all taxation should be levied out of the *produit net* of the agriculturists, and that all other classes should go free.

They denied that commerce or manufactures can enrich a nation; because, they alleged, in commerce equal values are always exchanged for equal values—and if the values exchanged are always equal, how can there be any profit on either side? They held that the only use of commerce is to vary and multiply the means of enjoyment, but that it does not add to the national wealth; or, if it does, it is only by giving a value to the products of the earth which might otherwise fail in finding a market. They contended also that, as all exchanges are merely equal value for equal value, the same principle also applies to sales, and therefore that the gains, which traders make, are no increase of wealth to the nation.

With such views they held that internal commerce conduces nothing to the wealth of the nation, and foreign commerce very little. They called foreign commerce only a *pis aller*. One very important truth, however, they perceived. They saw that money is the most unprofitable merchandise of any to import, and that merchants never import money when they can import products. Therefore they called the import of money only the *pis aller* of a *pis aller*.

They contended that the labour of artisans in manufactures is sterile or unproductive, because, though this labour adds to the value of the product, yet during the process of the manufacture the labourer consumes his subsistence; and the value added to the product only represents the value of the subsistence destroyed during the labour. Hence there was a transference of the value of the labourers' subsistence into an equivalent value of another kind; but no production of wealth.

They held that all the costs of trafficking come out of the profits of the producers and the consumers, which, though gains to them, are not profit to the nation; and therefore that the State ought not to tax them.

All classes of the community, except the agriculturists, they denominated sterile or unproductive.

These are the doctrines which the Economists maintained, with long and repeated arguments, in defiance of all opposition; but how men of the ability of the Economists could maintain that a country cannot be enriched by commerce or manufactures, with the examples of Tyre, Carthage, Venice, Florence, Holland, England, and hosts of others before them, is incomprehensible. With such patent glaring *facts* before them, it is surprising that they were not led to suspect the truth of their reasonings. It is one of those aberrations of the human intellect which we can wonder at, but not explain.

These doctrines provoked a reaction: men who were labouring in all sorts of vocations were roused to indignation, by being stigmatized as sterile and unproductive. Men were astounded to hear that a nation cannot be enriched by commerce or manufactures.

Nevertheless, the doctrines of the Economists seemed to be logically unassailable, provided that their fundamental dogma was right. But the consequences they drew from it were so startling, and so contrary to patent undeniable facts, that clear-sighted men began to inquire—Is it true that in commerce neither side gains?

Two writers entered the field against the Economists— Condillac in France, and Adam Smith in England. Both published their works in the same year, 1776. They overthrew the doctrine that in commerce neither side gains, and maintained that in commerce *both* sides gain—a truth that was seen by anticipation by the great Emperor Frederick II, in the thirteenth century; and by Boisguillebert, the morning star of Economics, in the beginning of the eighteenth century. In this brief sketch we have no space to say much about Condillac, because his explanation is not very satisfactory, and his work never attracted the slightest attention till very recently.

This, then, was the real origin of Adam Smith's work. He was neither the founder and creator of Economics nor of free trade. Economics, as a science, sprang out of the misery and calamities of the French people, and the Economists were the first to perceive and declare that there is a positive and definite science of Economics; and that, consequently, it must be constructed by exactly the same methods by which all other sciences have been created— namely, by settling its fundamental general concepts and definitions; by a strictly accurate statement of facts and phenomena; and by reducing all the phenomena to a single general law. Economics is the science of exchanges, or of commerce; and therefore the details of commerce are the phenomena of Economics. Nor was Adam Smith the founder of free trade. The Economists published their code of doctrine in 1759, in which free exchange was asserted to be one of the fundamental rights of mankind; and there were numerous and powerful advocates of free trade in Italy and Spain fifteen years before Adam Smith published a line. Turgot carried out immense reforms in the direction of free trade in 1774. How did these writers and statesmen learn the doctrines of free trade from Adam Smith, when his work was not published till 1776? The fact is that Adam Smith did not attempt to disprove the theory of protection and prohibition; he *assumed* free trade as the doctrine approved of by all enlightened minds. Adam Smith has done sufficient services himself to Economics, and his reputation does not require the advances and services done by other persons to be attributed to him.

Adam Smith, then, attacked the doctrine of the Economists, that in commerce *neither* side gains or loses. By a course of masterly reasoning, far superior to that of Condillac, but too long to be set out here, he demonstrated that in commerce *both* sides gain; and, therefore, that nations, in multiplying their commercial relations, multiply their profits and multiply wealth. Even if Adam Smith had never done anything else for Economics than this, he would have been entitled to immortal glory. By this single demonstration he brought about a change in public opinion and in international policy which has for ever removed a perennial source of war from the world. Nations learnt that instead of destroying each other, and trying to ruin each other's commerce, it was their interest to promote each other's prosperity and to multiply their commercial relations with each other.

Adam Smith next proceeded to demolish the doctrine that neither commerce nor manufactures enrich a nation. He demonstrated that both commerce and manufactures are productive of wealth, and enrich a nation.

Furthermore, he burst the bonds of the narrow dogmatism of the Economists, that the material products of the earth alone are wealth. For under the title of fixed capital he includes the 'natural and acquired abilities of the people'; and under the title of circulating capital he includes bank notes, bills of exchange, &c., which are mere abstract rights or credit, and types of vast masses of other incorporeal property. Hence he fully recognized the existence of the *three* orders of economic quantities, as the ancients had done.

But the utility of his work is sadly marred by the total want of clear, distinct and uniform fundamental concepts or definitions. He entitles his work, *An Inquiry into the Nature and Causes of the Wealth of Nations*; but he nowhere gives a clear and distinct definition of what wealth is. In the Introduction he says that the real wealth of a country is the annual produce of 'land and labour.' But he entirely omits exchangeability, which was the quality which the Economists, in agreement with the ancients, recognized as the essence of wealth. But Smith's definition is ambiguous. It is not clear whether he means the produce of land and the produce of labour, or the produce of 'land and labour' combined. It is probable that he meant the last; and so he has been generally understood. Now, such a definition is manifestly too wide and also too narrow; because there are multitudes of things which are the produce of 'land and labour' which are not exchangeable, and therefore not wealth; and there are multitudes of things which are exchangeable, and therefore have value and are wealth, which are in no way the annual produce of 'land and labour.'

Thus, after proceeding some length, he classes the 'natural and acquired abilities of the people' as fixed capital and as national wealth. How are the 'natural and acquired abilities of the people' the annual produce of 'land and labour'? Further on he classes bank notes, bills of exchange, &c., as circulating capital. How are these, which are mere incorporeal rights, the annual produce of 'land and labour'? It is evident that these ideas are absolutely incongruous. This indefiniteness of view we might have shown at much greater length; but these instances are sufficient to prove that his ideas of wealth in different parts of his work are absolutely inconsistent.

Furthermore, after inculcating for several hundred pages that value and wealth require the combination of 'land and labour,' he admits that if a thing is not exchangeable it is not wealth. He says that if a guinea could not be exchanged for other things it would not be wealth any more than a bill upon a bankrupt. Thus, after all, he recognizes that exchangeability is the real essence of wealth. By this single sentence he upsets the whole theory which he had been so elaborately building up.

Keen observers have long ago seen that the first half of Adam Smith's work is entirely inconsistent with the latter half; because in the first half labour is considered as the essence of value and wealth, and in the second half exchangeability, i.e. demand, is admitted to be the real essence of value and wealth.

Ricardo adopted the first half of Adam Smith's doctrine, and founds all his ideas of value upon labour. Whately adopted the latter half, and adopts exchangeability pure and simple, and says that Adam Smith's title only denotes the subject-matter of his work; but that Economics is the science of exchanges, or of commerce.

Adam Smith's first two books are upon production and distribution; but he explains that that means commerce, and he says that his purpose is to examine the causes of the price of things; in other words, the theory of value; and McCulloch says in a note that it might be called the science of values.

An acute writer pointed out long ago that the great defect of Adam Smith is the total want of unity of doctrine, and the want of uniformity of principle. He never had the least idea that the phenomena of value must be reduced to a single general law; but he catches at any theory which seems to explain the cases which for the moment he is considering. The consequence is that his theories are utterly inconsistent with each other; and of course, as they are a series of contradictions, they must sometimes be right. Moreover, though his work abounds with shrewd observations, it is entirely wanting in the very first requisite of every work of science, a clear and accurate definition of its subject-matter. Consequently, though Adam Smith did great and solid services in overthrowing the prejudices and errors of his own day, his work is in no way fitted as an exposition of the actual science at the present day; in fact, most of the great and complex problems, which are of pressing importance at the present day, had not arisen when he died.

Now, from the foundation of Economics as a science up to the time of Whately, who was Professor at Oxford in 1830, there was in this country a perfect uniformity of opinion as to the general nature of the science. The Economists expressly declared that it is the science of exchanges, or of commerce, or the theory of value: and so it was understood to be by the writers in France who did not enrol themselves in the sect of the Economists; by Condillac, Adam Smith, Ricardo, McCulloch, Whately, and all persons who were interested in it. And, however imperfect it might have been, or however many defects it may have had, these were all capable of being rectified. If this concept had been steadily adhered to, and the same labour had been bestowed upon it, to rectify and develop it, by the same methods by which all other sciences have been created, it might long ago have been erected into a positive and definite science, like any of the physical sciences.

But, most unfortunately, the science was thrown into utter confusion, and its progress retarded for a long time, by a distinguished French writer, J. B. Say, about the beginning of this century. He adopted the second and alternative definition of the science which the Economists most unguardedly and unadvisedly suggested. Moreover, he completely changed the meaning of its fundamental terms; by which he ruined Economics as a science, and has been the cause of all the subsequent confusion and of the deplorable state in which it is at present. From this state of chaos it has only begun to recover in recent times. Those who have examined the matter closely are beginning to see that the system of J. B. Say is absolutely unworkable as a practical science, and that in order to construct Economics as a positive science it is indispensable to revert to the original concept of it as the science of exchanges or of commerce.

While the Economists declared that the expression 'production, distribution and consumption' of wealth is one and indivisible, and meant nothing but exchange, or commerce, J. B. Say broke it up into its constituent terms and completely changed their meaning. While the Economists defined production to mean bringing the rude produce of the earth into commerce, Say defined it to mean bestowing value on a product. While the Economists defined distribution to mean the intermediate operations between production and consumption, and those only, Say treats of distribution in such a nebulous way that it is difficult to make out distinctly what he means by it. The Economists and Adam Smith used the word consumption (*consommation*) to mean purchase pure and simple, or demand; Say defined it to mean the destruction of value, and says that all consumption is a destruction of value. The absurdity of this is patent. When a person purchases (i.e. consumes, in the language of the Economists and Adam Smith) a diamond ring, a piece of plate, a picture, a statue, or a book—does he thereby destroy them? The fact is that consumption, which Say defined to mean destruction, is no part of Economics at all. For Economics is limited to the phenomena of exchange.

The Economists steadfastly refused to admit that labour and credit are wealth. But on the first page of his work Say classes *titres de créance*, bank notes, bills of exchange, the funds, &c., as wealth; and further on includes many other kinds of incorporeal property under the title of wealth. These are all abstract rights. Say also, like Adam Smith, includes all the industrial faculties of the people under the definition of wealth and capital.

Now, how can we speak of the 'production, distribution and consumption' of bank notes, bills of exchange, the funds, shares in commercial companies, copyrights, patents, and the other forms of incorporeal property?

How can we speak of the 'production, distribution and consumption' of labour of different kinds, of knowledge, and other intellectual qualities, and of personal credit?

Whereas we speak of the supply and demand, and the

value of all these things; and they are all the subjects of exchange or commerce. The whole operations of mercantile credit—the colossal system of banking—and the foreign exchanges—are all sales, or exchanges, and integral departments of commerce: but how can their mechanism and phenomena be explained under the expression the 'production, distribution and consumption of wealth'?

This separation of the component terms of the expression 'production, distribution and consumption,' and their treatment in separate chapters, utterly destroys the character of Economics as a science, and utterly breaks the back of the theory of value, which is the very essence of Economics.

Say's books abound in valuable observations, but his system of Economics is absolutely unworkable for any practical purposes. Say totally forgot to observe that the expression 'production, distribution and consumption of wealth' was rigorously restricted by the Economists to the exchanges, or commerce, of material products only, and, even as applied to them, was a very awkward concept; and that labour and credit were entirely excluded from it. But when labour and credit are admitted to be wealth by Adam Smith and Say, and introduced into Economics by them, the expression becomes mere unintelligible jargon.

J. S. Mill was the friend and pupil of J. B. Say, and modelled his ideas very much on those of Say. Nevertheless, he has considerable divergences from him. He saw that consumption, in the sense of destruction, is no part of Economics; and he divides his work into production, distribution and exchange. But production and distribution, in the language of the Economists and Adam Smith, was exchange—so that Mill's work is really simply exchange and exchange.

But as the basis of the whole science is the word wealth we have to see what meaning Mill gives to it.

In his preliminary remarks he says that it is no part of the design of his treatise to aim at metaphysical nicety of definition where the ideas suggested by a term are already as determinate as practical purposes require, and that every one has a notion sufficiently correct for common purposes of what is meant by wealth. It somewhat surprises us to hear this. For many centuries nations have been quite unable to agree as to what wealth is; and many bloody wars have been waged because of quarrels which rose directly out of a mistaken conception of its meaning; vast quantities of mischievous legislation have been enacted as the result of erroneous theories as to its nature and origin; and at the present moment the widest differences of opinion prevail among Economists as to what should be included under the term.

One of Mill's definitions is as follows: 'Everything forms part of wealth which has power of purchasing.' This exactly agrees with the definition adopted 1,300 years ago by the ancients, and includes everything which can be bought and sold, or exchanged, whatever its nature or form may be; and evidently comprehends all the three orders of economic quantities.

Now, let us see how far Mill is consistent with himself. After giving this wide and general definition he shortly afterwards attempts a second, and identifies the 'production of wealth, the extraction of the instruments of human subsistence and enjoyment from the materials of the globe.' Mill admits that industrial qualities are wealth. Now, how are industrial qualities extracted from the materials of the globe? Mill admits that personal credit is wealth. How is a merchant's or banker's credit extracted from the materials of the globe? Mill admits that a credit given by a solvent banker or merchant is of the same value as gold, and therefore wealth. How is a credit—a mere abstract right of action—extracted from the materials of the globe? Elsewhere Mill speaks of wealth as being the product of land, labour and capital; but how are personal qualities and abstract rights the product of land, labour and capital? We might point out several other self-contradictions of Mill on the nature of wealth; but that would be too wearisome for our readers. Mill says that every one has a sufficiently correct knowledge of the meaning of wealth; and now it is seen that he has no consistent ideas on the subject himself.

The fact is that Say and Mill have brought the science to a complete *impasse*. The expression 'production, distribution and consumption of wealth' was expressly restricted to the commerce, or exchanges, of material products only; and when we introduce personal qualities and abstract rights into the science, as Adam Smith, Say and Mill have rightly done, it throws the whole subject into irremediable confusion. There is no possibility of erecting the 'production, distribution and consumption of wealth' into any sort of scientific system; if we are to attain that end we must revert to the concept of Economics as the science of exchanges, or of commerce, as the most advanced Economists are now doing: and then we have a body of phenomena as capable of being erected into an exact and definite science as astronomy, optics, or any other.

We shall now see the bearings of the doctrines of the Economists and Adam Smith on free trade.

The Economists established it as one of the fundamental rights of mankind that they should be allowed to exchange their products and services freely with one another. Now, it is evident that when men agree to exchange their products and services, the arrangement of the price, or value, of the reciprocal products and services exchanged should be left entirely to the mutual agreement of the parties, the buyer and the seller. Who can tell so well as they what is the real value of the product or service to them? Now, when the price of the product or service is agreed upon and settled between the sole parties who are interested in it, suppose that some artificial force is suddenly directed against one of them, beyond what arises from their natural position, to oblige him to yield up more of his property to the other than he would do if the arrangement were left perfectly free—such a force suddenly put at the disposal of either party, whatever its nature be, whether moral or material, would clearly be unjust in its very nature, and would be nothing more than a license enabling one party to rob the other.

It may be asserted in the broadest possible terms that

it is the natural right of every man to employ his industry and the talents which Providence has given him in the manner which he considers to be most for his own advantage, so long as it is not to the injury of his neighbour. He has the natural right to exchange the products of his industry with those of any other person who will agree to such exchange, to buy from whom he will, and to sell to whom he can. A law which seeks to check the course of this free exchange is inherently wrong, and, because inherently wrong, inherently mischievous. And, though it may be permitted to take something from him for the necessities of the State, which is the guardian of the interests of all, a law which deprives one class of the community of a part of their property in order to bestow it upon another class is an intolerable violation of natural justice. If a person forcibly takes away a part of his property from another person without any equivalent it is simply robbery. In the same way if a man wishes to sell any article and can by any means force the buyer to pay a higher price for it than he otherwise would, it is simply despoiling him of part of his property, and appropriating it to himself.

Let us put this in a familiar way. Suppose that Richard Stubble lives in the country and grows corn, and that his friend John Smith carries on his business in town. Having some corn to sell, Richard proposes to have a transaction with his friend John. The free marketable value of the corn is 40s. per quarter. But suppose that Richard has about a hundred times more influence over the legislature than John has, and he gets them to pass a law by which he can compel John to pay him 50s. for what he could buy elsewhere for 40s. In that case he deprives John of 10s., representing so much of his industry, for which he gives him no equivalent, and takes it to himself. In the mediaeval ages great lords and barons used to keep armed retainers whom they employed to plunder any unfortunate travellers who came within their power. In the nineteenth century the governing classes passed laws by which they forced traders to surrender to them a considerable portion of their property against their will. Where is the moral difference between the two cases? When one man forcibly and unjustly deprives another man of his property, the precise method he may adopt for his purpose does not materially affect the moral aspect of the thing.

It is no argument to say that till comparatively recent times the protective system was established in this country, that it is still in force in foreign countries, and that it was supported and adopted by men of unblemished character and integrity. It is absolutely necessary that we should not suffer our estimation of the moral character of men to influence our view as to the soundness of their opinions. There never prevailed a pernicious error in the world which was not supported by the authority of men of eminent personal virtue. It is, unfortunately, through the very excellence of the men who adopted them, that most of the erroneous principles which have done so much mischief in the world derived their fatal influence. The real question is, not whether the men who hold certain opinions are estimable, but whether the opinions themselves are right or wrong. The fact is that questions are examined with greater care and more searching criticism nowadays than ever they were before; and by this more comprehensive investigation new considerations and relations are discovered. Arguments drawn from equity, sometimes well founded, sometimes the reverse, are every day obtaining greater influence in legislation; and many of the most beneficial reforms of the present day have been to abolish and set aside the partial and unjust laws which encumbered the statute-book. It is not so very long ago that public opinion in this country tolerated the slave trade, and men of eminent piety saw no harm in stealing men from their homes and transporting them to foreign countries to labour for the benefit of their masters. But public opinion became convinced of its abomination, and not only put it down but declared it to be a great crime. What was considered to be legitimate traffic at the beginning of the century is now declared by law to be piracy, and Englishmen who engage in it are liable to be dealt with as pirates. Little more than one hundred years ago, if a gale came on, it used to be the custom to pitch the negroes overboard like cattle, and this was related in a court of law without eliciting the slightest comment. Now, at bottom there is not much difference in the idea involved in protection and the slave trade. They both seek to effect the same object by somewhat different methods. They are both for the purpose of enabling one set of men to appropriate to themselves the fruits of their neighbours' industry—the one by the coarse method of force, the other by the somewhat more refined method of fraudulent taxation.

Lord Macaulay remarks that the two greatest and most salutary social revolutions which have taken place in England were those which, in the thirteenth century, put an end to the tyranny of nation over nation; and which, a few generations later, put an end to the property of man in man. To these we may venture to add a *third*, not less great and not less salutary than the other two—that great revolution in the ideas of the age which, in the nineteenth century, abolished for ever the property of one set of men in the *industry* of another.

The protective system is, therefore, nothing more than a method by which producers endeavour to force consumers to pay a higher price than they otherwise would do for their commodities. Now, let us consider a different case.

Suppose that the legislature, being entirely composed of consumers, should pass a law forbidding the farmers to sell their produce above a certain price, or to export it to foreign countries, where they might find a better market for it: or suppose that laws were made to prevent workmen demanding above a certain rate of wages: or compelling producers to bring their products to market and accept a price for them much below what they would fetch if there were no such law. This would be a case on the part of consumers precisely analogous to what protection is on the part of producers.

This form of injustice did formerly prevail to a certain extent in this country; but it never acquired a distinctive name in our language as it did in France. During the height of the horrors of the French Revolution in 1793, when the insecurity of property had scared away almost all sorts of produce from the market, the French Convention passed the severest laws to limit the price of commodities, forbidding persons to sell their produce above a certain fixed price, whence they were called the laws of the *maximum*. As might have been foreseen, these laws only aggravated the evil; and their disastrous effects are set forth with great minuteness in the third, fourth, fifth, and sixth volumes of Alison's *History of Europe* (seventh edition); though the author overlooks the fact that the very same objections apply against the system of protection, of which he is so strong an advocate.

Each of these systems, then, is erroneous, but in opposite directions; that of protection, by which the producer obliges the consumer to buy from him his produce at a price above its natural value; that of the maximum, by which the consumer obliges the producer to sell to him his produce at a price below its natural market value. Now, every law which interferes with the natural course of trade, which attempts to regulate the wages of labour, or the price of commodities, which attempts to meddle with the free exchange of industry or products between man and man, must necessarily fall under one of these forms of error. Every such law sins against natural justice, more or less, in one direction or the other, either as it assumes the form of protection or the maximum; and it is just as clear as the sun at noonday, that the only true, just and proper course is to establish and maintain absolute freedom of exchange.

The fact is, that both of these erroneous systems—protection and the maximum—are forms of socialism; they are both especially designed for the very purpose of interfering with the natural value of commodities. Consequently, whichever of the parties is enabled to compel the other to part with his property at a different rate than what he would, if unconstrained, is able to appropriate to himself a portion of the other's property. And this is the very essence of socialism. Protection is the socialism of producers; the maximum is the socialism of consumers. And nothing is more natural to find than that where the one doctrine is popular with one party the other doctrine is popular with the other party. Of this we may see examples in foreign countries where protection is the creed of the State, and socialism is the alarmingly increasing creed of the people.

Now, the idea which was at the root of all this legislation was that cost of production should regulate value, and that those who had produced articles had the right to have remunerative prices secured to them by law. This idea was a very natural one to occur to producers; and when we think of the condition of Parliament when this species of legislation was in fashion it is not surprising that it prevailed. In the last century, it is true, there were at various times laws enacted for disturbing the natural course of commerce; but the corn laws, which lasted, with various alterations, until Sir Robert Peel abolished them, were made in 1815. Now, what was the state of Parliament at that time? One branch was entirely composed, as it still is, of agriculturists; the other principally of agriculturists, and the nominees of agriculturists, as well as great manufacturers, great merchants, great shipowners, and great producers of all sorts. It was entirely a Parliament of sellers, a vast close and corrupt combination. The great body of the people, i.e. the consumers, had very little influence in the House of Commons. The sellers had a complete monopoly of law-making; and their legislation is exactly what might have been expected. All the producers in turn were permitted to plunder the public for their own benefit. It was nothing more than a gigantic conspiracy of all the sellers against all the buyers. These laws were a striking proof that no single interest can be entrusted to frame laws for the whole community in a spirit of justice; but, to insure that, all interests must have a voice.

These considerations are, we think, sufficient to place the doctrine of free exchange on an impregnable moral basis: and we have now to consider the effect of Adam Smith's demonstration that in commerce *both* sides gain. This, of all the services he has done to Economics, may be considered his chief achievement, one which alone, from its stupendous effects on national policy, would entitle him to immortal glory.

The essence of Adam Smith's doctrine is that the wider and more extensive commercial intercourse is among nations, the more prosperous and wealthy they all become. Every one, in seeking his own advantage benefits others as well, because if a man wants to acquire any object, he must have to offer in exchange for it something which other people want. Different countries have different advantages for producing commodities for the enjoyment and satisfaction of mankind. It is the interest of the whole world that all commodities should be produced in those places where they can be obtained best and cheapest, and exported to those places where they can only be produced of inferior quality and at a greater cost. Thus the whole world will obtain the greatest amount of enjoyments and satisfactions at the least labour and cost. Thus absolute freedom of commerce and exchange throughout the whole world is the true nature of things. But when hostile tariffs are interposed they act at once as a barrier, and diminish the commercial intercourse of nations to their mutual loss and impoverishment. Protective tariffs are expressly made for the purpose of forcing commerce out of its natural course and development, and that alone is sufficient to condemn them. This is so obvious that we need not dwell on it further.

It is, however, necessary to correct an assertion which is by no means uncommon. It is well known that Cobden in his wonderful campaigns many times declared that if England would lead the way other nations would quickly adopt free trade. At that time there seemed every prospect that this hope would be realized. The success of free trade legislation in England gave an immense stimulus to free trade doctrines in France, the birthplace and cradle of Economics and free trade. In 1846 and 1847 numerous Economists, among whom Michel Chevalier and Frederic Bastiat were the most conspicuous leaders, got up an association and agitation in France on the model of the Anti-Corn Law League in England, and excited immense enthusiasm. The movement had the best prospect of success, when the French Revolution of 1848 broke out and quickly spread all over Europe. That of course extinguished all hopes of free trade. When thrones were rocking to their foundations, and crowns were tumbling in the dust, statesmen could give no attention to Economics. *Inter arma* Economics *silet*. And instead of Economics the wildest socialism got the upper hand. The socialists knew instinctively that true Economics was their deadly enemy, so they abolished all the chairs of Economics in France. Under the fatal advice of Louis Blanc they established the *Ateliers Nationaux* (of which I have given an account in my *Dictionary of Political Economy*), where every workman was to be provided with work out of the resources of the State. But though the State could pay workmen to produce articles, it could not provide purchasers to buy them: so that, to prevent bankruptcy, the *Ateliers Nationaux* had to be suppressed at the cost of the most terrible civil war ever waged in any city.

Napoleon III, with the advice and assistance of Rouher, Chevalier, Cobden and Mallet, negotiated a commercial treaty with England in 1860 which considerably relaxed the protective system then established. But this treaty was carried by the autocratic power of the Emperor, and was utterly distasteful to the great mass of the French people, who were now mainly protectionist and socialist, which are one and the same thing. And alas! France, which in the last century was the beacon to spread the light of free trade throughout the world, is now enveloped in the deepest darkness of protection and socialism: nor does there seem any immediate prospect of her emerging from it.

Now, a considerable number of persons, seeing that other nations not only have not followed the example of England, but on the contrary have retrogressed, and are now even more protectionist than they were in 1847, and that, up to this time, Cobden's hopes have been falsified, have maintained that what Cobden regarded only as a hopeful prospect, was in his view the necessary corollary of England's adoption of free trade: and that as other nations have plunged deeper and deeper into protection and socialism, England should do so likewise. They clamour against what they are pleased to designate as one-sided free trade. And under the specious names of reciprocity and fair trade, they are calling for England to retaliate by enacting protective tariffs against those nations which have enacted protective tariffs against her, and so to do unto them as they do unto her. If this were carried out, England would have to revert to the darkest days of protection.

It has been frequently said that if Cobden were alive now, and saw the falsification of his hopes, he would advocate reciprocity and fair trade, as they are pleased to term it. But those who say so never studied Cobden's doctrines. Constantly and uniformly he inculcated that England ought to adopt free trade whether other nations did so or not, and even if all the world were against her, as is pretty much the case at present.

Having a perfect recollection of the great free trade discussions, I have no hesitation in saying that Cobden would have done nothing of the sort which the reciprocitarians and fair traders would attribute to him. His constant maxim was that *the true way to fight hostile tariffs is by free trade.*

No doubt all these hostile tariffs are extremely exasperating: they inflict incalculable injury, not only upon the wealth and prosperity of England, but upon the nations which enact them, and on the rest of the world. But if, as some hotheaded and inconsiderate persons urge, England were to resort to reciprocity and retaliation, she would merely double the mischief. If the present hostile tariffs destroy an incalculable amount of commercial intercourse, a resort to reciprocity and retaliation would destroy it infinitely more. As Sir Louis Mallet pithily said, 'If one tariff is bad, two are worse.' If foreign nations smite us on one cheek by their hostile tariffs, if we followed the advice of the reciprocitarians and retaliated, we should simply smite ourselves very hard on the other cheek.

Retaliation is not to be thought of. England may justly

fume and fret, but she must keep her temper and possess her soul in patience. There is no remedy but time and patience. When protectionist policy once gets the upper hand the natural tendency of its advocates is to strain it till it cracks. When protectionists do not reap the benefits they expect from protection, their constant cry is for more protection. We see this in Russia, Germany, France, Italy, and most conspicuously in the United States. In this last-named country there are evident signs that the people see that they have bent the bow too far, and the present Government is strenuously bent on relaxing it to a considerable extent; but how far it will succeed time only can show. But, whatever other nations may do, England must endure to the end and steadily keep the light of free trade burning amid despondency, gloom and darkness, in the hope that time, experience and reflection will bring other nations to a better frame of mind. One example alone is sufficient to prove the wisdom of this policy. Even in former times, when all nations were protectionist, there were always a certain number of free cities, and their wealth and prosperity, while all nations were weighed down with protection, completely establish the truth of Cobden's doctrine. If so be, England must continue to the end as the free port and market of the world.

Thus we see how true Economics throws a clear and steady light on the path of national policy.

We have now to consider the influence of economic speculation, true or false, on that new form of protection which, under the name of socialism, has in these last few years become so increasingly prevalent, and which is assuming more alarming and portentous influence every day.

Adam Smith, as we have shown even in this brief and cursory sketch, did immense services to Economics; but, alas! he also did infinite mischief by his self-contradictions and confusion on the nature and causes of value.

Aristotle said—'Value is the relation which anything bears to other things.'

The Economists were perfectly clear and consistent in their

doctrine of value. Le Trosne says—'Products acquire, then, in the social state which arises from the community of men among each other, a new quality. This new quality is value, which makes products become wealth.

'Value consists in the ratio of exchange which takes place between such and such a product, between such a quantity of one product and such a quantity of another product.' And in this the Economists were unanimous. Now, it is evident that if value is a ratio, there can be no such thing as intrinsic value; and also that a standard of value is impossible by the very nature of things. Value, like distance, necessarily requires two objects or quantities.

Aristotle also showed that the cause of all value is demand—χρεία. The word χρῆμα, which is one of the most usual words in Greek for wealth, comes from χράομαι, to want or demand: and the ancients showed a thing is χρῆμα—wealth—only where and when it is χρήσιμον—wanted and demanded: and that where and when it is not χρήσιμον—wanted and demanded—it is not χρῆμα—wealth. In the ancient dialogue we have referred to above, Socrates shows that money is wealth only in those places where it will purchase other things, and he instanced several examples of local moneys which were valuable and were wealth in certain places, but which had no value and were not wealth in others, where they had no power of purchasing. All the Economists of France and Italy showed that value proceeds entirely from the wants and desires of men. The Economists were quite unanimous that all value proceeds from *consommation*, or demand; and that where things are not *consommés*—demanded—they are no better than so much rubbish. Now, as all commerce or exchange proceeds from the mutual wants and desires of men, it is quite evident that value requires the concurrence of two minds, and that it proceeds from *reciprocal demand*.

Our great philosopher Locke was, unfortunately, the originator of all the confusion which has done so much to blight the progress of English Economics. Locke maintained that all differences of value arise from differences of labour. Locke's abstruse works are very little known, and if this fatal dogma had lain *perdu* in them there would have been very little harm done.

But, unfortunately, this idea was taken up in the early part of his work by Adam Smith, though quite discarded in the latter part of it, and his fifth chapter has been the ruin of English Economics.

Of this chapter that distinguished Economist and statesman Francis Horner says—'We have been under the necessity of suspending our progress in the perusal of the *Wealth of Nations* on account of the insurmountable difficulties, obscurity and embarrassment in which the reasonings of the fifth chapter are involved . . . . the discovery that I did not understand Smith speedily led me to doubt whether Smith understood himself.'

We shall now lay before our readers the cause of all this confusion.

In this unfortunate chapter Smith begins by saying that the value of any commodity is equal to the quantity of labour which it entitles him to purchase. Hence if we denote labour by l, we have

$$A = l, 2l, 3l, 4l \ldots$$

He then says that this is the same thing as saying that it is equal to the *produce* of labour which it enables him to purchase. On denoting produce by p, we have

$$A = p, 2p, 3p, 4p \ldots$$

Then he says that the value of anything is more frequently estimated in money than either in labour or commodities. On denoting money by m, we have

$$A = m, 2m, 3m, 4m \ldots$$

Now, although it has been pointed out that these modes of estimating the value of a quantity are by no means identical, we observe that in this passage Smith defines the value of a thing to be something *external* to itself. Hence the value of A must vary directly as l, p or m. The more of l, p or m that A can purchase, the greater is the value of A: the less of l, p or m that A can purchase, the less is the value of A. It is also perfectly clear that if any change takes place in the relation between A and these quantities, the value of A has changed.

Hence Smith admits that value, like distance, requires two objects. If any change takes place in the position of these two objects, the distance between them has changed, no matter in which the change has taken place. So if any change takes place in the relation of two quantities, their value has changed, no matter in which the change takes place. Hence it is clear that there can be no such thing as *invariable value*. Nothing whatever can have invariable value unless its exchangeable relation with everything else is fixed. Hence we can at once see that, by the very nature of things, there can be no such thing as an invariable standard of value by which to measure the value of other things, because by the very nature of things, the very condition of anything being invariable in value is that nothing else shall vary in value, and that there shall be no variations to measure.

Nevertheless a very large body of Economists have set out upon this wild-goose chase, this search for an invariable standard of value, which it is utterly contrary to the nature of things should exist at all. Directly after the passage we have referred to, Smith commences the search for that single thing which is the invariable standard of value. He says that gold and silver will not do because they vary in their value; sometimes they can purchase more and sometimes less of labour and commodities. Then he says—

'But as a measure of quantity, such as the natural foot, fathom or handful, which is always varying its own quantity, can never be an accurate measure of the quantity of other things, so a commodity *which is itself continually varying in its own value* can never be an accurate measure of the value of other commodities. *Equal quantities of labour at all times and places may be said to be of equal value to the labourer.* In his ordinary state of health, strength and spirits, in the ordinary degree of his skill and dexterity he must always lay down the same portion of his ease, his liberty, and his happiness. *The price which he pays must always be the same whatever the quantity of goods which he receives in return for it.* Of these, indeed, it may sometimes purchase a greater, and sometimes a smaller quantity, *but it is their value which varies, not that of the labour which purchases them.* At all times and places that is dear which it is difficult to come at, or which it costs much labour to acquire, and that cheap which is to be had easily, or with very little labour. *Labour alone, therefore, never varying in its own value, is alone the ultimate and real standard by which the value of all commodities can at all times and places be estimated and compared.* It is their real price; money is their nominal price only.

'*But though equal quantities of labour are always of equal value to the labourer,* yet to the person who employs him they appear sometimes to be greater and sometimes of smaller value. . . .

'*Labour, therefore, it appears evidently is the only universal, as well as the only accurate measure of value, or the only standard by which we can compare the value of different commodities at all times and places.*'

The utter confusion of ideas in these passages is manifest. A foot, or a fathom, is an absolute quantity, and of course may increase or decrease by itself: but value, by Smith's own definition, is a *ratio*, which requires two quantities: and therefore we might just as well say that because a foot which is constantly varying its own length cannot be an accurate measure of the length of other things, therefore a quantity which is always varying its own *ratio* cannot be an accurate measure of the *ratio* of other things. This is utter confusion of idea. We may measure a tree with a yard, because they are each of them single quantities; *but it is impossible that a single quantity can be the measure of a ratio.* It is manifestly impossible to say that

$$a : b :: x.$$

It is manifestly absurd to say that 4 is to 5 as 8, without saying as 8 is to—what? just as it is absurd to say that a horse gallops at the rate of twenty miles, without saying in what time.

But Smith says that 'equal quantities of labour are always of equal value.' What? If a man is paid five shillings for a certain amount of labour, is his labour of the same value to him as if he were paid £1,000? This certainly is a very comfortable doctrine for the employer, because, if he pays his workmen one shilling a week, according to Smith their labour is of just as much value to them as if he paid them twenty shillings a week. We doubt whether the workmen would acquiesce in this view.

Smith himself says that gold and silver vary in their value because they sometimes can purchase more and sometimes less of other things. But when labour sometimes earns more wages and sometimes less wages, does it not also vary in its value? How, then, can its value be invariable? How is its value to be determined on principles different from those which govern the value of gold and silver?

The fact is that Smith's dogma that labour is an invariable standard of value is a pure mare's nest. Neither labour nor any other single quantity can be a standard of value; and to suppose that it could, is only to betray utter ignorance of the mathematics of ratios.

The term value has been so confused by Economists that it will aid much in showing the confusion of Smith's ideas to translate them into mechanical language, substituting the word *distance*, which has not been so befogged in popular language, for value, thus—

'As a measure of quantity, such as a foot, which is always varying its own length, can never be an accurate measure of the length of other things, so an object which is always varying its own *distance* can never be an accurate measure of the *distance* of other objects. But the sun is always at the same *distance*. And though the earth is sometimes nearer to the sun and sometimes further off from it, the sun is always at the same *distance*. And though the earth is at different distances from the sun, the sun is always at the same distance from the earth: it is the distance of the earth which has varied, and not that of the sun: and the sun alone never varying its own *distance* is the ultimate and real standard by which the distances of all things can at all times and places be estimated and compared.'

Such is a fair translation into mechanical language of Smith's ideas on value, merely substituting *distance* for *value*. Smith practically contends that if a railway station is fixed, and a train approaches, or recedes from it, the distance of the train from the station varies; but that the station is always at the same distance from the train! Can we wonder at the language of Horner? The cause of the confusion is obvious. Smith begins by holding the value of a product to be the quantity of *other* things it will purchase: and then he suddenly changes his concept of value to the quantity of labour embodied in obtaining the product itself: and he has not the slightest idea that these are utterly inconsistent ideas.

Exactly the same confusion runs through the whole of Ricardo. His conception of value is vitiated by the same utter want of unity.

Ricardo's work is avowedly a treatise on value. Now, Bacon and common sense show that before a person begins to theorize on a subject he must first make an exhaustive collection of the facts relating to it, even the most minute; because a single fact which is irreconcileable with a theory is fatal to it. Ricardo excludes immaterial and incorporeal quantities from his investigations, which Adam Smith in conformity with the unanimous agreement of ancient writers included: he confines his inquiry solely to material things: and of these he excludes all but those which are the product of human labour. Now, material commodities which are the product of human labour, are one subdivision, and that by no means the largest, of material commodities, which are wealth by unanimous consent. Ricardo then attempts to found a general theory on a single subdivision of one class of commodities which have value: by this method he omits about eighty per cent. of the facts of the case. The veriest tyro can perceive that such a method of philosophizing is absolutely inadmissible.

He also falls into exactly the same confusion on value that Adam Smith does. He begins by saying—'The value of a commodity, *or the quantity of any other commodity for which it will exchange.*' Also—'The exchangeable value of these commodities, or the rule which determines *how much of one shall be given in exchange for another*': and several other passages to the same effect.

But he very soon slides into the same pitfall as Smith does; and he calls the 'quantity of labour bestowed on a commodity under many circumstances an invariable standard indicating correctly the variations of other things.'

He then maintains that, 'if a commodity could always be produced by an invariable quantity of labour, its value would be invariable, and it would be eminently well calculated to measure the varying value of all other things'; and in a subsequent part of his work he says: 'The labour of a million of men in manufactures will always produce the same value. That commodity is alone invariable which at all times requires the same quantity of toil and trouble to produce it.' Now, Ricardo's doctrine is that when manufactures have been produced they are of exactly the same value, whether they sell for a large sum of money or cannot be sold at all. We doubt whether the manufacturers of Manchester would acquiesce in this doctrine.

He then says: 'I cannot agree with M. Say in estimating the value of a commodity by the abundance of other commodities for which it will exchange.' Thus Ricardo, in this last sentence, not only disagrees with the whole world, but he flatly contradicts himself.

Ricardo, then, having excluded all commodities from his inquiry which are not the produce of human labour, roundly declares that labour is the foundation of all value.

Ricardo gives an instance, which is indeed the logical consequence of his doctrine, which will enable plain persons to judge of the value of his system. As he contends that labour is the sole cause of value, he alleges that as fine weather, the warmth of the sun, and copious showers, are the free gift of nature, they add nothing to the value of the crops.

If this be so, it is obvious that bad weather, storms of rain and wind, can in no way damage their value. If Ricardo's dogma be true, the value of the crop reaped cannot be greater than the value of the seed sown; because with the ploughing of the land, the sowing of the seed, and manuring the ground, human labour ceases, all the rest is the agency of nature. Surely the naked statement of Ricardo's doctrine is sufficient to show that his whole system is fallacious.

McCulloch is the bondslave of Ricardo; he also asserts that labour is the sole cause of value. Carey, the American Economist, says: 'Labour is the sole cause of value,' and he adds, it is so in nine hundred and ninety-nine cases out of a thousand; and if there be one case in a thousand where there is value without labour it is just the exception which proves the rule. Carey had queer notions of natural philosophy, for it is an axiom of natural philosophy that if there be a single case which is irreconcileable with a theory it is fatal to it.

Now the superlative importance of this doctrine is that it is the foundation of socialism and all its consequences. Socialists avowedly base their doctrines on Adam Smith and Ricardo, and just as the astounding consequences which the Economists drew from their doctrine, that in an exchange neither side gains or loses, caused Condillac and Smith to inquire into its truth; so the portentous consequences which the socialists draw from the Smith-Ricardo doctrine, that labour is the cause of all value, demand the strictest inquiry into its truth, because it has become a very prevalent dogma among working men, and a good many others besides, that working men are the creators of all value and of all wealth.

In the brief space at our command it would be impossible to give a full examination of the dogma commensurate with its superlative importance and its consequences. We can only touch upon a few leading points; but if any of our readers care to examine it more minutely, we may refer them to our *Theory of Credit*, in which it is investigated exhaustively.

Let us now test the dogma that working men are the creators of all value and of all wealth.

We may premise that by the term wealth, in accordance with the argument contained in an earlier portion of this paper, we mean anything whatever whose value can be measured in money; anything which can be bought and sold; anything which has purchasing power.

Now let us take a few examples of wealth:

(1) The simple space of ground upon which a great city stands has enormous value and is wealth. Did working men create the ground upon which a city stands and give it value?

(2) Herds of cattle, sheep, pigs, fowls, and other animals fit for food have value and are wealth. Did working men create all these kinds of animals and give them value?

(3) Timber trees standing on the ground, which no human being ever touched, often have very great value, and are bought and sold. Did working men create these timber trees and give them value?

(4) A whale was stranded on the shore of the Frith of Forth. As it lay on the beach it was sold for £70. Did working men create the whale and give it value?

(5) An aerolite fell in Sweden. The curator of the national museum bought it for £84. Did working men create the aerolite and give it value?

(6) Mr. Buckland says that at the Zoological Gardens the *dejecta* of the snakes sold for nine shillings the pound. Did working men create the *excreta* of the snakes and give them value?

(7) The manager of a great commercial company, such as a bank or a railway, often earns by his business capacity an income of several thousand pounds a year. His business qualities, therefore, have great value, and are wealth to him. Did working men create his business qualities and give them value?

(8) To professional men, advocates, physicians, surgeons, engineers, and many others, their capacity often brings them an income of many thousands of pounds a year. Their

capacity has therefore great value and is wealth to them. Did working men create their professional ability and give it value?

(9) Mill says justly that everything is wealth which has purchasing power. Merchants and traders purchase commodities almost exclusively with their credit, i.e. by giving a promise to pay at a future time; and these promises to pay have value, because they will be paid at maturity. Merchants and traders make a profit by trading with their credit: their credit has great value to them and is wealth. Did working men create the credit of our merchants and traders and give it value?

(10) The express purpose of a bank is to create credit, i.e. to issue promises to pay several times the amount of cash they hold in reserve. The floating rights of action issued by all the banks in Great Britain, and at present in circulation, are about £1,000,000,000. These thousand millions of circulating credits have all the effects of an equal amount of gold. They have value and are wealth. Did working men create the credit of our great banks and give it value?

We must now say something about credit, because the dogma that labour is the cause of all value has made the subject absolutely unintelligible.

We shall first explain what credit is.

When one person has the legal right to compel another person to pay or do something for him he is termed a creditor; the person who is legally bound to pay or do that something is termed a debtor; and the right of action which the creditor has against the debtor is termed indifferently a credit or a debt. It is to be carefully observed that this credit or debt is not the right to any specific material chattel; the creditor has no right to any part of his debtor's property; that is absolutely intact; it is simply the right against the person of the debtor to compel him to part with some part of his property in exchange for this right of action, credit or debt, at a fixed time. It is, therefore, a pure abstract right. But the creditor can sell his right of action to any one else for money; and it may be bought and sold any number of times like any material chattel. And because the right of action may be bought and sold, the Roman jurists termed it *pecunia, res, bona, merx;* the Greek jurists, χρῆμα, πρᾶγμα, ἀγαθόν, οἶκος, οὐσία, οὐσία ἀφανής; and English jurists, goods, chattels, vendible commodities, merchandise, incorporeal property, incorporeal wealth. So Mill acknowledges that the promise to pay of a solvent merchant or banker is of the value of gold, which is very clear, because the gold is the value of the promise.

Thus the whole mass of circulating credits or debts is a mass of exchangeable property just like any other, such as gold, silver, corn, manufactured goods, or any other. These credits, debts or rights of action have value for exactly the same reason that any other commodities have value, because at the proper time they will be exchanged for money or its equivalent. The whole commerce of the country is now carried on by them, except only to an infinitesimal degree, and the aggregate of money and all these credits under various forms constitute the circulating medium, or currency of the country, or the measure of prices.

The whole system of credit is based upon this principle—that every future profit, from whatever source arising, has a *present value*, and that this present value may be bought and sold like money or any other chattel.

Few persons have any idea of the enormous magnitude of this species of property in this country. In a return laid before Parliament by an eminent city firm it was shown that out of £2,000,000 of payments and receipts by the firm only £40,986 were made in gold, silver and copper; all the rest in different forms of credit; and some bankers found that in banking only four per thousand, or ·0025 per cent., were paid in coin; all the rest in credit. Thus if we say that ninety-nine per cent. of the transactions of this country are carried on by credit, and only one per cent. by coin, our statement will be well within the mark, and we may obtain a very rough approximate estimate of the actual amount of this circulating credit, because the best estimates of the actual coin in the country place it at about £110,000,000; now if we multiply this by ninety-nine we shall find the result to be £10,890,000,000, as the proximate actual quantity of credit in all its different forms in this country. Thus it is seen of what supreme importance it is to comprehend the great principles and mechanism of credit, if we would understand the commerce of the country, and the theory of prices. Now, in no sense can it be said that working men created these ten thousand millions of credit and gave it value.

Thus we see that the whole basis of socialism, founded on the Ricardian doctrine of value and incorporated as the leading idea of Karl Marx's *Capital*, is utterly overthrown.

Labour, like everything else, has value in so far as it is exchangeable. Attempts to raise the price of labour by artificial restrictions on its sale are destructive of the mechanism of exchange, from which alone value is derived. The theory of Economics here developed contains a complete vindication of the equity and beneficence of the principle of free exchange as applied to all forms of wealth, to Labour, to Credit, and to material commodities.

English Economics can never emerge from its present deplorable state until we utterly discard the doctrine that labour is the basis of value, and dismiss from our mind the concept of Economics as the 'production, distribution and consumption of wealth,' by which it is impossible to create it a science. When we shift the basis of value to exchangeability, and revert to the original concept of Economics as the science of commerce, or exchanges, scientific order succeeds to chaos, everything becomes clear and simple, and we have a definite, positive, and intelligible science. Economics is the theory of value, which, next to civil government, is the most important thing in human affairs. It may be summed up in words which M. Michel Chevalier did me the honour to say contained the best definition of the science which has yet been proposed—'*Economics is the science which treats of the laws which govern the relations of exchangeable quantities.*'

HENRY DUNNING MAC LEOD.

II.

THE COMING INDUSTRIAL STRUGGLE.

WILLIAM MAITLAND.

II.

THE COMING INDUSTRIAL STRUGGLE.

WE frequently hear now that the Manchester school of political economists is dead, and that the doctrines it inculcated are extinct. That this should be so seems to be considered a subject for general congratulation. Its policy is described as narrow and selfish, unsuited to the more enlightened and philanthropic times in which we live; while its professors are accused of want of patriotism and, strangely enough, of having sacrificed the interests of the whole nation to those of one particular class. Those, however, who have read the inaugural address of President Cleveland—perhaps the most remarkable declaration of policy ever delivered by any man in any country, though it has attracted far less attention in England than it deserves—may come to the conclusion that the Manchester school is not dead; but that, like a large part of the population of this country, it has emigrated to America, and taken its principles with it. This is, perhaps, not to be wondered at. We are a very great and a very intelligent nation, and for the last twenty-five years we have been lecturing the United States, in season and out of season, on the folly of protection, and the advantages to be derived from a strict adherence to sound economic principles. We have pointed to the marvellous development of our own industries, and to the rapid increase of wealth and enlightenment among every class of the community, as the best proof of the soundness of our advice; while we even ventured to predict for them an almost similar advance, if they would but follow our example.

How far we were honest in proffering this advice it is difficult to say. The followers of the Manchester school could consistently do so; for they believed that their policy must be for the advantage of every country adopting it, and that every advance in prosperity made by one nation must be for the advantage of every other. On the other hand, many believed that American manufactures were solely kept up by protection; and that, if the United States could be induced to open their markets, their own manufacturers could not compete with ours, and we should obtain an almost complete monopoly. Even Mr. Gladstone, who claims to be one of the last survivors of the Manchester school, in a controversy with the late Mr. Blaine, in the *North American Review*, some years ago, on the subject of free trade and protection, wrote as if it were the special mission of the United States in the universe to provide raw material for our manufacturers and food for our operatives, forgetting that he was addressing the representative of one of the largest manufacturing countries in the world. However, America is now going to adopt a free trade policy, possibly because of our advice, but much more probably from her own bitter experience of protection, which has ruined her agricultural classes, has tended to accumulate wealth in the hands of a few, and has led to a system of making concessions to every class of the community which had influence enough to exact them, to the detriment of those who had no such power.

This departure is far more important than at first appears. It may be said that America is only one country, and that most continental nations are still protectionist; but not only is America the most important of all as regards wealth, territory, population and resources, but she is also the only nation which can really claim to be protectionist in the fullest sense of the word. She alone is raising a revenue far in excess of her requirements. France, Germany, and all other protectionist countries, may gild the pill and endeavour to persuade their people that this form of taxation is a benefit, but every farthing raised is urgently needed for the support of their enormous armaments and the interest on their debts.

They probably find it easier to raise their revenue in this form than in any other. But the United States, practically without an army, a navy, or a public debt, had a revenue far in excess of what she could require, even after allowing for many illegitimate drafts made upon it; and, perhaps for the first time in the history of the world, the enormous accumulation of wealth in the public treasury became a pressing danger to the State. It was this condition of affairs which gave rise to the abuse of the pension fund, and led to the reckless extravagance, to call it by no stronger term, of the last Administration, which culminated in its defeat at the last election. But, opposed as I am to protection in every form, there is no doubt that more can be said in favour of it for America than for any other country. America is very nearly, if not altogether, self-supporting. With the exception of tea and coffee, and perhaps a few drugs, she can produce everything she requires in the way of food for her population, or raw materials for her manufacturers. If protection has failed in such a country, what can be said for it elsewhere? It has failed, and America is now pledged to a policy of free trade.

While this change has taken place in the United States, the very reverse is going on among ourselves. Our farmers and manufacturers, or rather those who profess to speak for them, clamour for protection. Workmen are to be protected against their employers; the unemployed against those who do not employ them. We are to be protected against working too many hours, against getting drunk, against old age, against incapacity, against everything, except, perhaps, small-pox, by these new reformers. All this will require money; and, enormous as our taxation is, especially in view of the present condition of trade and commerce, this appears to present no difficulty. Government is to pay for all the proposed benefits, and the necessary taxation can be raised from the capitalists. Coexistent with this public extravagance, as is always the case, there is the most wild and reckless private expenditure the world has ever seen among all classes of the community, while both public and private extravagances are held up as proofs of our marvellous prosperity. For years the old watchword of the Manchester school—Retrenchment—has never been heard here, and it now sounds strangely in our ears, as it comes to us, across the Atlantic, from the lips of President Cleveland, as he preaches public and private thrift and frugality, individual freedom, and independence of all government support and protection.

The object of this paper is to forecast, as far as possible, what will be the effect of this change of policy; and what each country will gain and lose by it. But, before entering on this subject, and to show how wide the lines of divergence already are, I propose to place in juxtaposition a few statements from the speech of Mr. Cleveland, in which he lays down the fundamental principles of good government, and some of the utterances of prominent statesmen in this country, belonging to all parties—unless, indeed, there still be a party representing the Manchester school.

President Cleveland.

'While every American citizen must contemplate with the utmost pride and enthusiasm the growth and expansion of our country, the sufficiency of our institutions to stand against the rudest shocks, the wonderful enterprise of our people, and the demonstrated superiority of our free government, it behoves us constantly to watch every symptom of insidious infirmity that threatens our national vigour.

'It cannot be doubted that our stupendous achievements as a people, and our country's robust strength, have given rise to a heedlessness of those laws governing our national health, which we can no more evade than human life can evade the laws of God and Nature.

'... We should be wise and should temper our confidence and faith in our national strength and resources with a frank confession that even these will not permit us to defy with impunity the inexorable laws of finance and trade.

'Closely related to the exaggerated confidence in our country's greatness, which tends to the disregard of the rules of national safety, another danger confronts us not less serious. I refer to the prevalence of a popular disposition to expect from the operation of our Government especial and direct individual advantages... This is the bane of republican institutions—a constant peril to our Government by the people. .... It perverts the patriotic sentiment of our countrymen, and tempts them to a pitiful calculation of the sordid gain to be derived from their Government's maintenance. It undermines the self-reliance of our people, and substitutes in its place dependence on governmental favouritism.

'The lesson of paternalism ought to be unlearned, and the better lesson taught that, while the people should patriotically and cheerfully support their Government, its *functions do not include the support of the people.*

'Acceptance of this principle leads to a refusal of bounties and subsidies, which burden the labour and thrift of a portion of our citizens....

'It' (that is, the neglect of this principle) 'leads also to a wild and reckless *pension* expenditure, which ... prostitutes to vicious uses the people's prompt and generous impulse to aid those disabled....

'Every thoughtful American must realize the importance of checking at its beginning any tendency to extravagance in public or private stations, and to regard frugality and economy as virtues. The toleration of the idea of extravagance results in waste of the people's money by their chosen servants, and encourages prodigality and extravagance in the home life of our countrymen. Under our scheme of government, waste of public money is a crime against the citizen, and contempt for the character of our people for economy and frugality in their personal affairs; and it deplorably saps the strength and sturdiness of our national character. It is the plain dictate of honesty and good government that public expenditure should be limited by public necessity, and that this should be measured by the rules of strict economy. It is equally clear that frugality among the people is the best guarantee of the contented and the strong support of free institutions.

'The existence of immense ... combinations ... formed for the purpose of limiting production and fixing prices is inconsistent with the fair field which ought to be open to every independent activity. Legitimate strife in business should not be superseded by an enforced concession to the demand of combinations that have power to destroy. Nor should the people ... lose the benefit from the cheapness which usually results from wholesome competitions. These ... combinations frequently constitute conspiracies against the interest of the people [1]. ...

'When we proclaim that the necessity for revenues to support the Government furnishes the only justification for taxing the people, we announce a truth so plain that its denial would seem to indicate the extent to which judgement may be influenced by familiarity with the perversion of taxing power. When we seek to reinstate self-confidence ... by discrediting abject dependence on governmental favours, we strive to stimulate those elements of the American character which support the hope of American achievement.'

Sir William Harcourt.

'I have already pointed to the growth of expenditure in the last seven years, and I have nothing to say on the subject of that expenditure. I am not going to enter into any controversy with reference to it, or to condemn it, but this, at least, I may say—that those who have authorized, encouraged, and insisted upon it—I am speaking now entirely without distinction of party, for it has not been one party alone—are bound to provide the means of defraying it. I know there was once in this country an economical party (laughter); but there is no economical party now, and I believe that the Prime Minister and myself are the only survivors of it (laughter). There has been attributed to me a saying

---

[1] Mr. Cleveland here refers to the great trusts and monopolies which have ruled the markets for some years past; but his words are equally applicable to combinations in this country which have attempted and, to some extent, succeeded in forcing the Government to conform to their demands.

that every one is a Socialist now. I do not know that I ever said it; but this I will say—there are no economists now. Financial economy has gone the way of political economy (ironical cheers). A chancellor of the exchequer preaching against extravagance is nowadays a voice crying in the wilderness. We hear much of the stinginess of the treasury; I only wish the treasury had power to be more stingy than it is. A chancellor of the exchequer may hold up his hands in despair, like the old steward in *The Rake's Progress*; the money is spent, or, as the French say, the wine is drawn, and you must pay for it. After all, the causes of this are not far to seek. Economy was possible, and even popular, in former days. Governments were compelled to be economical, for the people demanded it, and the House of Commons supported it. Sir Robert Peel was an economical minister. At that time the country was poor, capital was deficient, trade was bad, the weight of our debt was crushing, and taxation relating to the resources of the people was enormously heavy.

'The people were obliged to attend to the pence because they had no pounds to look after. Now the nation has grown rich, taxation, compared to the resources of all classes, is relatively light, and probably, in proportion to its wealth, this is the most lightly taxed country in Europe. Therefore, it is not unnatural that when any one comes forward with a proposal for increased expenditure he should be received as if he were the discoverer of a new pleasure (laughter). Private members with large hearts and small responsibilities take up favourite schemes for some favoured class of the community. They demand higher wages and greater pensions, and they desire that the State should undertake new duties, fresh responsibilities and larger expenditure. We create new empires here, and annex fresh territories there; we are anxious to reduce postal charges all over the world, to relieve more rates, to undertake lifeboats, &c. For these things the country is well agitated, and interests are well organized, the House of Commons is well canvassed, and one afternoon, in the gaiety of our hearts, we pass a resolution unanimously which is to cost a few millions when it comes into operation a few years hence. This is the cause of the increase of public expenditure.

'I pointed out the other night, with reference to a motion of this kind, that it meant £25,000,000; but the House of Commons said, Only £25,000,000! How cheap! Let us have it at once (laughter and cheers). *I do not condemn these things*—they are all excellent in their way, there is a great deal to be said for them, and very little to be said against them; but the time comes, and it has come, when you must pay for them.... I belong myself to the old school, and I would gladly see a good deal less spent, for, in fact, a good deal of it is wasted (cheers); and, if I might reverse the old saying, I would say that those who call the tune must pay the piper. The wealth of this country has increased, and is increasing, year by year. You may find yourselves in temporary straits, *but there is no occasion for apprehension and disquiet.* The condition of your affairs is sound, solid and prosperous. The resources of the country are ample, and they are always at command.

'He (Mr. Goschen) then proceeded to show that while public attention was fixed on the great staple industries of the country—the cotton, coal and iron industries—there is a mighty trade going on, there is wealth being rolled up—wealth of which no public statistics exist, but which is nevertheless accumulating and adding to the capital of the country. He pointed out that the profits of the cotton trade were less than the aggregate profits of the medical profession, and that the profits of the coal mines were still less than those of the lawyers (laughter).'—(SIR WILLIAM HARCOURT, Budget Speech, April 25, 1893.)

MR. ARNOLD MORLEY.

'The market rate of wages referred to was not a standard a government, or any other large employers of labour, ought to be guided by, and, he thought, the Post Office ought to set an example to other large employers of labour.'—(Reply to Deputation of the Unemployed, December 2, 1892.)

Sir John Gorst.

'The principle he was anxious to lay down was, that, whenever the public was the employer of labour, and the workers were working either for the general public or for the public in any division of the United Kingdom, the employers should so regulate all the conditions of the employment as to make themselves model employers of labour. . . . The whole matter was in the hands of a Government department, who were under no obligation to make any profit out of the work which they turned out; who had no foreign competition to rival them, and who were only under the necessity of seeing that the work was good. *It really did not much matter what it cost.*'—(Debate on Labour in Dockyards, March 6, 1893.)

Mr. Campbell-Bannerman.

'With regard to wages, the Government did not shut their eyes to the change that had come over the public mind in this matter. A very few years ago it would probably have been regarded on both sides as a perfectly sufficient answer if he had said, "We get men enough at the wages we offer. If our doors are open, there is a constant stream of men coming in; and, if they are shut, there is a mob outside wishing to come in; therefore, why in the name of common sense should we wish to raise our wages?" He did not use that answer, he did not believe in it.'—(Debate on Labour in Dockyards, March 6, 1893.)

Mr. John Burns.

'No better method of attempting to solve the question of the unemployed, which grew more serious every year, could be found in large districts where Government establishments existed than for systematic overtime to be abolished, a week of forty-eight hours established, and men from the ranks of the unemployed engaged in the arsenals and dockyards on *reproductive* work,' &c.—(Debate on Labour in Dockyards, March 6, 1893.)

These quotations show how wide apart the lines of divergence already are; and I propose to consider, in the first place, how the United States will be affected by this new departure. Briefly stated, Mr. Cleveland declares that the government of the country must be carried on with extreme thrift and frugality, and that all taxation beyond what is actually required for revenue is alike impolitic and unjust. Protection, therefore, will gradually disappear; and those who believe that this step will give us a monopoly of the American markets, will, if they are right, see their desire consummated. I am of opinion, however—and I write with a long experience of America—that they will be grievously disappointed, and that the very reverse will be the case. Americans are at least as good manufacturers as we are; and, so far from protection having aided in the development of their industries, its effect has been to restrict them. I am not going to discuss here whether protection may not, in the first instance, have helped to establish these industries; that is now beside the question; for all the most important of them are now firmly established, and are ready for any further development. Many may feel inclined to dispute my assertion that Americans are as apt manufacturers as ourselves; but, if they will remember that the first consequence of protection is to raise the cost of production, and that of free trade to lower it, and that, notwithstanding this, there are already many articles in the production of which the United States not only compete with us, but in which we are quite unable to compete with them, they will find it difficult to explain this fact on any other hypothesis.

It is interesting to examine the cause of this exceptional position of some articles, as it has a very direct bearing on the future of industry in the United States. It will be found that when a very large home demand for any article has existed in America, a demand as great as, or perhaps greater than, the whole of the home and export demand of any other country, the manufacture of that article has been in the end confined to America, the extra cost of production there being met by improvements in labour-saving machinery, &c., while the larger quantity turned out enables the manufacturer to accept a small profit. Let us take an example. Rifles and pistols are much more common in America than here, and there are probably five hundred Americans who own one or both of these weapons for one person who does so in this country. For this reason, American rifles and pistols are common enough in England, while English weapons are practically unknown in America. I am, of course, not speaking of the very finest weapons, but of those for which there is a popular demand. The same holds good of farming implements, tools of many sorts, clocks and watches, railway carriages, type-writers, sewing and many other labour-saving machines used in factories, &c., &c. It is, above all, in the manufacture of labour-saving machinery that Americans are pre-eminent, and, good manufacturers as we are, we cannot lay claim to equal inventiveness or equal mechanical skill of this kind.

The iron and steel industry is also, to some extent, a case in point, for—although, so far, there has been little or no export—the home demand for railway and other iron and steel is so enormous as compared with that of any other country, that prices have been reduced until they are perilously near those current in England; and any further reduction in the cost of production, such as may be expected from the promised revision of the tariff, is likely to bring the United States into our home and foreign markets as a competitor with us, for the first time, in one of the great staple industries.

This points not only to great manufacturing capacity, but to the immense advantage her large and increasing home market will give America over every other country. A home demand is always a much more important factor in industry than an export demand, as it is more steady and more to be depended on. I think, therefore, I am not wrong in saying that Americans are, at least, as good manufacturers as we are, and that men who have been able, notwithstanding the enhanced cost of production, whenever any exceptional circumstances were in their favour, not only practically to exclude us from their markets, but to compete with us in our own, will, in the future, when they meet us on equal terms, be able to do the same with many other and much more important products. For it must not be forgotten that while protection—and even the last and crowning phase of it, the McKinley Bill—has succeeded only partially in excluding us from the American markets, it has, with the few exceptions referred to, absolutely shut American manufacturers in, and prevented them competing with us, either in our home or in foreign markets. In his address to the London Chamber of Commerce, towards the close of last year, Sir John Lubbock showed very conclusively that America had damaged herself far more than she had hurt us by her protective policy, and especially by the McKinley Bill; but it is easy to go a great deal further, and to demonstrate that to American protection, more than to anything else, we owe our still undisputed commercial and industrial supremacy, and that it will depend on the policy adopted by this country whether we are in future to retain our fair share of it or are to lose it beyond all hope of recovery.

No one will dispute that protection raises the cost of production and that free trade lowers it, and it is to this alone that we owe our present immunity from American competition. If protection is now abolished in that country, the cost of production will be reduced, and American manufacturers will then start on equal terms with ourselves. But will the terms be equal? I am inclined to think not. Assuming, however, that American manufacturers are not better than our own, that their energy and activity have not been stimulated by the adverse conditions under which they have hitherto worked, that they are not more inventive and have not greater mechanical skill—even then it will be seen that they have every advantage we can claim, and many we can lay no claim to. They have plenty of good and most efficient labour, and can get as much more as they require; they have an abundance of iron and coal; in many places they have natural gas, available both for lighting and fuel; they are far ahead of us in the use of electricity; and they have unlimited water-power, which is likely to become a very important factor in the future of industry, in the production of electricity. But, besides all these, they have three special advantages which far surpass all the others—they have the home demand of a rapidly increasing population of already seventy millions; they produce nearly all the raw material for their manufacturers; and, above all, they produce all the food for their operatives. We are already dangerously dependent on our foreign trade, and must, to a large extent, import our raw material and food. Is it likely, then, that with all these advantages in their favour, and with a reduced cost of production, free trade is going to give us a larger share of the American markets than we have hitherto had? Those who think so know very little of the energy, the activity and the eagerness of Americans in business. On the other hand, is it not evident that free trade will exclude us from American markets much more effectually than protection has ever done? It will not stop there, however; for, if they can compete with us successfully in America, they can equally compete with us here in our home markets, in India, in China and the East, in our own Colonies (all the more successfully if the latter still adhere to their fatal policy of protection), and in Africa, when we have succeeded in colonizing that 'most distressful country.'

Take as an example one of the most important industries, the manufacture of cotton goods. This industry is already firmly established in America; and, with nothing to feed on but a demand practically limited to the home market, it has advanced with leaps and bounds, and is ready for any further developments. America grows the best cotton in the world and grows much more than all the rest of the world. At present we import the bulk of this cotton at a great cost, manufacture it, and, after deducting what we require for our own use, export the balance, much of it back again to America. We know that India, where trade is as free as it is here, now retains a large part of the cotton produced in that country; and, by manufacturing that cotton, which is much inferior to American in quality, has almost monopolized the trade for all the heavier and coarser cotton goods, not only in the Indian, but in all the Eastern and East African markets, leaving us to supply the demands for the finer goods made from American cotton, or from a mixture of the two. This has not really hurt us, for the prosperity which this and other large industries have produced in India has created such an increased demand for the finer goods that our exports are larger and relatively more valuable than they were. But if America now retains her cotton, and can manufacture it as cheaply as, or more cheaply than, we can—is there any reason to doubt that she will succeed, at least as well as India, hampered as that country always is by an excessive burden of taxation? And, if so, what will be the condition of Lancashire? Surely the moment is ill chosen for imposing restrictions and regulations which can in any way hamper the free action of our manufacturers—whether capitalists or operatives—when a struggle is before them, on the result of which their very existence may depend.

I may be told that the high wages in America will prevent all this coming to pass; but here again I believe that those who differ from me are mistaken; I do not believe that the real cost of labour is higher in America than here. The apparent excess in wages merely represents greater efficiency. But assume for the sake of argument that wages are higher, much higher, if you like, in America than here—does it follow that they will remain higher, or, what is the same, that wages here will remain lower? We are all aware that there has been now for many years a vast emigration of our people to the United States, some twelve millions having gone there in the last fifty years; and the same emigration has been going on from every country in Europe. Few of us, however, know that of this large emigration not much over one per cent. has been skilled labour. Our operatives have not gone to any great extent, and the reason is not very far to seek. They knew, some had probably learnt from experience, that employment in industries which are dependent on, and strictly limited to, the demand for the home markets, and which have no other outlet for their surplus, is apt to be less regular than employment for a market which commands both a home and an export trade; that, while they may receive higher wages so long as they are employed, they are much more liable to be thrown out of work than in a country which has the whole world for its customer; and that, therefore, at the end of a year, or a series of years, they are worse and not better off than they were at home. But if this new departure in America also attracts the whole world as her customer, the objection to emigration on the part of skilled labourers at once disappears; and in its place they will see the great advantages active, energetic men have in a new and rapidly developing country for the investment of their savings and the opportunity it affords them of raising themselves and their families to a much superior condition. It is the pressure of population to a very great extent which leads to emigration; and, so far, it has been the lowest class of unskilled labour which has emigrated, while the skilled labour has remained. The moment, however, that our operatives begin to see that America holds out inducements to them which the older country cannot offer, they will emigrate in increasing numbers; the pressure will be relieved, and the unskilled labour will remain to fill their places as best it can. There is one way, and, as far as I can see, only one way, in which we can hold them—we can give them higher wages, wages at least equal to those obtainable in America; and to do this we must be able to afford it. If we find it impossible to retain our skilled labour, other consequences will follow of immense importance to both countries. No one who has watched the emigration to the United States for many years past can doubt that it has been far from an unmixed benefit, and it may have been an unmixed evil, to that country to receive the continuous stream of emigration which has poured into it—the most miserable, the most ignorant, and the most discontented population from the poorest agricultural countries in Europe, almost unmixed with any better element. Its departure was a benefit to the country it left, but a danger to that which received it. If these conditions are now reversed—if the better class of labour leaves us, and the less competent remains, the emigration of a large part of our population every year may cease to be the blessing to this country it has hitherto been.

This is no wild, incoherent prophecy, dead though the Manchester school may be, and oblivious though we may have become of the most fundamental principles of political economy. Admit only that free trade will lower the cost of production, which protection has raised, and it will be evident to any one who will carefully consider the whole question, that every one of the changes foreshadowed must follow as a necessary consequence.

If it were not that we see so many indications that the country is deserting its old policy of freedom of trade and freedom of enterprise, we could look forward to the future with perfect equanimity. If our adoption of the principle of free trade has in the past led to most marvellous prosperity at home, which has reacted on every part of the world, and if so great an advance has been made by the action of a small country like England, what may we not expect from the same action in a country with the immense and varied resources of the United States, capable of supporting a population at least ten times as large as England? Even during our greatest prosperity we could not maintain the increased population which that prosperity produced, and, during all those years, millions emigrated to people America and other countries for whom we had no room at home. At least one half of our increase we had to send abroad to maintain our prosperity. Can we suppose that it will be no additional advantage to America and to us, no additional security to the permanence of worldwide prosperity, that, for far more years than we need look forward to, overpopulation there must be impossible; that every soul born in that country will be one more worker, one more customer for the trade of the civilized world, instead of being, as is so often the case here, a drag on the rest of the community which must be got rid of?

We should remember, however, that while America has so many advantages over us, we have at least one advantage over her, and that a very important one. We are in possession; and, before she can wrest our present industrial supremacy from us, she must dislodge us from the position we now occupy. It must be years, it may be many years, before she can stand on as strong an industrial footing as we now hold. Time is in our favour; and if we are wise we can so fortify our position as to render it wellnigh impregnable. Those of us who are convinced free-traders do not believe in or care for exclusive commercial supremacy; the very phrase is a contradiction in terms, for trade is in its nature not exclusive but reciprocal. Further, we believe that Nature, if her laws are not interfered with by artificial restrictions imposed by the ignorance or folly of mankind, will give supremacy in the future, as she has always done in the past, to that part of the world, and to that nation, which, for the time being, can use it most for the benefit of the whole human race. We believe also that the most efficient and economical distribution of industry is that which takes place under free trade; and that, if from any cause we lose any of our more important industries, others, perhaps now unthought of, will spring up to take their places. We believe that every country and every nation will under freedom be guided to its true path of development, and can retrograde and become extinct only through its ignorance, its folly, or an overweening and ill-founded belief in its own greatness.

When, however, we look at home we are filled with misgivings. While we see America embarking on a course which, judging from our own experience, must lead her on to fortune, we see England rapidly retracing her steps. The whole air is redolent of protection, which now comes to us under many new disguises, most of them strangely enough described as reforms. This new school of self-styled reformers (I do not know if they also profess to be economists) has many and most wonderful panaceas for the improvement of mankind, for there is scarcely a measure proposed by them that is not a restriction of individual freedom. And yet the great fight of the old school of reformers was for freedom, not alone of trade, but for the individual freedom of every man to use the powers given him for his own advancement, well knowing that no man could improve his position without at the same time adding to the well-being, not only of his own nation, but of all humanity. The fight against governmental extravagance and the demand for retrenchment were scarcely even an extension of this principle. It was believed then that every man was entitled to the fruits of his labours, and that Government had not the right to ask him to contribute from these more than was absolutely requisite for carrying on that government with the strictest economy. We have changed all that now. Sir John Gorst and Mr. Arnold Morley appear to belong to the same school of political economists (if they will excuse my applying so mean an epithet as economist to gentlemen with such liberal ideas)—for the one believes it does not matter how much a warship costs so long as the Government foots the bills, and the other considers that the market rate of wages is not the standard which ought to guide the Government or any other large employers of labour. Mr. Arnold Morley does not tell us what the new standard he has discovered is, but I presume it to be sentiment. I wonder if he ever remembers that there are many small employers of labour, who pay their wages out of their own pockets, and not out of the pockets of the taxpayers, who will be ruined by the introduction of his new standard, and that their ruin will entail ruin upon thousands of working men, every whit as deserving as his letter-carriers.

The occasion on which Mr. Arnold Morley delivered himself of this sentiment furnishes us with perhaps as good an example of the change which has come over us in recent years as can be found. A deputation of the unemployed, having nothing better to do, arranged to pass a part of their day with Mr. Arnold Morley. Instead of entering into their own woes, as he probably expected they would do, they read him a severe lecture on the duties of Government in general, and of the Postmaster-General in particular, towards those whom they employ. These gentlemen evidently belonged to the same school of political economists as Sir John Gorst and

Mr. Arnold Morley himself, for they shared their belief that the more money Government expends on wages, the more there will be for outside employers of labour to pay as wages to their workpeople, and the more with which to give employment to the unemployed themselves. If Mr. Arnold Morley will refer to the life of his most distinguished predecessor, the late Mr. Fawcett, he will find that, on a somewhat similar occasion, that gentleman laid down an exactly opposite rule; and Mr. Fawcett not only spoke with authority as a political economist, but he did more during his term of office, by affording the public greater facilities for the transmission of parcels, &c., to increase in a legitimate way the employment given to the working classes by the Post Office than any other Postmaster-General in our time.

Mr. Arthur Balfour tells us that the failure of Mr. Cobden's teaching is due to his having fought against the aristocratic and landed classes solely in the interest of the manufacturers. No doubt Mr. Cobden did oppose the landed classes, and the fight was a bitter one; but there was at least as much bitterness on the one side as on the other. It was that class which had imposed and maintained the disabilities under which all the other classes of the community suffered; and it was for the repeal of these disabilities, in the interest of all classes, that Cobden fought, and fought successfully. What is there in Mr. Cobden's life to show that he would not have fought as stoutly against the restriction of labour as he did against the restriction of trade; and that in doing so he would not have believed he was acting in the best interests of the working classes themselves? To the last hour of his life Mr. Bright remained unconvinced as to the advantage of factory legislation; and it suits those who are opposed to his views on that subject to point to this as a proof of the selfishness of the policy in furtherance of which he spent his life. But Mr. Bright's conduct in this, as in all else, was perfectly honest and consistent. He believed, not in helping or protecting people, but in teaching them to help and protect themselves. It is true he was a manufacturer; but, as such, he probably knew more of the working classes than most of those opposed to him, and he knew that the conditions which gave rise to the cry for this special legislation would, if things had been left to work themselves out, have taken another form, and these people would have protected themselves, as responsible human beings ought to do, and can do, more effectually than any government can ever hope to do for them. In the last fifty years two men stand out conspicuously as the champions of the working classes, two men of blameless life and noble character, who spent their lives in the service of their fellow-men—Lord Shaftesbury and Mr. Bright. The one, a great nobleman, taught that it was the duty of the upper classes and of the Government to protect those whom he believed to be weak and incapable of helping themselves. I yield to no one in my admiration of the single-heartedness with which Lord Shaftesbury devoted a long life to the cause which he had at heart; but I am convinced that his action has been disastrous, and to none so much as the working classes, by teaching them to look for help elsewhere than to themselves. Mr. Bright, on the other hand, was a man of the people, who knew them well, and believed in them. He spent his life trying to awaken the working classes to a sense of their rights and responsibilities; and, having done that, he had no misgivings as to their being able to protect themselves. Mr. Bright's teaching has been, I believe, all for good; but then I belong to the extinct Manchester school.

Perhaps the best exposition of the policy of the new Liberal party is that presented to us by Mr. Chamberlain in his article in the *Nineteenth Century* of last November. Mr. Chamberlain says a few half-complimentary words over the grave of the Manchester school. It was useful in its day, he thinks, but its day is passed; and he then proceeds to introduce to his audience our old enemy protection in a number of new disguises, under the name of 'Constructive Legislation.' He enumerates some, possibly all the measures which he thinks may be advantageously passed for the amelioration of the condition of the working classes. There are two characteristics common to all these measures; they all require a great deal of money and the interference of

Government. Neither Mr. Chamberlain nor any of those who agree with him have ever been able to tell us where all this money is to come from, nor, I fear, will they succeed in doing so until they have solved the greatest economic problem of all time—how you can both eat your loaf and have it. The pockets of the capitalists and manufacturers have, it is true, been suggested; but Mr. Chamberlain knows full well that they never have much money in their pockets, and have none at all when they are most prosperous. They can then employ it to better purpose. It cannot be taken from the wealth realized by past production, for three reasons—the first, because that wealth has been largely re-employed in industry; the second, perhaps a childish reason, because it would be misappropriation; the third, because, as the fund would soon be exhausted, it could not provide a permanent provision for the objects in view. It must, therefore, be taken from the current industry. It must come from the manufacturers' profits, where they still exist. Even admitting that all manufacturers are still making a profit, it is not a very large one; and it is clear that the profits in every industry must vary according to the special advantages possessed by some manufacturers as compared with others. The larger and wealthier among them can, as a rule, make money when those less favoured can barely make both ends meet. It is evident, therefore, that any readjustment of the division of profits between employers and employed, or any provision made out of profits for the latter based on what the larger and wealthier manufacturers can afford, must tend to the extinction of the smaller men, and that with their extinction a large number of operatives will be thrown out of work. These will, I presume, join the ranks of the unemployed, for, according to Mr. Burns, Government is to find *reproductive* work at a full rate of wages in our dockyards and arsenals. It seems to escape our new reformers that in process of time all the population which has not already left the country will be occupied in the manufacture of war material; for it is evident that the wages paid to every man engaged in the building of warships and guns, which, Mr. Burns notwithstanding, is not reproductive work, means the withdrawal from really reproductive industry not of one man but of many men. If we know anything, we surely know by this time that money raised by taxation, and expended by Government, does not go nearly so far and is not applied to as good purpose as the same sum expended in private enterprise. Moreover, these ships and guns once made must be manned; and the evil does not stop there, for then we must get up a little war just to see how well, or how badly, they work. There is one sense, however, in which these works are reproductive. When finished, they are so imperfect, that the supposed necessity for them requires us to produce others to take their place; and in these we reproduce the same or as great defects. The difference between building a war vessel and a merchant vessel is, that every man engaged either in the construction or the maintenance of the former is a drain on the resources of the country; while every man engaged on the latter is contributing to find employment for many others at home and abroad, and is thus, not only occupied in work which will in time reproduce itself out of the profits it makes, but is adding to the wealth and prosperity of the nation at large. Our new reformers seem to take a totally different view of the situation from President Cleveland; and consider that, while it is the duty of the Government patriotically and cheerfully to support the people, it is in no wise one of their functions to support the Government, or, in other words, themselves. Those manufacturers who are left after the extinction of their smaller and less wealthy competitors will, for a time at least, do an excellent business, even after they have deducted from their profits their share of what is required for the support of the unemployed. It is wonderful how clearly we see the mote which is in our brother's eye, for I should be afraid to say how many English homilies I have read in the last ten years, addressed to the benighted American people, proving most conclusively that the protection of industry must create huge monopolies which oppress the people, and especially the working classes. We fail to recognize the fact that the protection of labour must accomplish the same result even more surely. It is the same with every measure proposed, if we follow it to its logical conclusion; it is the working classes who must, as Sir William Harcourt says, pay the piper; and this is, perhaps, only fair, for it is they who call the tune.

These would-be reformers are entirely sceptical as to the capacity for progress possessed by a really free society, and they map out the future course of progress by means of their own foot rule. A reference to the many proposals for the provision of old age pensions from the rates will explain my meaning. It is clear that the rate of pension must bear some proportion to the rate of wages current at the time the measure is proposed, the more so if the prospective pensioner is to contribute towards the amount required. To-day we fix the pension at five shillings a week, and in forty-five years a working man now aged twenty will come into the enjoyment of that income. Supposing, however, a similar measure had been passed forty-five years ago, half-a-crown a week, or less, would probably have borne about the same proportion to the rate of wages then current as five shillings does to-day. In the meantime, we have taken away from the young man, during the best years of his life, the greatest incentive to thrift—the necessity of making provision for old age—and we have misled him into relying on a pension at sixty-five, which, when that time arrives, proves to be no provision at all. What reason is there for thinking that the rate of wages will now stand still, and that forty-five years hence five shillings will satisfy the legitimate ambition of a working man any more than half a crown does to-day?

I have often wondered what an American working man would say if any one suggested he might have a pension of five shillings a week when he was sixty-five. I should not advise any one to make the proposal to him, except at a very safe distance.

'God knows,' said Mr. Gladstone, in his interview with the coal-miners, 'that eight hours is long enough for any man to work underground.' Mr. Gladstone generally weighs his words very carefully, and, in speaking thus, he must have done so either to add impressiveness and solemnity to what he was saying or because he considered it incapable of contradiction. It is evident, however, that God cannot have come to two absolutely contradictory conclusions; and I would ask if God does not also know that there is far more suffering of the cruellest kind among the poor from cold than there is among the colliers from overwork, and whether legislation which could in any way add to that suffering would not be wellnigh criminal? We know from experience that, where a policy of free trade prevails, the tendency is always to the maximum of production consistent with a reasonable profit to be divided between employers and their workpeople. A maximum of production must necessarily lead to a maximum of employment and a maximum purchasing power for the wages earned. The regulation of industry must as certainly lead to its restriction, to a decreasing amount of employment available for the working classes, and to a lower scale of real as opposed to nominal wages. The former policy leads to a state of great national prosperity and an increasing demand for all the necessaries and luxuries of life; the latter to continual contraction of production and the misery to which it must give rise.

England and America can be very useful to each other, and in no way more so than by teaching each other what to avoid. The whole history of American protection provides us with an object lesson which we cannot study too carefully. At first it was a tax for revenue and, as such, possibly accomplished its object as well as any other form of taxation; then it was to establish their industries, and this it may have helped to do; but it was found that this system had no inherent strength. The older these industries grew the greater was their need of protection. Tariff was piled on tariff, and still the believers in protection cried Give! give! and at last the climax of absurdity was reached when the McKinley Bill was passed. Protection is unsound in theory, but it is far more unsound in practice. It is not equal protection which is wanted; but each section of industry intrigues to be specially protected at the expense of every other section. Wealth and poverty being merely relative terms, a good protectionist has no desire to advance only with the rest of the population, and calls on his fetish to pass him on a little ahead of the others. It generally happens, however, that there is some class which cannot be protected, and the larger and more simple this class, the longer will it be able and willing to support all the rest of the community. In the United States this was the agricultural class, and on it fell the entire burden of taxation. Naturally its powers of endurance were limited; but the crash was averted for long by loans made to the farmers on mortgages of their properties by the other sections of the community which they supported, and, unfortunately, to a large extent by investors in this country. The financial crisis through which America is now passing is purely agricultural, and neither commercial nor industrial, as seems generally to be supposed. Of the bank failures which have taken place, 85 per cent. have occurred in the Western States, 10 per cent. in the South, and only 5 per cent. in the Eastern States, which alone can lay claim to any industry not immediately connected with agriculture, excepting, of course, mining, through which, however, banks could not become directly involved. And the end of the crisis is not yet, for the mortgages on agricultural lands are held principally by the savings banks, which have the right to require six months' notice of withdrawal from their depositors, and this, it has generally been supposed, would give sufficient time to enable them to foreclose, should that be necessary. In every announcement of the failure of a bank it has been stated that the assets were amply sufficient to cover the liabilities; and no doubt they are, if the same level of value at which these mortgage loans were made can be maintained. This, however, remains to be seen, and must depend on the proportion of mortgages they hold, as compared with other securities. It is evident that anything like general foreclosure is impossible.

With this picture before our eyes, it is wonderful that we should rush so madly after the chimaera protection. Like the Americans, we think we have discovered the class which can support all the others; and this class we fondly believe is the capitalist. Unfortunately capitalists, unlike the American farmer, are neither very simple nor very enduring; and we may find that they, or at least their capital, have taken wings for other countries where they will be less interfered with. In the end, we shall find that the burden must be borne by the whole nation, and that the working classes, who form by far the larger part of it, must suffer the most severely. We cannot fight against natural laws; and, in the end, we must awaken to a sense of our madness; but my fear is that, in the interim, we may lose our present strong commercial and industrial position beyond all hope of recovery. In his speech of June 10, on one of the Home Rule amendments, Mr. Chamberlain, speaking as the representative of the working classes, pointed out that, if less costly and less restrictive State regulation of industry is adopted in Ireland than is in force in Great Britain, Irish manufacturers will be able to work on such favourable terms, as compared with their English competitors, that an agitation will at once be set on foot to repeal these regulations. Now, except one comparatively small part of it, Ireland has never been, and never can be, under ordinary circumstances, a great manufacturing nation, yet if, notwithstanding this, Mr. Chamberlain believes that Irish competition is a real danger, does he see no danger threatening us from the enormous resources and natural advantages of America, a country which has no State regulation or restriction of her industries at all? How does Mr. Chamberlain propose to meet this difficulty? Or does he believe that America is a less dangerous industrial competitor than Ireland?

We may be told that America also has her labour troubles, and that the working classes there will also insist on having State regulation. The first part of this statement is true, no doubt; but it must be borne in mind that American labour troubles have been different from ours. The labour agitations there have generally been directed against great artificial monopolies, which were either directly protected or the outcome of protection. When Labour found its partner, Capital, pillaging the agricultural classes, it is not to be wondered that Labour should have tried to insist on having her fair share of the plunder. So far, the labour agitations in America have been directed against protected monopolies; although many of those who took part in them may not have recognized the fact. I am convinced that the American working man will never tolerate any attempt on the part of the State to interfere with his right to do what he likes with his labour. He will continue to work how and when and for as many hours as he likes. He looks forward to something a good deal more substantial than a pension of five shillings a week, and he is not going to allow the State to interfere with the attainment of the object which he has in view.

In a recent speech delivered in Hyde Park, Mr. John Burns spoke of Labour as crucified between two thieves, Capital and Machinery. Now America, with its vast resources requiring development, and a relatively small population, ought to be an ideal country for the new trades unionism. Clearly if ever there was a country in which labour should be able to fix its own wages it is America; and yet here is to be found a production out of all proportion to the population, when compared with that of any other country, and yet wages are not much higher than they are in this country. Making use of Mr. Burns' somewhat question-begging illustration, we may find an explanation which is simple enough. Capital is not so dependent on labour as he had supposed; and, when driven to it, perhaps without being driven to it, it can reduce its wages bill by the introduction of labour-saving machinery. Hence the crucifixion of which Mr. Burns complains, and from which he will find that the working man has only two means of escape; he may subside into a state of pauperism and dependence, or, becoming self-reliant, he may accept Capital and Machinery as his partners and become as independent as either of them.

If Mr. Burns and his colleagues will only consider the question calmly and dispassionately, and take a somewhat wider view of the whole matter than they are wont to do, they will find that, so far from legislation being able to do anything for the improvement of the condition of the working classes, exactly the reverse is the case. Much of the money received by Government is, and always will be, wasted, while the balance is expended so extravagantly that it does not go nearly as far as it would in the hands of private individuals, and, consequently, cannot afford as much employment for the working classes. We cannot impress upon ourselves too often, or too strongly, that every farthing raised by taxation is taken from some industry where it is directly affording employment to labour of a useful and profitable nature.

Apart from this, moreover, we shall find that under no circumstances can a country hope to wall itself in, and become independent of the rest of the world, by protective or restrictive legislation. America has tried and failed; and yet America was more independent of foreign supply and foreign demand than any other country on the face of the globe. Such a policy may for a time give an appearance of great prosperity, which is, however, purely fictitious, and at last ends in disaster. England, however, is in a very different position. We have long passed that stage of our development in which we could rely on our own resources and be independent of other countries. On them we depend, to an almost unexampled extent, for our supplies of raw material, for our food, for the sale of our products, even for the absorption of our surplus population. If the labour party will only recognize this surely very patent fact, they will see that we may pass all the Acts we like; we can make our Government departments model employers of labour, and thus raise the rate of wages against other employers; we can limit the hours of labour, give every man an insurance against old age and accident, establish councils of arbitration with compulsory powers to give effect to their decrees—but all this legislation must be in vain if the United States adopt a free trade policy and their working men determine that each man shall retain the power to dispose of his labour as he sees fit.

In the case of labour, whatever it be with regard to other things, it is not the worst or the least favourably situated which determines the value, but that which is most efficient and enjoys the greatest advantages. If this were not so, we should not have seen wages advancing as they have done during the last fifty years; nor should we have been able to maintain our industrial supremacy in face of the competition of other countries where wages are much lower, and whose industrial progress has been relatively greater than our own. Clearly it is the country which possesses the greatest natural advantages which must determine the margin of profit for which it will work; and, fortunately, there is always a tendency to raise the standard of subsistence, which not only leaves a sufficient margin for other less favoured countries, but by creating an increased demand, not merely for the necessities, but also for the comforts and luxuries of life, leads to a great extension of industry all over the world, and to the general well-being of the human race.

If labour is well advised it will leave its cause to the action of natural laws instead of trusting to human legislation, which must in the end prove a broken reed. The worst feature about all forms of protection is that it always requires further protection to support it; and, unless we are warned in time, we shall find that labour is making greater demands on industry than can be satisfied, and that other nations are beginning to monopolize our trade. Each decadent trade will then demand protection against its foreign rivals, and we shall see a huge edifice of protection raised in our midst, which must in the end, from the want of any sound foundation, crumble to pieces and destroy those who built it up. It is surely evident that, if America has greater natural industrial advantages than we possess, from the day she appears in our foreign and colonial markets as our competitor (which her system of protection has till now practically prevented her becoming), the working men of America will fix the rates of wages and the hours of labour for us, as well as for themselves, in defiance of all the laws we may pass with a view to controlling them.

But, while working men can do nothing by protective legislation to improve their condition, there is one way in which they can do much. They can protest against national extravagance, instead of demanding it; and they can insist on retrenchment. Our public expenditure is now close upon £100,000,000 a year; and if Government goes on as it has been doing for years past, acceding to every fresh demand made upon the treasury by every section of the community, this amount will soon be largely exceeded. It is in consequence of this enormous unproductive expenditure, more than anything else, and perhaps also not a little to the private extravagance to which, as is always the case, it sets the example, that our industries are depressed and our workpeople to a large extent without employment. If the labour leaders will make use of the power now vested in their hands, and will insist on the most thorough-going retrenchment in every department of Government, they will find abundant scope for their energies, and will do more to ensure the prosperity, not only of the classes they directly represent, but of the nation at large, than any other leaders of the people since the days of Mr. Cobden and Mr. Bright. They need not fear that they will be spoiled by overpopularity, for the economist is never a popular character. Nor need they fear that the task will prove unworthy of their strength, for the great spending departments of Government are as strong as, or stronger than, they ever were; and where Mr. Cobden and Mr. Bright failed, or succeeded only for a time, they will do wisely not to overrate their strength. But if the task is no lighter than it was, the necessity for some one undertaking it becomes greater every day.

We build great navies and maintain large armies, and we are told that the main object of these is to protect our trade from the possible attacks of other nations. Have we no reason to fear an attack far more dangerous from the United States, which will be carried on by industrial armies and merchant fleets, and which, if we continue in our present course, will find us weakened and unable to resist? We have recently been having an arbitration in Paris with the United States. Some of the incidents in the dispute are worth attention. We had one of our numerous fleets lying in British Columbia, and the United States, practically without a navy at all, sent a revenue cutter—a mere naval police-boat—and arrested every British ship she found sealing in Behring Sea. The Commission has decided that this was little else than an act of piracy, and yet we neither bombarded New York nor San Francisco nor annexed Alaska nor marched an army to Boston, simply because we knew that America never interferes except in what is, or what at least she believes to be, her own business; and, although in this instance she may have been technically wrong in the action she took, the regulations now laid down by the Commission for the future conduct of sealers show that she was to some extent justified. We hear a great deal about our prestige, and spend millions to maintain it. Surely a nation which can boast that she can maintain her prestige with a single revenue cutter is in a most enviable position. Clearly dignity and moral strength are not the prerogatives only of nations armed to the teeth with engines of destructive warfare. True, America now seems anxious to follow the burdensome European fashion, and acquire a navy; but even in this she is different from European nations. The real origin of her navy was the necessity of finding an outlet for her overflowing treasury, and now that that has been somewhat depleted, wiser counsels are likely to prevail.

Unfortunately there are 'jingoes' in America as everywhere else, who wish to have the pleasure of paying for an army and navy, and to annex every conceivable continent and island under the sun; but they receive very little support from the bulk of the nation. Only the other day the American residents in the Hawaiian Islands deposed the native government, and practically annexed the islands to the United States; but the Federal Government absolutely declined to confirm their action. Yet Hawaii is much more closely connected with the United States than many islands and other parts of the world which we have annexed were with England. By a commercial treaty existing between the two countries each had agreed to admit the products of the other duty-free, and the sugar industry of the Pacific States, the largest foreign industry they possess, was dependent on Hawaii; but America has not yet discovered that apparent expediency gives her any right to commit an injustice, and it is to be hoped that for her own sake, as well as for that of other nations, she may never make this discovery. The best reason for America not having a large and costly navy is that she does not require one, and, such being the case, she could not man it, for her people are too profitably employed at home to spend their time sailing the seas in search of quarrels.

We, on the other hand, are so entangled in the meshes of European and Eastern politics that all parties in the State seem agreed on the necessity of submitting to the grievous burden of our military and naval armaments. Great wars are happily so rare that we are entirely in the dark as to the value of the huge and costly experiments which we are making in naval construction. We do not know whether in time of war our ships can be successfully manœuvred, whether they will prove seaworthy and shot-proof, and we are not without apprehension that they may turn out to be as great a danger to each other as to an enemy. We maintain an army at an enormous expense, and yet it is admittedly insufficient, without the aid of very untrustworthy alliances, to meet the demands which may be made on us. We attempt to conciliate one nation in the hope of securing it as an ally, and by doing so we arouse the suspicion and jealousy of some other nation, and so almost precipitate the catastrophe we seek to avoid. Is not the position of America, I repeat, in many ways enviable? Is it impossible for Europe to learn a lesson from her example?

Our Colonies, unhappily, have committed many errors; but they have none of them been drawn into the stupendous folly of wishing to entangle themselves in our complicated European politics. Ambitious and sentimental schemes of Imperial Federation have dwindled down to a mere proposal for protection, a Zollverein, which is to open colonial markets to our manufacturers and home markets to colonial products, to the exclusion of other countries. The proposal is too ridiculous to bear much discussion. How, for instance, would it suit Canada to be shut off from trading with the seventy millions of the United States, her nearest and best customers, in exchange for the very trifling advantage to be gained from trading with Australia and her small and probably decreasing population of three millions? Or is it likely that Australia will care to involve herself in war with the United States for the sake of a few sealskins coveted by British Columbia? If our Colonies have done nothing else by incurring the enormous load of debt which now weighs them down, they have at least discovered a new protection against annexation. The Colonies have now neither men nor money to spare; so they are not likely to prove valuable either as markets or recruiting grounds for many long years; and until they follow the example of America, and, paying off their debts, determine to contract no more, they will find that the surplus population of this and other countries will prefer the United States as a field of emigration.

These, I am well aware, are unpopular sentiments; but in the changes which must follow on the adoption of free trade by America, England will be brought face to face with a great dilemma. We have an enormous population absolutely dependent on our foreign trade. If we wish to retain our share of that trade and to save our labouring population from the suffering involved in a long, continuous, and ever-increasing depression of trade, we must insist on some relaxation of the burden of taxation. We have staggered along till now because America has handicapped itself with protection and because we have only been opposed by European States as heavily burdened as ourselves. In the future we are to face a young and vigorous competitor, which is laying aside the errors of protection and preparing to run its industrial course without encumbrances. The question is not, Are these sentiments popular? but, Is the danger real? England has a proud roll of achievement in the service of humanity. No greater addition could be added to her fame than that it should be given to her to take the initiative in the disarmament of Europe.

There is another way in which more economical public administration and greater freedom of enterprise would materially assist industry. Of late years vast sums of money have been sent abroad to Argentina, to Australia, to Africa, and to every part of the globe. A very large part of this might just as well have been thrown into the sea; it is hopelessly and irretrievably lost. This money would have been much safer at home; and, if our industry were not hampered with heavy taxation, obstructive regulations and with fear of what is known as the 'labour trouble,' it would remain at home, and give employment to labour in the extension of industry.

One might write much without exhausting the lessons to be learnt from America; but these I have mentioned must suffice. No one reading Mr. Cleveland's inaugural address inculcating thrift and self-reliance on his countrymen, and warning them against overconfidence in the future because of their achievement in the past, and then turning to the somewhat boastful harangue of Sir William Harcourt, can doubt where the real strength and wisdom lie. Both of these men presumably represent a majority of their countrymen and of public opinion. The one represents a country where development has little more than begun, and whose prospective wealth is greater than has ever been dreamed of for any nation in the history of the world—a country not only practically without a debt, but which has just, by an unparalleled effort, repaid an enormous debt, so repugnant to it was the very idea of indebtedness—a country without an army because it fears no other nation, with no liabilities beyond her own frontiers, and no complicated foreign relations such as in European States may at any moment give rise to a struggle for existence: and to this country her President preaches public thrift and frugality, and deprecates overconfidence in her own powers. Sir William Harcourt, on the other hand, sees great and increasing depression in all the most important industries of this country; but he bids us be of good cheer, as there is no occasion for apprehension or disquiet. A mighty trade is going on, wealth is being rolled up, capital is accumulating; and the two industries to which he refers are the medical and legal professions, which, according to him, produce wealth faster than either cotton or coal.

These comforting assurances do not reassure. Turning

from Sir William Harcourt's easy, confiding optimism, we see on every side leaders of party renouncing the duty of leadership, ostentatiously abandoning every principle of economy in a headlong race to catch the votes of the most ignorant class of the electorate—a class which, to do it justice, is amenable to reason and appreciative of courage, if those who profess to be our leaders had the boldness to speak out. We see that freedom of enterprise which is the foundation of England's greatness, and the support of her vast population, threatened on all sides by the unreproved clamour of ignorant empirics. We feel ourselves burdened by a large imperial debt of which we have repaid only a fraction and by a local indebtedness which increases by leaps and bounds, while during the last twenty years we have spent on our armaments nearly enough to have paid off the national debt. We have got rid, it is true, of an oppressive protective tariff, but we are fettering our industry by debt, by taxation, by strikes, and by innumerable vexatious and costly regulations. Meanwhile, we see a great nation of our own kith and kin about to adopt that principle which has been the secret of our success, and which we in our folly are now throwing away. We cannot, under these conditions, look forward without apprehension to the inevitable and rapid transference of the centre of trade to the other side of the Atlantic. It means to our poorer classes long and dark years of suffering, till our population can transport itself to freer fields of industry or becomes reduced by decimation to the needs of an industry shrunk to the narrowest dimensions.

If, by reason of the very obviousness of the danger, we are warned in time, not we alone, but all Europe, will have to thank America. That country, fearing no other, and at peace with all, will begin to monopolize the trade of the world. The nations of Europe will then, when they find their resources dwindling away, discover, perhaps when it is too late, that they have devoted too large a proportion of their wealth and the flower of their manhood to preparations for wars which rarely come, and would never come at all without these preparations. Then, when they will find themselves sinking beneath the burden which they have allowed their rulers to impose upon them, despite the opposition of officialism and of the classes interested in keeping up this extravagant expenditure, they will insist on following the wiser and better example set them on the other side of the Atlantic.

WILLIAM MAITLAND.

III.

NATIONAL WORKSHOPS.

ST. LOE STRACHEY.

III.

NATIONAL WORKSHOPS.

I.

'WE are tired of abstractions. Let us come to realities.'—That is the cry of the modern Socialists when they are confronted with the disquisitions of the older school of Economists. So be it. Let us try and test Socialism and its theories, not by counter theories but by facts. The Socialists have a great many doctrines and counsels of perfection, but their essential principle of practice is contained in the formula which declares that society will only be successfully and happily organized when the sources of wealth and the machinery of production are in the hands of the State—when, that is, the machinery of production is either nationalized or municipalized, and when the community, not the individual in competition, undertakes the production of all the things which man needs, from his clothes to his daily newspaper. When we are confronted with this theory, with the declaration that it ought to be put in practice, and with the demand that it shall be combatted, if it is combatted, with facts, not abstractions, the first thing we must ask is, What does the experience of the past teach on the subject?—has the plan of making the community the producer and the manufacturer the owner of the machinery of industry and production ever been tried before? The answer is Yes. It has been tried, and was a failure. When did that trial take place? In Paris in 1848, when, under the supervision of the Provisional Government, which accepted the doctrines of modern Socialism, a serious and practical attempt was made to inaugurate the era of State employment and State production. The history of the national workshops of 1848 is, then, whatever its teachings, of the utmost importance to those who are anxious to consider, fairly and reasonably, as I trust I am, the proposals of the Socialists of to-day. If the proposals of the Fabians would solve the social problem, abolish poverty and misery, and build a new heaven and a new earth, I, like every one else I ever heard of, would be a Socialist, and would adopt the doctrine of the nationalization of the sources of production. 'God hates the poor, and justly punishes them for their wickedness,' is not a doctrine that has ever been seriously held, though it is, I am aware, often represented as the Anti-Socialist's gospel. The question is, Would the realization of Socialism mend matters, or would it not rather make them worse? That is the problem which I propose to consider in the light of the experience of the national workshops of 1848.

II.

Perhaps it will be said that the Parisian experiment of forty-five years ago is no guide, because the men who set up the *Ateliers Nationaux* did not really adopt the Collectivist theory, or because, even if they did, they did not apply it properly, i.e. give the scheme a fair trial. Therefore, it will be urged, the doings of 1848 throw no light on the subject. I accept the challenge. If the precedent is to apply, the intention must have been genuinely Socialistic, and the experiment must have been made consciously and deliberately, and not merely haphazard. Before, then, beginning to read a lesson from the national workshops, it is necessary to show (1) the Socialistic intent of the founders of the *Ateliers Nationaux*, (2) the fact that they did their best to make the workshops a success. The readiest way of establishing the truth of the first of these propositions is to quote verbatim the Decree of the Provisional Government, in which they laid down the principles that guided them in their dealings with the social problem. Here is the Decree:—

PARIS,
February 28, 1848.

IN THE NAME OF THE FRENCH PEOPLE.

Seeing that the revolution made by the people should be also for the people;

That it is time to put an end to the long and iniquitous sufferings of the workers;

That the question of work is of supreme importance;

That there is no question greater or more worthy of the consideration of a republican government;

That it specially behoves France to carefully study and to solve a problem at this moment before every industrial nation in Europe;

That means must at once be devised to guarantee to the people the legitimate fruits of their toil;—

The Provisional Government of the Republic decrees:

That a permanent Committee, to be called *Government Committee for Workers*, shall be nominated, with the express and special object of watching over the workers. To show what importance the Provisional Government of the Republic attaches to the solution of this difficult problem M. Louis Blanc, one of its members, will be nominated President of the *Government Committee for Workers*, and another of its members will be chosen as Vice-President— M. Albert, workman. Workmen will be called on to sit upon the Committee.

The meetings of the Committee will take place in the Palais du Luxembourg.

THE MEMBERS OF THE PROVISIONAL GOVERNMENT.

III.

No doubt some of the men who signed this document only half believed that the experiment would be successful, and after its failure declared that they knew all along that it was hopeless. No one, however, who reads the records of the Revolution of 1848, and notes how greatly charged the air was with Socialism, can doubt that the Government as a whole were genuinely determined to give the Socialistic principle a fair trial, and that many of them, and especially those charged with the conduct of the workshops, at whose head was Louis Blanc, a convinced Socialist, entertained the highest hopes of success. Even Lamartine, who in 1844 wrote that the best governments were those that did not interfere with liberty of action in industrial affairs, signed the Decree, and for the time plunged deep into Collectivism. That the experiment was fairly made, and that there was no determination, conscious or unconscious, to show that the national workshops were a piece of Utopia, is clear from the account of the undertaking written by M. Émile Thomas, their director and president, and published only a month or two after the collapse. M. Émile Thomas was a practical man of business, who was entrusted with the superintendence of the work by the Government. Though not a Socialist by conviction, it is clear that he did everything in his power to 'run' the workshops successfully, and that if any one could have organized them into efficiency it was he. That, at any rate, is the impression which I believe will be produced upon any one who reads the *Histoire des Ateliers Nationaux considérés sous le double point de vue politique et social; des causes de leur formation et de leur existence; et de l'influence qu'ils ont exercée sur les événements des quatres premiers mois de la Republique suivi des pièces justificatives. Par Émile Thomas. Paris: Michel Levy Frères*, 1848. The proof that Thomas did his best for the workshops is to be found in the fact that Louis Blanc, armed with virtually absolute powers, superintended the undertaking, and could, if he had thought the work was being mismanaged, have dismissed Thomas. Perhaps, however, the best way of showing the bona fide character of the experiment is to describe the actual organization of the workshops and to note what they accomplished. In doing so I shall adopt, with some slight alterations, dictated by the desire to economize space, the account given by Mr. Nassau Senior in an essay in the *Edinburgh Review*, since republished by his daughter, Mrs. Simpson ('Journals kept in France and Italy:' H. S. King and Co., 1871). It must be remembered that Senior visited Paris directly after the Revolution, that he was on terms of intimacy with many of the men who were responsible for the *Ateliers Nationaux*, and that he had talked with those who had seen the workshops in full swing. In a word, he is a firsthand authority on a subject in which he took a profound interest. The actual details of his account are drawn directly from Thomas's book, which is primarily a reprint of the official documents.

IV.

Before, however, summarizing Senior's account of the workshops I will give the Decrees formulating the *droit au travail* and establishing the *Ateliers Nationaux*.

Here is the Decree which stated the right to work, or more scientifically—the right to wages (*le droit au salaire*):—

PARIS,
February 25, 1848.

THE FRENCH REPUBLIC.

The Provisional Government of the French Republic binds itself to guarantee the existence of the workman by means of work;

It binds itself to guarantee work to every citizen;

It recognizes the right of the workmen to unite, to enjoy the fruits of their toil.

The Provisional Government gives back the million which will fall in from the civil list to the workmen to whom it belongs.

THE MEMBERS OF THE PROVISIONAL GOVERNMENT.

Here is the Decree under which the *Ateliers Nationaux* were actually established:—

PARIS,
February 26, 1848.

IN THE NAME OF THE FRENCH PEOPLE.

The Provisional Government of the Republic decrees the immediate establishment of national workshops. The minister of public works is charged with the execution of the present Decree.

THE MEMBERS OF THE PROVISIONAL GOVERNMENT.

V.

The effect of this Decree was the immediate opening of national workshops. Their organization was as follows. I adopt Senior's abstract of Thomas's account.

A person who wished to take advantage of the offers of the Government took from the person with whom he lodged a certificate that he was an inhabitant of the Département de la Seine. This certificate he carried to the *mairie* of his *arrondissement*, and obtained an order of admission to an *atelier*. If he was received and employed there, he obtained an order on his *mairie* for forty sous. If he was not received, after having applied at all of them, and found them all full, he received an order for thirty sous. Thirty sous is not high pay; but it was to be had for doing nothing, and hopes of advancement were held out. Every body of eleven persons formed an *escouade*; and their head, the *escouadier*, elected by his companions, got half a franc a day extra. Five *escouades* formed a brigade; and the brigadier, also elected by his subordinates, received three francs a day. Above these again were the lieutenants, the *chefs de compagnie*, the *chefs de service*, and the *chefs d'arrondissement*, appointed by the Government, and receiving progressively higher salaries. Besides this, bread was distributed to their families in proportion to the number of children. 'The hours supposed to be employed in labour were,' adds Senior, 'nine and a half. We say supposed to be employed, because all eleemosynary employment, all relief work, all parish work, to use expressions which have become classical in Ireland and England, is in fact nominal.' M. Émile Thomas tells us that in one *mairie*, that containing the Faubourg St. Antoine, a mere supplemental bureau enrolled, from March 12 to March 20, more than 1,000 new applicants every day. On May 19, 87,942 had altogether been enrolled, and a month later, 125,000—representing, at four to a family, 600,000 persons—more than one half of the population of Paris.

VI.

Such are the facts of the organization. I have no desire to moralize as to the abstract futility of these arrangements. I merely desire to call attention to the actual results of M. Louis Blanc's experiment, under the nineteenth and thirtieth Decrees. The first witness I will call is the Correspondent of the *Economist* newspaper, who was in Paris in 1848, and saw with his own eyes what he describes:—

The greatest experiment made by Louis Blanc was the organization of tailors in the Hôtel Clichy, which, for the purpose, was converted from a debtors' gaol into a great national tailors' shop. This experiment began with peculiar advantages. The Government made the buildings suitable for the purpose without rent or charge; furnished the capital, without interest, necessary to put it into immediate and full operation; and gave an order, to commence with, for *twenty-five thousand suits* for the National Guard, to be followed by more for the Garde Mobile, and then for the regular troops. The first step taken was to ascertain at what cost for workmanship the large tailors of Paris, who ordinarily employed the bulk of the workmen, and performed Government contracts, would undertake the orders. Eleven francs for each dress was the contract price, including the profit of the master tailor, the remuneration for his workshop and tools, and for the interest of his capital. The Government agreed to give the organized tailors at the Hôtel Clichy the same price. Fifteen hundred men were quickly got together, with an establishment of foremen, clerks, and cutters-out. It was agreed that inasmuch as the establishment possessed no capital to pay the workmen while the order was in course of completion, the Government should advance every day, in anticipation of the ultimate payment, a sum equal to *two francs* (1s. 7d.) for each man in the establishment, as 'subsistence money'; that when the contract was completed, the balance should be paid, and equally divided amongst the men. Such fair promises soon attracted a full shop; and when we visited the Hôtel Clichy, upwards of fifteen hundred men were at work, and apparently were not only steady, but industrious. The character of the work they were upon at the time, the urgency of the ragged Garde Mobile for their uniforms, formed an unusual incentive to exertion; the foreman told us that notwithstanding the law limiting the hours of labour to ten, the '*glory, love, and fraternity*' principle was so strong that the tailors voluntarily worked twelve or thirteen hours a day, and the same even on Sundays: they seemed to forget the stimulus of the expected balance which each was to receive at the conclusion of the contract. What was the result? For some time many contradictory statements were put forward by the friends and opponents of the system. Louis Blanc looked upon it as the beginning of a new day for France. He had already arranged that as the tailors were the first to begin, the cabinet-makers should next be organized, and one by one all the trades of France. He forgot that he would not have an order for the cabinet-makers to furnish half the houses in Paris to begin with: this, in his estimation, was no difficulty. He had in view public warehouses for the sale of furniture; and although not a chair or table had been sold in the existing over-stocked shops for two months, he had no doubt about customers. But the result of the experiment in the Hôtel Clichy has been fatal. The first order was completed: each man looked for his share of the gain. The riches of Communism, and the participation in the profits, dazzled the views of the fifteen hundred tailors, who had been content to receive 1s. 7d. per day as subsistence money for many weeks: no doubt every one in his own mind appropriated his share of the '*balance*'; for once he felt in his own person the combined pleasure of 'master and man.' The accounts were squared. Eleven francs per dress for so many dresses came to so much. The subsistence money at 1s. 7d. a day had to be deducted. The balance was to be divided as profit. Alas! it was a balance of loss, not of gain; subsistence money had been paid equal to rather more, when it came to be calculated, than sixteen francs for each dress, in place of eleven, at which the master tailor would have made a profit, paid his rent, the interest of his capital, and good wages to his men, in place of a daily pittance for bare subsistence. The disappointment was great when no balance was to be divided. The consternation and disturbance was greater when a large loss was to be discussed, for which no provision in the plans had been made. The customers—that is, the new National Guard and the Garde Mobile—were in a rage at the detention of their uniforms, and the whole attempt seems to have resulted in confusion and disappointment. Louis Blanc is not a match for the master tailors of Paris.—From *The Economist*, May 20, 1848.

The next witness is Mr. Senior—for, as I have said, he was cognizant of the facts at first hand. He entirely corroborates the testimony of the Correspondent of the *Economist*, and tells us, as above, that the work done in the *Ateliers Nationaux* was purely nominal—an exact counterpart of 'all Parish work'—i.e. the parish farms and parish houses of industry which Senior had seen at work, or rather at idleness and waste, during his inquiry into the English poor law. In addition, however, to noting Senior's evidence in regard to the complete failure of the national workshops, I should like to quote the following very able reflections:—

> When the relations of the labourer and the capitalist are in the state which in a highly civilized society may be called natural, since it is the form which in such a society they naturally tend to assume when undistorted by mischievous legislation, the diligence of the labourer is their necessary result. As he is paid only in proportion to his services, he strives to make those services as valuable as he can. His exertions perhaps ought more frequently to be moderated than to be stimulated. A large proportion of our best artisans wear themselves out prematurely. In another state of society, which is also natural in a lower civilization—that of slavery—a smaller but still a considerable amount of industry is enforced by punishment. But in eleemosynary employment there is absolutely no motive for the labourer to make any exertion, or for the employer, a mere public officer, to enforce it. The labourer is, at all events, to have subsistence for himself and his family. To give him more would immediately attract to the public paymaster all the labourers of the country; to give him less, and yet require his services, would be both cruelty and fraud. He cannot be discharged—he cannot be flogged—he cannot be put to task work—since to apportion the tasks to the various powers of individuals would require a degree of zealous and minute superintendence which no public officer ever gave. When the attempt was made in Paris, men accustomed to the work earned fifteen francs a day, those unaccustomed to it not one.

Another witness is Victor Hugo, who boldly asserted in the National Assembly that the experiment was a failure. 'The national workshops,' he declared, 'have proved a fatal experiment. The wealthy idler we already know well; you have created a person a hundred times more dangerous both to himself and others, the pauper idler.... At this very moment

England sits smiling by the side of the abyss into which France is falling.' The pauper idler is a happy phrase and well describes the condition of the unemployable—the men who pass their lives looking for work and praying God they won't find it. Hardly less emphatic was the grave report of the Commission appointed by the French Government to inquire into the subject. While compelled to recommend the expenditure of further enormous sums of money, it felt bound to admit that 'the Revolution, which found the workmen of Paris contracted in their proper sphere, has been, by treating them like spoilt children, the cause of that change in their character which makes every one now dread the excesses of which they may be guilty.'

The next witness to whom I would refer is M. Émile Thomas, the Director of the *Ateliers Nationaux*, whose work I have named above. He shows how exceedingly difficult it is to do the thing which the Socialist assumes to be so easy, i.e. make people work, and how in spite of the most tremendous exertions to render the workshops a success, they broke down. His work, however, should be read, not merely quoted. He was a plain man of business, not a forger of epigrams, and he does not attempt to sum up the results of the experiment in any single passage. He tells the plain tale of what he saw and did quite plainly—a fact which makes the general drift of his history all the more impressive. His account of the workshops is the most convincing testimony possible that in 1848 Collectivist production had a fair trial and utterly broke down.

A word in conclusion as to what was the end of the national workshops. When the National Assembly found that the *Ateliers Nationaux* were rapidly bringing the State to a condition of bankruptcy they determined to close them. This they did, with the result that the workmen rose in insurrection, and that for four days and nights there was such street fighting as the world had never seen before. In putting down the insurrection caused by the dissolution of the great Socialist experiment, 12,000 men were sacrificed—the number of killed at Waterloo was hardly greater.

VII.

Before leaving the subject of the Socialistic experiments tried in Paris, I will put on record for purposes of reference the following extract from Thiers's *Rights of Property*, which describes another experiment in Collectivism:—

The owner of a great engine factory lent for a time his works to his workmen, so that there was no capital sunk in the formation of an establishment, and he agreed to buy at a stated price the machines or parts of machines they might construct. This price has been augmented 17 per cent. on the average. The associated workmen were to govern themselves, to pay themselves, and to share the profits among them. The master had nothing to do with them. He paid for the machines, or portions of machines, and naturally he was not to pay until the work was done.

The associated workmen remained divided, as they were before, in different departments (a great facility of organization, since they had only to continue the habits they had acquired); they placed at the head of each department or workshop a president, and a general president over the whole. They preserved the former classification of wages (another facility arising from acquired habits), except that they gave three francs instead of two-and-a-half francs to the lower class, that of common labourers, and they discontinued paying the skilful workmen (the *marchandeurs*, or middle-men) the high wages resulting from piece-work. These did not, like the rest, work all day; yet as they must be satisfied in a certain degree, they were accorded supplementary wages of ten, fifteen, and sometimes twenty sous, which, added to the four francs of average wages, gave five francs, at the most, to those workmen who had previously earned six, seven, or eight francs a day. These supplementary wages were given by the presidents of the workshops. After having thus raised the wages of the mere labourer, and lowered those of the clever workman, the following was the result of the three months' trial.

There was a daily tumult in the workshop. 'Tis true, tumult was pretty general then, and was not less at the Luxembourg, or the Hôtel de Ville, than in the manufactories. The men made holiday whenever it pleased them to take part in this or that demonstration, which, however, only injured the workmen themselves, for the proprietor paid only for the work when done. But they did not work much when they were present, and the presidents charged with the maintenance of order and the supervision of the labour were changed two or three times a fortnight. The general president, having no local supervision in the workshops, was subject to fewer variations of favour, being changed once only during the period of the association. Had they worked as before, they would have received a sum of 367,000 francs in these three months; but their returns were only 197,000 francs, although their prices were raised 17 per cent. The principal cause of this smaller production was not owing solely to the fewer number of days and hours they attended the workshops than before, but because, when present, they did not work with such activity. The piece-hands, who only received at the utmost a trifling supplement of a franc, were not very zealous in labouring for the association. The men whom they generally took with them when they were on piece, to whom they gave a small additional sum, and whom they superintended in person, were left to the almost negative supervision of the presidents of the workshops, and a thousand workmen out of fifteen hundred manifested that ardour with which men are animated when they do not work for themselves. In a word, 100 labourers received half-a-franc a day more; 300 or 400 workmen received their ordinary 300 or 400 francs, but during fewer days, for they took more holidays; and the 1,000 clever mechanics, who formerly worked by the piece, were deprived of the advantage due to their exertions, which had raised their daily wages to seven, eight, and ten francs. Accordingly, the good hands were all determined to leave the establishment, and when the three months assigned to the association had expired, it came to an end without a single protest. It was a kind of insolvency, for it owed many hours which had not been made up, and had swallowed up the little capital of a benefit fund instituted by the owner of the establishment previously to this philanthropic administration.

Ten sous more a day, to a hundred labourers out of 1,500; the wages of 300 or 400 more kept at the same point; those of 1,000 clever hands diminished; the whole body much poorer in consequence of absences, representing 32 per cent. of time lost; 197,000 francs of work, instead of 367,000 in the same period; all the good workmen disheartened; and finally, the association itself insolvent after three months' existence, although there was an establishment already prepared by the owner—this was the result.

Compare in this context the Report of the Surveyor who in 1893 superintended Mr. Shaw Lefevre's attempt to pull down a part of Millbank Prison by means of the unemployed. When these men worked with the knowledge that their pay would vary according to the work done, they did twice as much as when they knew that whether they worked or idled their pay would be $6\frac{1}{2}d.$ an hour. While the cost of cleaning and stacking bricks by the unemployed, acting as the pensioners of the State, averaged from 12s. to 13s. a thousand, the same men when employed by piece managed to earn higher wages than before, although the rate agreed on was only 7s. a thousand.

VIII.

Perhaps it will be said that the national workshops failed because they were set up in France, and that Collectivism would do much better in England. That is a strange argument considering the natural aptitude for being ordered about officially possessed by our neighbours. Still I will try to meet it. We possessed till the Reform of the Poor Law a good many experiments in Socialism in the shape of Parish

Farms and Houses of Industry, where the poor were, in accordance with the Statute of Elizabeth, 'set on work.' These experiments have lately been examined in a very able and moderate article by Professor James Mavor (*Nineteenth Century*, October, 1893). The conclusions he arrives at are that all the attempts were failures:—

> The conclusions from this survey of attempts 'to set the poor on work' cannot be said to afford much substantial ground for optimism regarding the probability of success of modern attempts in the same direction. It is quite evident that the parish farm hitherto has not afforded a means of relief to the respectable artisan out of employment, but that it has been occupied solely by the vagrant and the beggar. It would seem to be a well-established fact that these two very distinct classes will not mix together in parish farms or anywhere else. The history of the parish farm shows that while it is costly and highly susceptible to the evils of bad management, it may be adapted to the needs of the beggar; but there is no evidence to show that the respectable artisan would be likely ever to enter it so long as the beggar is there.

IX.

Before I leave the subject of Collectivism tested by experiment, I desire to say a word on the general question, and for that purpose will resume some portion of what I have written elsewhere on the subject (i. e. in *The Liberal Unionist* in 1891). I admit as fully as any Socialist can that the ideal is to get a better, fairer and more equal distribution of the world's goods. Two solutions are offered of this problem—one by the Socialists, the other by those who follow in the footsteps of Mr. Cobden and Mr. Bright. The Socialists in effect say, 'Make the State the universal proprietor and the universal employer of labour, and you will have solved the problem and produced a community where misery shall have ceased to exist.' On the other hand, the advocates of Free Exchange, not less zealous nor less religious in their own faith, say, 'Free trade and labour from all shackles, put an end to the ruin and waste of war, and of the armaments maintained for the purpose of war, stop all unnecessary absorption by the State of wealth which should belong to the individual, and you will make human labour so valuable that every man willing and able to work will be able to command material comfort.' I have no hesitation in saying that I believe the solution offered by the advocates of Free Exchange is the true solution. Socialism, which has existed as an aspiration since the world began, has in bygone times been carried into practice, but always with one result—the enslavement and misery of people. When the Spaniards tore down the veil behind which the Peruvian State had developed secluded from all intercourse with the outside world, they found a community arranged on the most approved Socialistic model. The State owned the land, the flocks and herds, the houses, and finally, the bodies of the inhabitants. What was the result? The Peruvians were a nation of slaves, living a life which was little better than that of well-kept, well-fed animals. Again in Paraguay the Jesuits produced a Socialistic state. The *infantes barbati*, or bearded children of their Reductions—the name given to the communities in which the Indians were collected— were ideal Socialist citizens. They possessed no property. No family was richer or more esteemed than another, and all individual effort was suppressed. Yet who will venture to assert that Paraguay under the Jesuits is a model which ought to be copied in the regulation of human society? The case against Socialism is, indeed, conclusive in every particular. Socialism can be proved unsound both economically and historically; and, further, it can be shown to be in conflict with the strongest impulses and instincts of human nature. It may be said, perhaps, that if Socialism can be shown to have failed it cannot be shown that any system based on Free Exchange has ever succeeded. No doubt no State has yet been civilized enough to adopt the principle of Free Exchange in its entirety. It can, however, be proved that those States which have approached most nearly to that ideal are the most prosperous, and their inhabitants least miserable. England has gone further than any other country in the direction of Free Exchange, and unquestionably the people of England are better off than those of any country whose conditions as to debt and geographical position make the comparison a fair one. Wages are better, prices lower, and the standard of comfort higher in England than in any country of the Continent. That this is due to the partial adoption of the principle of Free Exchange, I do not doubt for a moment.

X.

I will end by giving what I believe to be the plain reasons why plain men should not be Socialists. It is not because Socialists are innovators or agitators or preach things contrary to the Book of Daniel, or are this, that, or the other, but simply and solely because Socialism is nonsense. Let me try then to put my reasons for not being a Socialist in the simplest possible form—the form which is patronizingly called suitable for children and uneducated persons, but which in reality is the form in which everyone reasons out a subject in his own mind.

Should those who desire, above all things, an improvement in the condition of the labourer become Socialists?

No.

Why not?

Because Socialism, if carried out, would injure, instead of benefiting, the labourer.

Why would Socialism injure the labourer?

For the following reason: If the condition of the working men is to be improved, that is, if they are to have more food, more room in their houses, more clothes, more firing, more of everything they desire, it is evident that there must be more of all these things in the world. That is, there must be more wealth, for these things make up wealth. But in order that there shall be more wealth, i.e. more of the things men need and desire, more must be produced. If ten men have only five loaves between them, and need one each, the only way they can be made comfortable is by getting five more. It follows, therefore, that nothing which decreases the total wealth of the world, which diminishes, that is, the corn grown, the wool clipped, the houses built, the cotton spun, or the coal dug, can improve the condition of the poor. If, then, Socialism would diminish the production of the things needed by mankind it would be injurious.

But would it diminish the wealth of the world, and so make less to go round?

Yes.

How?

In this way. The great stimulus to the production of wealth of all kinds is self-interest. American farmers who increase the wheat supply of the world, by working hard throughout the year, do not do so out of love for their fellows, but because they want to get rich, and be able to spend money in the manner most pleasing to themselves. In the same way the man who throws up a life of comfort, and works from morn to night till he has made a discovery which will enable the manufacturer to turn out double the amount of woollen cloth without increased expenditure, does so because he has the incentive of self-interest before his eyes— the incentive of knowing that success will be rewarded by the fulfilment of his desires. Throughout the world the motive force of the machinery which produces wealth is self-interest—not self-interest in a bad sense, but the natural and legitimate desire for reward and enjoyment. Destroy this motive force, give men no rewards to strive for, and each individual, unless compelled, will do no more than is necessary to keep himself and his family from starvation. But this is exactly what the Socialist intends to do. He proposes to take away the incentive, under the influence of which more and more wealth is added to the world's store, and to deprive men of the rewards in order to obtain which they now labour. The Socialist would confiscate all private property, and dole out to each individual a subsistence portion. But in order that there shall be something to dole out the inhabitants of the Socialistic state will be compelled to work. Compulsion in a word will become the ultimate motive force of the machinery of production under Socialism, just as under our present system it is self-interest. Which is likely to be the most successful? Who works best, the slave or the labourer, at weekly wages who, if he finds his work irksome, can at least gratify his own tastes in his own way? All experience shows that compulsion produces less than pay.

Convict labour is a synonym for waste and inefficiency. Socialism, then, based as it must be on compulsion, would diminish the wealth of the world. But if the total wealth of the world is diminished there will be less to go round, and, therefore, the share of each person will be less. That is, Socialism would injure instead of benefiting the poor.

St. Loe Strachey.

IV.

STATE SOCIALISM AND THE COLLAPSE IN AUSTRALIA.

HON. J. W. FORTESCUE.

IV.

STATE SOCIALISM AND THE COLLAPSE IN AUSTRALIA.

The literature of State Socialism is ever increasing, though it is but rarely enriched by the addition of such a volume as that written by Dr. Pearson under the title of *National Character*. Possibly it might seem a depreciation of the value of this book to rank it in so narrow a category as that of State Socialistic literature. The scholarship, the wide culture, the encyclopaedic study and research which show themselves on every page, have been duly recognized by critics far more competent to appreciate, though not less ready to admire, than the present writer; and praise from such quarters might reasonably be held to claim for it a higher place. None the less, however, is it certain that Dr. Pearson's book is an inquiry into the working of State Socialism— a forecast of its probable effects on human character—to which the writer, by his own admission, has felt himself impelled by 'twenty years' residence under the Southern Cross.' In other words, we owe this book to the inspiration of Australia; and this is a highly significant fact.

'The history of the English Colonies in Australia and New Zealand is particularly instructive because it shows what the English race naturally attempts when it is freed from the influence of English tradition. The settlers of Victoria and, to a great extent, of the other Colonies, have been men who carried with them the English theory of government; to circumscribe the action of the State as much as possible; to free commerce and production from legal restrictions; and to leave every man to shift for himself with the faintest possible regard for those who fell by the way. Often against their own will the colonists have ended by a system of State Socialism that rivals whatever is attempted in the most bureaucratic nations of the Continent. The State employés are an important element in the population; the State builds railways, founds and maintains schools, tries to regulate the hours and wages of labour, protects native industry, settles the population on the land, and is beginning to organize systems of State insurance. . . . Planted in Australia the Englishman . . . is rapidly creating a State Socialism, which succeeds because it is all embracing and able to compel obedience, and which surpasses its continental State models because it has been developed by the community for their own needs, and not by State departments for administrative purposes.' Of course it does not follow that they are right; but 'it is surely safe to say that political experiments which half a dozen self-governing British communities are instinctively adopting deserve attention as an indication of what we may expect in the future.'

This quotation gives the key to Dr. Pearson's design. State Socialism 'succeeds' in Australia: Dr. Pearson will work out for us the probable results of its success in the civilized world at large. The argument is developed briefly as follows. It seems absolutely certain that the higher races—i.e. those that are held to have attained the highest form of civilization—are confined within certain unchangeable limits by the influence of climate. Australia is a country in point, half of it being, so to speak, 'a white man's country,' half of it distinctly not so. Having established his position as to the 'unchangeable limits of the higher races' (a most valuable and interesting chapter, by the way, on a sadly neglected subject), Dr. Pearson passes on to consider how confinement within those limits is likely to affect those races—how, in fact, they are to survive, or rather think they are to survive, restriction within their own climatic borders, the increasing competition of the inferior races, the consequent closing of the outlets for trade and energy. He answers—and he gives good ground for his answer—By resort to State Socialism! Englishmen, for instance, losing faith in themselves, will fall back on the State and State Socialism, and resign themselves to a stationary order in society—wealth and population ceasing to increase. From such stationary order is likely to result increase of standing armies, of great cities, and of national debts—the first by no means an unmixed evil, which is more than can be said of the other two. The nation is bound to remain the unit of political society, because the interests and feelings of different races and countries are too discordant to be harmonized under a central government. The future of society will, then, depend very much on the perpetuity of national feeling. Given that perpetuity of national feeling, and with it the exaltation of the State to the highest place in the minds of men, we may expect—what? The millennium? No; 'the decline of the family and the decay of character.'

Such is the conclusion to which Dr. Pearson is irresistibly led by his review of the prospects of State Socialism as a success; and we cannot sufficiently admire the practical courage and candour wherewith he has given it utterance. He holds no brief for or against State Socialism; he accepts it as inevitable; examines it in an impartial spirit and pronounces judgement without flinching. Not unnaturally, therefore, his work has been branded by many as pessimistic—after the usual fashion of those who strike unpleasant arguments with a label and therewith declare them slain. Personally I cannot see that it is more pessimistic than optimistic; for surely it is an optimistic assumption that State Socialism will successfully fulfil the functions that are generally prescribed for it. Moreover this assumption, as it seems to me, is rather more than the mere acceptance of an hypothesis for the sake of argument. 'In Australia State Socialism *succeeds*,' are Dr. Pearson's own words. Does it succeed? That is a question to be examined rather than begged.

In a chapter—the most optimistic chapter in his book—on the advantages of an enhanced national feeling, Dr. Pearson has much to say of the hold that a State, which confers innumerable benefits on its citizens, should thereby acquire over them. Such enlargement on the topic is pertinent, because it is on the perpetuity of national feeling (according to Dr. Pearson) that society depends in the future. A few quotations will make the matter clearer.

'Whatever may have been the case in old days, a child's obligations to the State are now infinite. The State watches over the infant from birth; provides that the growing child shall not be stunted by excessive toil, is properly clothed and fed, and so educated as to have a fair start in life; it assures the adult against starvation, protects him against tyrannical employers and from the criminal classes that prey upon property; it secures him liberty of thought and faith; and it offers him the means of safe and easy insurance against illness or death.'

Again: 'The love of any man speaking the English tongue for his country is now for a land that can give him ampler protection than his fathers ever dreamed of, that invests him with the privilege of a dominant race, that adjusts his public burdens so as to be least onerous, that gives him the right to assist in the making of laws, that protects him against his own weakness, and offers him the means to start on equal terms in the race for honour or wealth.'

And yet again: 'It is now the State which is fascinating every family by proffering the *bâton de maréchal* to its children as it forces upon them an education that will fit them to rise to wealth or dignity . . . The broad fact remains that human co-operation for political ends is yearly becoming more fruitful of good purpose, and more successful in its attempts to relieve want . . . Neither is it only material benefits with which a great country endows its citizens . . . the citizens of every historic State are richer by great deeds that have formed the national character, by winged words that have passed into current speech, by the examples of lives and labours consecrated to the service of the commonwealth. The religion of the State is surely as worthy of reverence as any creed of the churches, and ought to grow in intensity year by year.'

'*It is, however, the note of every true religion that if it promises great good it demands proportional sacrifices.*'

It is in this last sentence that the difficulties of State Socialism really confront us. I am not concerned to dispute that in the religion of the State, as outlined by Dr. Pearson, there is much that may elevate and ennoble; nor that the State, as apparently the less unintelligible abstraction, may command readier and more willing worship than Humanity. But abstractions are abstractions, and no profusion of capital letters will make them concrete. We are forced to ask, What is the State? With Dr. Pearson we must set it down at something higher than merely 'the casual aggregation of persons who find it to their advantage to live in a certain part of the earth'; and if we desire to appraise it at its highest—as worthy of its capital letter—we must treat it as an abstraction, and a remarkably vague abstraction. But human creatures who, like the Australians and, indeed, the majority of English-speaking peoples, have a decided bias, temporary or permanent, towards materialism, are somewhat impatient of vague abstractions. Even three hundred years ago the framers of the Anglican Articles of Belief thought it expedient to define the visible Church. There is no such formula, so far as I know, for the visible State. Such phrases as 'a congregation of faithful men in which the pure gospel of State Socialism is preached and salaries are received according to Act of Parliament,' are insufficient and out of date. Men seek for something terse and tangible, and accordingly objectify the State in the Government for the time being; and in that Government seek for the outward manifestation of those hidden qualities, which, by their hypothesis, are comprehended in the abstract idea of the State.

There is one divine attribute, and one only, that is assigned by its devotees to the State—namely, omnipotence. It is thought that the State, in virtue of some mysterious and unexplained qualities, can do for men what they cannot do for themselves—enjoys, in fact, powers that are practically superhuman. Even Dr. Pearson, soberest of writers, seems to lend countenance to this astonishing doctrine when he employs such loose expressions as that 'the State offers a man the means to start on equal terms in the race for honour and wealth.' That the State may profess to make the offer is likely enough; but herein it arrogates superiority to Fate, which, in my judgement, is not a tenable position. This omnipotence of the State is, however, assumed, as I have said, and in common with other attributes finds objectification in the reigning Government. It is, moreover, by no means surprising that the faith therein is never stronger than in a democracy. For democracy (to employ Dr. Pearson's excellent definition) seems really to mean the vesting of power in the people in such a way that their changes of purpose may have instantaneous effect given to them. It is the peculiarity of a democracy that it never believes that a Government cannot do a thing: it believes only that it will not do it. So if one Government declines to give instantaneous effect to one change or another of its purpose, it seeks another that undertakes the duty; and some party can always be found to make the undertaking. Hence the eternal cry of the disappointed agitator—'We can expect nothing from *this* Government. But wait a little; a time will come.'

Nor can it be denied that to a superficial observer the State seems to possess some attributes that are generally accounted divine. To the mass of mankind material considerations are paramount—it is not sweetness and light, but fullness and warmth, that signify happiness. If the prayers of the world for a single day could be summarised it would be found, I cannot doubt, that the commonest and most constant petition is for the grant of material benefits. The Lord's Prayer itself contains the material clause, 'Give us day by day our daily bread.' Those, however, who utter it in other than a merely formal spirit rarely hope to see a raven fly in with provisions through the window, or to find an angel at the door with a bread-basket. They trust that the prayer may be answered according to the inscrutable wisdom of a Power that has allowed men to starve before now; and they are stimulated by their trust to individual endeavour. Not so with the State. The State undertakes immediate and direct supply of material benefits. Men go to the State and ask, if not for bread, at all events for work—and they get it. They ask higher wage for that work—and they get it. They ask for reduction of hours of work without corresponding reduction of pay rate—and they get it. They ask for relief from the burden of educating the children which they have begotten into the world—and they get it. They ask for protection against the consequences of their own folly—and the State undertakes to grant it. They ask for an equal start in the race for power and wealth—and the State promises it. They ask for the moon—and the Government, or objectified State, binds itself to give the demand its most serious consideration.

For it is the peculiar attraction of the deity of the State that it is never absolutely inexorable. In fact it is a deity that can be coerced. Jehovah may be adored or blasphemed; the idol of the savage may be feasted or whipped by the helpless and the starving; and the food supply is not thereby visibly affected. The State, on the contrary, in its objectification as the reigning Government, can always be squeezed. Nor does it object to such pressure. Ministers of the State wherein State Socialism prevails are as vain, as ambitious and as arrogant as the high priests of any church; and they rejoice in every new appeal to their authority as fresh evidence of the faith that is reposed in them. They borrow prestige from the mysterious abstraction, of whose bounty they are held to be the dispensers; and they know that every addition to the prestige of the State is an addition to their own. To this source may, perhaps, be traced the ever increasing intensity and passion of the struggle for the government of men. All great rulers, from Moses onward, have testified to the thanklessness of this task of government. Cromwell would sooner have kept a flock of sheep; Danton would rather have been a poor fisherman; but still men press and hustle each other in the race for authority to rule. The State is omnipotent; with such omnipotence at their back they can seize the reins with a light heart.

Now if the faith, alike of ministers and citizens, in the

omnipotence of the State be taken as the test of success, then assuredly Dr. Pearson has some reason to claim success for State Socialism in Australia. Everything that the devotee of the State chose to demand from his idol has practically been granted or promised. The State has provided, in one or other or in all the Colonies, all the cherished privileges that were enumerated a few pages back. Moreover, it has made the provision of work doubly attractive, in the eyes alike of worker and onlooker, by declaring the work to be reproductive—in fact, to pay for itself. Thus, a railway not only furnishes employment and wage during its construction; but, when constructed, assumes the guise of a national benefit, and, more curious still, of a national asset. Moreover, in Australia the State grants all these privileges unconditionally, without demanding any service from its citizens in return. The logical complement of State Socialism is compulsory military service; a subject on which Dr. Pearson's remarks are well worth reading. But, from the point of view of national defence, Australia has no occasion to compel military service. Her defence is undertaken by England, and depends on the British fleet, which was specially increased for the purpose at British expense, and is maintained at no greater cost to the six Australasian Colonies than an annual payment of £125,000, divided between them. Thus, in all its doings, the State in Australia omits to train its citizens to the idea of sacrifice. Noting, no doubt, how thoroughly the citizens appreciated the duty of the State towards themselves, it counted on them for as thorough an appreciation of their duty toward the State; in fact, it calculated (if it thought about the matter at all) that multiplicity of benefit would breed infinity of obligation.

Finally, therefore, as the crowning attraction and supreme revelation of its omnipotence, the Australian State bestowed all these benefits upon its citizens, apparently free of charge, by the simple expedient of borrowing scores of millions of pounds from the British capitalist. It is true that taxes were levied; but very largely in the form of protective customs duties, which are always popular among those who seek an easy life; and, indeed, it is pretty evident from the latest developments that the State virtually provided the citizens with money to pay taxes withal. Of course the amount of the debt always appeared as an offset against the national prosperity; and here the fiction of the 'reproductive' works came usefully into play. If the British capitalist happened to observe that he had lent the State ten, twenty or forty millions, the high priests waved their hands towards railways and irrigation schemes, and said, loftily, 'There are your millions; not idle, but breeding new millions.' So the prestige of the State grew and waxed great; and therewith that of the ministers also; for they needed but to wave their hands, and the land was filled with plenteousness. And they looked upon the work of their hands, and saw that it was good. And Mr. Froude journeyed to Australia to see the wonderful things that were there; for the fame thereof had reached his ears in his own country. And he saw the ministers of the State, and communed with them; he saw their work also, and blessed it. And his blessing is a curse unto Australia unto this day. And passing over to New Zealand he saw there George Grey, the seer (which had formerly been of the ministers, but was cast out), and he communed with him, and cursed New Zealand. Notwithstanding, his curse was changed into a blessing. And other men also came from England to see Australia, which blessed it, and gave glory to the State, not knowing what they did. Nay, there were that blessed it, not having seen it with their own eyes; and of all these the blessing is changed into a curse.

Undoubtedly, in the piping times of the 'eighties,' the Australian Colonies, judged by certain standards, were quite ideal States—paradises of the working man, and so forth. Their success was frequently quoted as conclusive evidence of the value of State Socialism and of the infinite power of the State for good; and they were consequently flattered and belauded to an extravagant degree. Nor were they backward to accept such homage. The Australian Colonies began to look upon themselves as decidedly superior communities;

and the men that directed them began to imagine themselves statesmen. To nourish the prevailing sentiment of national self-satisfaction, the Governments instituted that peculiar form of national advertisement which is known by the name of 'statistics'—statistics of 'realized wealth,' 'national resources,' 'national assets,' and the like—all designed to assure the world in general, and the people of England in particular, that the Australians were, for all their State comforts, the most energetic, industrious and enterprising folk in the world. Now, no one likes to be called energetic and industrious so much as the man who never does more work than he can help; and accordingly the Australian working man heard and was delighted. Nor was he altogether without justification. All official documents declared Australian prosperity to be phenomenal; and that prosperity was certainly due to some one's exertions—why not, therefore, to his own (as every one assured him), with the help and guidance of an enlightened abstraction called the State? Deity and devotee alike live on faith, and thrive with its increase. So the game went merrily on during the eighties, becoming fast and furious towards their close, till at last it culminated in the year 1888. That year was marked in Sydney by a great festival to celebrate the centenary of the arrival of the first two convict ships at Botany Bay; and in Melbourne by a great Exhibition to commemorate the fiftieth anniversary of the foundation of Victoria.

Shortly after, the tide began to turn. The first blow dealt at the omnisufficiency of the State was struck by an Australian newspaper, the *Melbourne Argus*, which discovered and gave publicity to the fact that the surplus shown by the Victorian Treasurer for the financial year just expired (1889) had no existence except in imagination. Further inquiry showed that the surpluses of some previous years had been obtained by a manipulation of the public accounts, which in a private firm would not have been considered straightforward. Though known and remarked in the Colonies, this incident of the sham surplus of 1889 was unheard of in England until Mr. Charles Fairfield made it public in the pages of *A Plea for*

Liberty. Other attacks followed Mr. Fairfield's, as the mysteries of Australian State Socialism were gradually unveiled; and at last the ministers took fright and began to admit, in Australia at least, that matters might not be in quite so satisfactory a state as could be desired. In England they continued, through their instruments, to puff the perfection of their system and to denounce the attacks of critics as persistently as ever. Still, the steadiness of the downward tendency was too strongly marked to make denials and denunciations of any avail. The Colony of Victoria, wherein Dr. Pearson made his principal study of the success of State Socialism, presents, perhaps, the most instructive picture of financial collapse—Victoria was the *enfant gâté* of the British State Socialist, the darling example of such critics as Sir Charles Dilke. Her decline and fall may be traced in the following brief statement.

July, 1889. The Treasurer announced a surplus of £1,600,000.

Nov. 1889. The Treasurer announced that the surplus of £1,600,000 had sunk to £142,000; and that there were liabilities of £5,600,000 to be met. Liabilities accordingly met by means of loans, and finance declared (by Mr. H. Willoughby, *Nineteenth Century,* Sept. 1891) to have been 'put straight without the slightest confusion.'

1890. Treasurer announces a surplus of £600,000 on the past financial year.

1891. Treasurer announces a deficit of £797,000 on the past financial year, reckoning to June 30; and of £1,418,000, reckoning to July 1; also that £1,700,000 had been borrowed from trust funds (Government Savings Bank deposits) in anticipation of loans. £3,000,000 were borrowed in London during the year, of which £900,000 were for conversion of a matured loan.

1892. Treasurer announced a deficit of close on £1,600,000 for the past financial year. £3,000,000 raised by loans during the year 1892.

1893. Estimated deficit of £2,500,000. Collapse.

There is no necessity to dilate further on the present financial condition of Australia—it has been all too sorrowfully brought home to hundreds of ruined Englishmen. 'When a State undertakes enterprises beyond its strength, it always does it at the risk of bankruptcy,' writes Dr. Pearson, very sagely; and bankruptcy is the fate that has overtaken Victoria, New South Wales and Queensland. Now it is agreed by common consent that finance is the principal test whereby the success or failure of a system of administration should be tried. Applying this test to Australia we are surely forced to the conclusion that State Socialism, so far from succeeding there, is a hopeless and disastrous failure. Now, the practical certainty of bankruptcy in these three provinces, and particularly in Victoria, has been patent to any man who chose to use his eyes, since the year 1890, if not from still earlier times. Dr. Pearson's book bears date 1893; and we must, therefore, assume that, at all events to the close of 1891, he still considered State Socialism to be a success in Australia. Consequently we can only conclude that he would not regard such a test as final, and would require further evidence to convince him that he was mistaken. I can hardly believe, I confess, that if his book were still unprinted he would leave the passage about the success of State Socialism in Australia unaltered. But his subject is a wide one; and he expressly disclaims the consideration of such possible contingencies as the trial of impracticable experiments, and the resort to such old failures of the past as unlimited issues of paper money by 'ignorant tribunes of the people.' We are, therefore, driven to apply some other test. It may, of course, be said, and indeed it has been said, that the financial collapse in Australia is due merely to a fortuitous concurrence of unfortunate circumstances; that it is merely transitory and superficial, and that it will be followed by speedy and solid revival. It has also been said that the collapse was due to the malicious attacks of English critics, who sought notoriety by uttering dismal prophecies of Australia's failure, and secured fulfilment of those prophecies by decrying her credit. But it would be as reasonable to attribute the outbreak of an epidemic of typhoid fever to the predictions of a doctor who condemns the sanitary condition of a town. The fact that it could be predicted is sufficient evidence that the collapse was due, not to unlucky mischance, but to simple and ascertainable causes. If, in spite of national bankruptcy, success can still be claimed for State Socialism in Australia, it can be upon one ground only—viz. that, though the State may have failed (let us say through excessive zeal) in its duty to the citizens, yet the citizens have redeemed such failure through their infinite devotion to the service of the State.

Now, I have already described, in Dr. Pearson's own words, the consummation which he hopes may be reached in the growth in each individual citizen of a proper sentiment of gratitude, loyalty and piety toward the State—I have sketched what the State has undertaken to do, and what it actually has done (no matter at whose expense), for its citizens in Australia; and it now remains to examine what return the citizen seems likely to offer to the State. 'It is the note of every true religion that, if it promises great good, it demands proportionate sacrifice.' 'What reward shall I give unto the Lord for all the benefits that He hath done unto me?'

The peculiar tendency to accumulate large debts, which present experience has shown to be characteristic of State Socialism, has not escaped so keen an observer as Dr. Pearson. His residence in Victoria cannot but have forced this danger upon his notice, and presented it to him as real and pressing. It is evident, indeed, that this peculiarity has puzzled and disturbed him not a little. 'The day may come,' he hopes, 'when a man who leaves an old and indebted State will be like the partner who peremptorily withdraws from an embarrassed firm'; but he admits that if thousands of citizens who have supported a policy of lavish expenditure leave the country when the burden of taxation becomes unpleasant, the very existence of the State may be imperilled. I have little doubt but that this latter sentiment was suggested to Dr. Pearson by (among other examples) what happened in New Zealand in the year 1888-9. New Zealand, it should be mentioned, at that time led the race of extravagant administration among the Australian Colonies; and, indeed, is still rather ahead of her sisters in the matter of certain State institutions—e.g. State insurance. Her career was, however, cut short in the nick of time by Mr. Froude's strictures in that delightful but inaccurate book *Oceana*. New Zealand gained a bad reputation in the English money market; the supply of loans was cut off; and she found herself on the brink of bankruptcy. Now, there can be no doubt whatever that the adventurous politician who initiated and encouraged the policy of extravagant borrowing in New Zealand was cordially supported by the mass of the people. To this day, I venture to affirm, there are many in the Colony who still swear by him. Nor is it altogether surprising considering that, as if by the waving of a magic wand, he flooded the country with money, and began an era of apparently unexampled prosperity. Let it be noted meanwhile that in New Zealand there was no concealment of the financial position by mishandling of the accounts. The annual balance sheets showed faithfully enough a deficit just about equivalent to the amount of the annual interest due on the loans; so that it was sufficiently patent to any intelligent man that the interest on old loans was discharged, not by the labour of the citizens, but by the complaisance of the British capitalist. No sane man could believe that such a system would last for ever; yet it was stopped, not by the unwillingness of the citizens to continue it, but by the refusal of the British capitalist any longer to support it. Now, innocent people might suppose that citizens under such obligations to the State as in New Zealand would have stood by her in the hour of her trial. Nothing of the kind. No sooner was the borrowing stopped than the 'working men,' the adult males, who are generally reckoned to be the cream of the population, streamed away in thousands to Australia. So far from making a sacrifice for the State, which had nursed them so tenderly, they not only forsook her, but in many cases left their wives and children behind to be a burden to her. Those who remained sought by every means in their power to shift the weight of their obligations to the State on to others' shoulders. Sir George Grey openly proposed that, under the form of an income tax, a fraction of the interest due to the English bondholders should be confiscated for the benefit of the State, which meant, in plain words, repudiation. The Government, without going so far as this, imposed this income tax upon the foreign holder of debentures in New Zealand companies; and has got into some trouble in consequence, though not with its own citizens.

So much for New Zealand. Sensible colonists who watched the exodus of the working man from that country on the cessation of the borrowing policy, predicted (not without bitter satisfaction) that he would soon return, a wiser creature than when he left. And so in fact it has turned out. Compared with the crashing collapse of Victoria, New South Wales and Queensland, the fall of New Zealand appears like a gentle subsidence. The 'working man' of Australia, sworn supporter of reckless extravagance, 'cleared out' directly there was a question as to the payment of the bill; and fled to New Zealand, South America or any country where he could hope to receive benefits without repaying them. Nay, a few hundred extremists, so we read in the papers, have started off to construct a Utopia which shall satisfy all their ideals; schismatics from the established State religion which once commanded their reverence in Australia, embarked on some parody of the *Mayflower*, bound on the welcome and simple mission of forming a fool's paradise. But the bulk of the emigrants, so far as I can gather, has made its way to New Zealand; deserters, some of single, some of double, some of triple dye, but all alike without shame. Within six months of their arrival they are entitled to a vote; and, with unconscious irony, will probably press for the imposition of heavy burdens on absentee proprietors and absentee lenders. Absentee debtors, of course, are not to be classed with such vermin. The devotee of the State has but two clauses to his prayer—'Give us day by day our daily bread, *and forgive us our debts.*'

It may be said that such citizens as these are no citizens. Possibly; but why, then, does the State so readily grant them the privileges of citizenship, asking at very most no more from them than an occasional service on a jury—a service, by the way, which, being properly within the domain of the State, not infrequently finds its way into private hands, to the great discomfort of justice? There is, I think, but one answer—the religion of the State encourages hirelings rather than shepherds.

Now let us consider the case of the citizens who remain faithful to the country of their birth or their adoption. Some, beyond all question, remain true to her from really high motives of sentiment and honour—the men who would never desert a companion in misfortune or disgrace, much less a country. But are such motives bred by the lavishment of material benefits? Surely not. Were the sharers of the *sportula* the men who stuck to their Roman patrons in their fall as well as their prosperity? I do not think so.

But there is a much larger body that stays from sheer inability to go away. These are mainly of two classes—salaried official employés of the State, too old, too strongly committed to her service, or too much narrowed in the discharge of the duties thereof to begin life over again; and the country people, who are attached, partly by sentimental, more often by commercial, ties to the soil—the working moiety of the population, which produces whatever wealth is produced in the country. The first is that over which the State has most immediate and complete control. They are simple dependents—the one class from which the State can extort sacrifices. As the easiest, they are always the first victims of retrenchment; and the first cry in a country where State Socialism has brought about financial embarrassment is 'Cut down the salaries of the Civil Service.' The ministers lend a willing ear: salaries are cut down, old servants are discharged, with or without an inadequate composition for the pension to which they were entitled by the terms of their contract; and the whole service is disheartened and demoralized. These men are among the few that have faithfully served the State; and this is their reward. Is it conceivable that such involuntary Abdiels should keep their loyalty, love and zeal towards so faithless and oppressive a taskmistress?

The people who work on the land are in rather a different position. Although from the mere fact of dispersion they cannot organize themselves to put pressure on the State like the townsmen, yet they have compelled the State in some measure to justify their faith in its omnipotence. Of course they have ever been the last to receive protection for their industries; but they would not consent eternally to pay through the nose for every tool, utensil and garment in order that the townsman might prosper and amuse himself; and accordingly, together with the privileges extended to every citizen, they have occasionally exacted special favours, such as bounties and the like. Now, these men have always felt a conviction (and quite justifiably) that they are the true Australian citizens—ready, it is true, to take anything that they could get from the State, but proud to think that they were not dependent on it, nor bound to it by a daily increasing sum of uncancelled obligation. To them the collapse must have been a more than ordinarily painful surprise. They know that they have worked on as usual, and yet they learn of failure after failure of banks and business firms—probably enough of the disappearance of their own earnings in such failure. They hear of public liabilities whereof the total seems ever to increase, of a public revenue that never ceases to fall, of business at a standstill, of a Government at its wit's end. They hear of imperative necessity for immense retrenchment and new taxation; reduction of the benefits granted by the State, increase of the burdens to be borne for her. Lastly, they hear that thousands of taxpayers have fled from the coming wrath, and that thousands more are preparing to follow them; and that they who have always worked must stay and work on, in difficulty and discouragement, to pay the piper to whose music the fugitives have danced.

Then they ask, Why this collapse? Who is responsible for it? And the answer is, The State. It was the State that promised to create universal prosperity and universal contentment; and to carry out its promise utilized, not its own resources, but money borrowed from other countries. The State had ideas of ready-made prosperity as of a ready-made suit of clothes. It seems so simple to take a man of fine physique, clap him in a borrowed suit of fine clothes, call him a millionaire, and bid him go play. But, the true workers rejoin, Why so sudden a collapse? Surely there should have been unmistakable warnings. We had no such warnings. The balance sheets and official information furnished by the State through its ministers were, at any rate till quite recently, most satisfactory and reassuring. The answer is, The State your god is a jealous god, and does not like its devotees to think that they can do without her, still less that she is wholly dependent upon them. It was a part of her policy to conceal from you that you were the only true workers in the country, and that without you she was nothing. It was equally part of her policy to conceal from the British capitalist the fact that he has hitherto paid the interest on the money that he has lent her out of his own pocket. Whether from unwillingness to lose faith in the omnipotence of the State or from fear of publishing the discovery which they had themselves made, that such faith was groundless, successive batches of ministers so garbled the financial accounts and returns of the State as to convey a wholly false impression. Hence a general feeling of distrust and uncertainty towards Australian State balance sheets at the present moment. In Victoria these balance sheets were presented with various suppressions and omissions according to the interest of the reigning Government in showing a deficit or a surplus, i.e. a deficit as the creation of their predecessors in office, a surplus as the production of their own talent. In New South Wales the dispensers of the riches of the State have recently made some very candid admissions. 'The Colonial Treasurer is practically powerless to control the finances; he is liable at any moment to have accounts to meet of the very existence of which he was unaware'—such is the confession of the present Treasurer. You ask, How about the 'reproductive public works?' wherein the borrowed money was invested; and you point triumphantly to the Victorian railways, which, according to official returns, paid not only the interest on the capital borrowed for their construction, but a small percentage of profit also. Well, by this time you must know that these official returns were misleading. Those railways never did pay that interest, and at the present moment are less likely to pay it than ever. In 1891 the earnings were avowedly £332,000 short of the interest on the capital outlay, and in 1892 £445,000. If you ask about another class of 'reproductive' public works, those constructed for purposes of irrigation for the benefit, at any rate ostensibly, of you in the country, I must point out to you that the aggregate arrears of interest due from local bodies on this account rose from £200,000 to £300,000 between 1891 and 1892, and that you may as well write off these sums and more as bad debts. It is of no use for you to say that much of the money spent on these reproductive works was wasted; that some of the railways, for instance, ought never to have been made at all; that many ought to have been delayed for ten, twenty or thirty years; that nearly all should have been constructed at much smaller cost; and that if you had had any idea of the haphazard fashion in which the affairs of the State were conducted you would have risen to put a stop to the system. All that is no doubt very true, indeed, has been admitted to some extent by ministers. You supposed, at any rate hoped, that all was right, and never dreamed that the ministers of the State were deceiving you. But you must remember that the ministers are but men, like you believers in the State, concerned to uphold its divinity, and therefore unwilling to profane its mysteries.

All this, though interesting, is but a digression from the most important point, namely, that the State looks to you and to your exertions to discharge liabilities incurred partly for your good, but chiefly for the good of others. You must not complain of this. You must not say that the State has done you more harm than good by attracting all labour away from you to its own works, and encouraging the population to do artificial work in the towns, instead of natural work in the country, and that its eternal interference has been the ruin of Australia. The interest on the debt must be paid, and you have got to pay it.

Can we believe that these citizens will feel gratitude and

devotion towards the State which has so deceived them? Will they not rather curse her for the injustice that she has wrought? For has not each man the perfect right to say that if the State had but openly shown him the true nature of her doings he would have renounced his allegiance and left the country while he could, without loss of independence, character or honour?

Meanwhile, the State has made a last effort to retrieve its damaged character. In the general distress the people, demoralized by long dependence on its bounty, call louder than ever on the State for help; and the State has responded. In Victoria it tried, besides other experiments, to avert the failure of banks, by declaring them closed for five days; which is as though a doctor should stop a man's breath to save him from breathing his last. Needless to say, the few banks that were confident as to their soundness refused to avail themselves of this enforced holiday; while those that knew their own unsoundness closed for five days, reopened—and failed—as it was inevitable that they should fail. In New South Wales and Queensland, the Governments, still filled with the omnipotence of the State, have undertaken, with no mightier engine to hand than an ordinary paper mill, to create money, under the name of 'Treasury Notes,' 'Treasury Bonds,' and so forth. This, of course, is no new thing. The State has set itself the same task at various periods in various countries; but it is significant that such 'money,' whether designated 'Treasury notes,' 'Cedulas,' or 'Assignats,' has never failed to fall into early disrepute. These 'State promises to pay' are in reality nothing more nor less than drafts on the credulity of those who believe in the omnipotence of the State; and human credulity finds its limits very swiftly, when pounds, shillings and pence are in question. Thus in two at least of the Australian provinces the State has fired its last shot. What may be the ultimate outcome of these issues of forced paper it is difficult to say. The issue, of course, is declared to be limited, and all reissue to be forbidden; so that at present the scheme does not come under Dr. Pearson's category of 'old failures'; but it is a disquieting reflection that issues of forced paper have a tendency to outlive the term originally assigned for their existence. In any case there is but one source from which these promissory notes can be redeemed, viz. the labour and production of the workers in the country districts, who are already sadly overburdened. The truth is that the State in the last resort can find neither help nor salvation except in the private enterprise, which in Australia it has done its best to extinguish; but this truth being unpalatable, both to itself and to its worshippers, the State leaves no means untried to disguise it. By the people these paper issues have been hailed with acclamation as a stroke of magical beneficence; in other words, neither Government nor people are alive to the fact that a State's promise to pay is a people's promise to work.

Looking, then, at the situation from both sides—from the side of the State in respect of the benefits which it has conferred upon the citizens and from the side of the citizens in respect of the obligations which they recognize towards the State—I find it impossible to justify Dr. Pearson's assumption that State Socialism succeeds in Australia. The experiment may have been interesting, but the result is failure; and the immediate products are a bankrupt treasury and a demoralized people. The reign of State Socialism in Australia has been a reign of gambling, pure and simple; and the tendency to gambling is of all tendencies that which an Australian Government should have been most careful to discourage. For the English have a natural passion for gambling only less intense than have the Chinese; and Australia is from the nature of the case a gambling country. So treacherous is the climate, with its alternation of heavy destructive drought and heavy destructive flood, that even the soberest work on the land partakes heavily of the nature of gambling. If the new settler begins with a good season, he makes money very rapidly; if with a bad, he is, for all his efforts, not less rapidly ruined. On this point all men with experience of Australia seem to agree—there is, as a rule, no medium between these two extremes. Then, as if this were not enough, the State aggravates the uncertainty of work on the land by continual tinkering at the land laws—now withholding the public land from sale, alleging scruples about 'alienating the national patrimony,' now disturbing the holders of land already alienated, now proposing to repurchase the 'national patrimony'; so that men can hardly tell what their rights in the land may be; while rabbits, by a strange irony, enjoy undisputed possession of thousands of square miles. Another natural stimulus to the gambling spirit was the discovery of gold; which, though commonly accounted a blessing, is in reality the greatest curse that can oppress a country—offering royal roads to wealth, and discouraging steady industry. As if this were not enough, the State floods the country with borrowed millions, thus obtaining and promoting, directly and indirectly, an unprecedented extension of credit for its citizens. Hence, as was to be expected, more and more gambling, culminating in the frantic speculation known as the Melbourne Land Boom of 1888; when the price of real property in Melbourne actually rose above that in the City of London; while the State, to keep the ball rolling, carelessly squandered a quarter of a million[1] of borrowed money on a great exhibition.

The prevalence of the gambling spirit, and the direct encouragement thereof through precept and example by the State, has, of course, left its mark on commercial morality. I must guard myself against misconception and the accusation of Pharisaism by saying at once that I do not think English commercial morality is much to boast of; and am rather inclining to the opinion that the old and extinct aristocratic prejudice against trade had its root in something greater and stronger than the mere pride and folly of caste. I am not concerned to deny, meanwhile, that the morality of the tradesman or merchant or banker has as good a right to distinct existence and special recognition, as such, as the morality of the advocate or the politician; for every profession and calling has its own ethical code—known to the

---

[1] The *net loss* on this exhibition exceeded £200,000.

outside world as etiquette, and to the initiated as business. But, making all these allowances, I do not think it can be disputed that the standard of commercial morality in Australasia is low, and lower than in England. The position can be illustrated by the different treatment of bankruptcy in the Colonies and the old country. Gambling and bankruptcy are intimately connected together—gambling being carelessness, indifference, contempt, but always at bottom defiance towards obligation; bankruptcy the admitted inability, from whatever cause, to fulfil obligation. The attitude of law and still more of society towards bankruptcy is a sure index to the standard of respect that is paid to the sanctity of obligation in any community. If any one will compare the bankruptcy laws of England with those, say, of New Zealand, I do not think he will find any difficulty in deciding which are the most stringent, or, in other words, make most for honesty. But the social attitude towards bankruptcy in the Colonies is even more significant. Bankruptcy is attended by comparatively few difficulties; and is accompanied by no stigma. Perhaps this may be more excusable in a new country than an old, but it is not less dangerous. Dr. Pearson justly says that 'in a new society a man goes on experimenting till he finds the career in which he works best; and that this facility has a great effect in promoting individualism.' I think that it has a great effect in promoting bankruptcy also; for, through the too lax acceptance of the principle, the liberty to experiment *ad libitum* is construed as the right to fail *ad infinitum*. Hence to have 'passed through the court,' as the phrase runs, is in the Colonies held to be rather an evidence of enterprise than a certificate of failure. It cannot astonish us, therefore, to find bankruptcy in high places in the Colonies. I take no such unfair test as a mere enumeration of the Australian premiers, past and present, who have been obliged to confess insolvency; for misfortune spares no man. I take the recent and significant case of a politician who quite lately held the office of premier. This gentleman, while yet in the first blush of bankruptcy and of intimate connexion with a business whose failure had justly or unjustly provoked severe criticism in the Colony, was actually selected for the appointment of Agent-General in England; and this at a time when his prime duty would have been to reassure British capitalists as to the safety of their investments in his Colony. The press, to its honour, opposed the appointment and forced the Government to cancel it. But conceive the selection of a bankrupt for such a mission; and consider the standard of commercial morality in a country where such a selection could not merely be thought of, but was only most reluctantly withdrawn, as much from policy as shame, in deference to the press. It is the standard reproach against two great rival English statesmen, that the one lived a gambler and the other died a bankrupt. If his marvellous talents and amazing personal charm cannot save the fame of Fox; if his lofty character and transcendent services cannot wholly efface the one stain on the memory of Pitt, surely it is a mistaken and unwholesome leniency to leave similar failings in Australian politicians wholly out of account.

Let us take another aspect of Australian commercial morality. It is constantly claimed on behalf of Australian ministers, that they have never diverted the riches of the State to their own personal gain. Let us freely grant that in some important English-speaking communities such virtue is all too rare; and let us give all honour to Australasian ministers for that they still hold it dear. But what are we to say to the publication of misleading accounts, false balance sheets and fictitious returns by authority of the State? It cannot be urged that ministers were unaware of the irregularity of their proceedings, for it was constantly brought to their notice by the auditors. It cannot be advanced that political exigency is sufficient excuse; for the ministers and their apologists expressly debarred themselves from any such plea. They asserted again and again that the money borrowed by the State was expended on commercial undertakings in accordance with business principles; and they must, therefore, be judged by the code, not of political, but commercial ethics. What, again, are we to say of the ministers who, after admitting, under the legitimate torture of press criticism, that a certain balance sheet was misleading, not to say false, none the less advised the Governor to countersign that same false balance sheet, and suffered it to pass into the English official returns as correct? What, further, shall we say of the people which, after the exposure of such a scandal by the press, allows the guilty ministry to remain quietly in office, and retire on its laurels? Lastly, what shall we say of New South Wales and of its present Premier? In the summer of 1892 that Premier, Sir George Dibbs, came to England to support the tottering credit of his Colony. He wrote a long letter to the *Times* in defence of Australian financial administration in general, and of New South Wales finance in particular; he succeeded in reassuring English investors to some extent (for he was received with honour in high places, and even knighted), and is said to have actually raised the New South Wales Government Stock one per cent. He then pressed the Chancellor of the Exchequer hard to open Colonial Government Stock to English trustees; most fortunately without success. Shortly after he returned to his Colony. Within six months he saw it sunk in hopeless financial collapse; within nine he had, by the establishment of a forced paper currency, virtually admitted its bankruptcy. Now, one would have thought that a Premier so ignorant of the financial condition of his Colony as to cry up its soundness and stability (and make a journey to England for the purpose) but half a year before a confession of insolvency—one would have thought, I say, that a minister so ignorant, would have been forthwith driven from office. On the contrary, he not only remains in office, but has received a public testimonial (£700 was, I think, the amount subscribed) for his eminent services to his country. Such sympathy with ignorance seems, at first sight, a little difficult to account for, in view of the free education so liberally supplied by the State to every citizen in New South Wales, though, to directors of shaky companies, and indeed, to debtors at large, it must be very full of encouragement and comfort. But surely it must be conceded that a community in which executive power and public feeling conspire to set at naught the sanctity of obligation, is, to say the least of it, in a very unsound condition. The whole fabric of State Socialism depends for stability and coherence on the due maintenance of mutual obligation between citizen and State. Yet the State, as we have seen, neglects to uphold it, even as between citizen and citizen; and if man keeps not faith with his brother, whom he has seen, how shall he keep it with the State, which he has not seen? Why, lastly, should men hesitate to abuse the trust of their fellow men, when the State itself, which is the pattern for all, does the like to a fellow State?

It may be replied that education is the means whereby such evil may be corrected. Now, we hear a great deal about education in Australia and of the consequent intelligence of its citizens; but the same fundamental mistake runs through the whole scheme of Australian State Socialism—namely, the grant of benefit without the exaction of sacrifice—and in the case of education shows itself as the imparting of knowledge without the enforcement of discipline. Mr. Gladstone recently said that the English are an undisciplined race; and the assertion contains so much truth that it is much to be regretted that it should have been spoiled by its context; for the English are at any rate patient of discipline, which is precisely the point at which the Irishman fails. The English, as compared with the Germans, are decidedly undisciplined; and the Australians, as compared with the native English, are even more decidedly undisciplined. The cause is not far to seek. A settlement in a strange land is not formed by the steady, the soberminded and the commonplace; these can do well enough at home; but by the discontented, the restless, the adventurous and the enterprising, who are attracted by the relief from discipline and restraint—by the liberty to fight the battle of life in their own way. Even after the settlement has become a colony the population is fed mainly by the influx of men of similar temperament; for the man who leaves his native land—whether as an emigrant to seek his fortune or as a colonist to make a new home—is plainly a man who is not satisfied with it and hopes to do better. Thus in all new countries there is, so to speak, a kind of hereditary predisposition to indiscipline, which shows itself mainly in the relaxation of parental authority. All the more reasons, it will be urged, why the State should take the rising generation in hand. The State has taken the rising generation in hand accordingly, and has absolved parents from all responsibility in respect of the making of citizens. The decline of the family, which is the fate that Dr. Pearson predicts for the civilized world, is rapidly accomplishing itself in Australia; but the rise of the State in its place is invisible, except to those who pretend to see it in columns of reckless expenditure. The ministers of the State have so little conception of the responsibility that the State has assumed that they ignore the necessity for inculcating obedience as the first of all lessons. In one Antipodean Colony which I know, it was proverbial that if a schoolmaster attempted to enforce discipline by proper punishment, the parents promptly complained to the member for the district, the member complained to the Minister of Education, and the schoolmaster ran great risk of dismissal. What wonder that the children kick up their heels at all authority, and grow up to become larrikins? Parents wash their hands of them as soon as they are old enough to be put in charge of the State; the State washes its hands of them as soon as school hours are over; and yet the children are expected to grow up good citizens. As to higher education, Dr. Pearson, who is a most competent witness, shall himself tell us how and why it is valued in Australia: 'In the English Colonies I have known the tendency is to tolerate University training as a necessity for professional men; but to regard primary school education, or something only a little above it, as sufficient for all the needs of practical men and men of the world. Indeed, high schools in Australia seem to be maintained chiefly because some people like their children to have the distinction of a rather costly training; because a few others intend to send their sons and daughters into professions; and because a good many find it convenient to keep their children of a certain age away from home during the day.'

Such is the spirit in which the citizens receive such gifts of the State as they consider to pass the needs of every day.

How, then, to recall Dr. Pearson's words already quoted, are they to gain knowledge of the immaterial benefits with which every historic State endows its citizens—the great deeds which have formed the national character, the winged words that have passed into current speech, the example of lives and labours consecrated to the Commonwealth? It is to historic England that the Australian owes whatever significance he may possess. What does he know of it? and in what light is that historic England displayed to him by the State? First, as a credulous and convenient loan agency, and latterly as a grasping and suspicious creditor. Whether it wished it or not, this is what the State in Australia has done; and for noble deeds, winged words and lofty examples the Australian must fall back on such men as Sir George Dibbs.

This is on the whole the blackest blot on the administration of State Socialism in Australia—it has corrupted the national character. If the situation were merely that of communities wherein a few rogues at the head of affairs had embezzled public money, borrowed on the public credit, and absconded therewith, then we might contemplate it with comparative equanimity and look with confidence for ultimate revival. But in Australia such a scandal in high places has been escaped only at the price of far greater mischief. The borrowed millions have been lavished on the people at large—every soul has had his share of the plunder—and the absconders are numbered by thousands. The colonists have played at work for so long that they have forgotten how to work in earnest; and industry and honesty have gone to the wall. And yet, if we forget (as we can afford to forget) the early days of penal settlement in Australia, and think only of more recent times, I think we must admit that there was plenty of good human material to the State's hand for the making of a solid and prosperous community. The deeds of the pioneers and explorers and early settlers are rightly enshrined as monuments of energy and enterprise; and it is not too much to say that the early traditions of Australia are of hard work, perseverance and self-help. Whatever of good there is in Australian life (and there is much) is due to these traditions and to the habits that grew up along with them. Colonial hospitality is proverbial—indeed, hospitality (as we understand it in England) is too weak a word to express this side of the colonial character. Colonial neighbourliness is another virtue which equally deserves to pass into a proverb. Indeed, I know nothing more beautiful to see than the spontaneous and unreflecting self-abnegation wherewith colonists come forward to share the burden of a neighbour's sickness or distress. Young clerks, for instance, who are busy at their desks all day and, it may be, have to prepare for an examination all the evening, relieve each other and keep each other company over a neighbour's sick bed—sacrificing pleasure, health, rest, and even prospects, without the slightest consciousness of performing more than the simplest neighbourly duty. Such virtues as these the State could not destroy if it would; but the old energy and self-reliance it has done its best to destroy, with a lamentably full measure of success. 'The Lord will provide' is a text with a dangerous double-edge; 'the State will provide' is an excuse for idleness and shiftlessness; 'the State will provide at another State's expense' is an irresistible exhortation, not only to idleness, but dishonesty. It has first corrupted the commendable and sturdy pride of the colonists in their young motherland into noisy, blatant conceit, and finally smothered it in shame.

Seeing, then, things as they are, I think we have at least as much right to take State Socialism in Australia for a failure as Dr. Pearson has to treat it as a success; and that we are justified in reasoning from this failure to other failures, just as he reasoned from this assumed success to other successes. Of course it may be urged, not without plausibility, that the experiment of State Socialism has not been fairly tried in Australia; that it is incomplete; that the system has broken down for the moment only; that the recuperative power of young communities is great; that one should not be in too great a hurry to rush to sweeping conclusions. That there may be some force in such objections I will not dispute. But I am obliged to ask, What is a fair trial of State Socialism? Are we to declare all trials unfair, until at last one be found, or claimed, to be successful? And when are we to declare the experiment complete, if not at the stage where the explosion of bankruptcy brings the whole laboratory about the experimenters' ears? As to the recuperative powers of young communities[1], these depend not upon mere natural resources, but principally upon the citizens, or, as we may now say, with thanks to Dr. Pearson for teaching us the word, upon national character. The national character in Australia has, I think, been sufficiently proved to have suffered very seriously from State Socialism. Where, then, is ground for hope of swift recovery?

Let us now, therefore, pass to the consideration of the question whether State Socialism is as likely to break down in other countries as in Australia. The Australian Colonies are under the rule of a democracy; and, as Sir Henry Maine pointed out many years ago, democracy is a terribly expensive system of government. Are we to look for a similar collapse of State Socialism in Germany, where administration is from long habit and tradition conducted on the most economical principles, and the people, from long centuries of suffering and misfortune, are drilled, disciplined and patriotic? And if not in Germany, are we to look for it in England, which represents the mean between these two extremes? I do not question for a moment but that in all cases the effect of State Socialism will in the long run be the same. For, whether under the guidance of an enlightened despot, of a hare-brained Kaiser or an ordinary demagogue, State Socialism seems to proceed on a false principle towards the fulfilment of an impossible task. At the core of the system is to be found the oft-exploded

---

[1] I am aware that two of the Australian provinces have recently succeeded in floating loans in London, and that it is now assumed that their principal difficulties are over. None the less I see no occasion to alter a word that I have written; for without going into detail I may say that I do not share the general confidence in such sudden resurrection from collapse; and am strengthened in my opinion by two recent enactments of the Parliament of New Zealand, which could only have been passed in the fear of a serious financial crisis, and are not justified even by that. If New Zealand's recovery be so slow and uncertain, how much slower and more uncertain must Australia's be!

fallacy that all men are equal; presenting itself in the still more preposterous notion that all men are equalizable. On what other possible hypothesis could Dr. Pearson have worked out his conclusion as to the decay of individual character? State Socialism is, in fact, the creation of the ever-increasing multitude of civilized men who are oppressed with the sense of the finality of this life. They have seen, from the teaching of history, that hitherto it has always been the fate of a large fraction of mankind to serve the remainder; that in fact history is simply the record of the struggles of individuals to pass from the class that serves to the class that is served, and of the efforts of communities to adjust the relations between the two to the current ideas of justice. Speaking generally, it can hardly, I think, be denied that the fraction of mankind that is served is superior to the class that serves it. It is not necessarily a question of merit in them; it is simply an exemplification of the unpleasant but incontestable truth that, broadly speaking, a lucky man for the purposes of this life is better than an unlucky man. The Church, while unable to resist the temptation to try and do something towards relieving the distress of the unlucky, always kept the promise of redress in a future life in reserve as a final resource, when all others should fail. The State is far bolder. It undertakes to make this life potentially endurable and pleasant to all—to say that henceforth there shall be no such division of men into servers and served; but that all men shall serve the State, and the State serve all. And this it hopes to accomplish by taking the human organism in hand almost from the cradle, passing it (to take an extreme case) through the State crèche into the State school, and from the State school into the State workshop, from the State workshop to the State asylum for the old, and from the State asylum to the State grave. But this is a process which costs money; and who is to provide the money? In Australia it was claimed for a time that this problem had been solved; but in truth it was only evaded. State Socialism there worked on the old lines—that there was a class to serve and another class to serve it. The class to be served was the colonist, and the class to serve was the British capitalist. But the British capitalist kicked; and the system broke down, with disastrous results both to capitalist and colonist; and now the situation is recognized in its true light as reversed, i.e. that the capitalist claims the service of the colonist.

In other countries the methods of State Socialism can be only superficially different. The savings of successful natives instead of those of foreigners will be appropriated for the supposed happiness of the unsuccessful, and the certain demoralization of all. This has been done even in Australia itself, where the Government Savings Bank deposits have in some cases been taken by the State to meet current expenses, and virtually form a portion of the national debt: indeed, in Victoria the *Melbourne Argus* openly says that they may as well be reckoned as such. Now, if a schoolmaster were to fix an arbitrary standard of marks, far below the 'highest possible,' for his pupils, and, deducting the excess gained over that number by the first boy, should add the difference to the marks gained by the last boy, we should call him an idiot, ignorant of the rudiments of his profession. Yet this is the process which under State Socialism the State proposes to pursue towards its citizens. The pace of a cavalry charge is (or rather was) supposed in theory to be regulated by that of the slowest horse in the regiment. Military men, by reputation the most precise and hidebound of pedants, have freed themselves without difficulty in practice from so absurd a restriction; for they recognized the value of the counter-proposition—that if every bridle could be cut at the supreme moment, a cavalry charge could not fail to sweep everything before it. Yet the pace of the slowest horse is the ideal which, consciously or unconsciously, State Socialism has perpetually before its eyes. The carthorse cannot gallop like the thoroughbred, so the thoroughbred must be hobbled to bring him back to the carthorse. It is claimed, of course, that State Socialism can, so to speak, raise the general average speed of the carthorse; and so conceivably it may, but, by Dr. Pearson's own confession, not by very much. But the point is that the ideal of the State, particularly of the democratic State, is the lowering of standards. The same influence is at work everywhere and is traceable with equal clearness in trades unions and would-be-intellectual society cliques, viz. the reduction of the standard of excellence to the shallowness of the meanest member's capacity; the claim that the best shall fare no better than the worst; the ostensible exaltation of all geese to be swans; the veritable attempted degradation of all swans to be geese.

Now, is it conceivable that such a system can endure? That the State will attempt to make it permanent I cannot doubt, for I have seen in Australasia with what desperate jealousy it will endeavour to throttle all private undertakings which it chooses to consider encroachments on its province; nor do I think it the least unreasonable to believe that, in its efforts to enforce it, the State may be as intolerant of the right of private judgement, and as ruthless in its endeavour to suppress it, as any church. But that the system will break down in bankruptcy long before it can be pushed to the limits now assigned to it seems to me to be inevitable. For from whence are to come the funds to support it? It is useless (as has been very frequently pointed out) to indicate the millionaire with one hand and the pauper with the other, and ask whether it is right that the one should have been permitted to make his million and the other to sink to starvation. If a country wants millions it must allow those that can to make them, or it will never get them at all; in a word, it must give the lucky men liberty to follow out their luck. If, while a man is trying to make his million, the State perpetually interferes to prevent him from making it, the million will never be made, by the State or the beggar or any one else. But this is exactly what State Socialism proposes to do, forgetting that though the State can make, and does make, beggars by the thousand, it cannot make a millionaire. Nor does it weigh in the slightest degree with the officials of State Socialism that a millionaire, when once he has made his million, as often as not hands back a large portion of it, of his own free will, to the service of the public. The making of a million is one way whereby a man can show his superiority to other men, if in no more than the art of thriving according to the material standard of this world; and demonstrated individual superiority is what State Socialism cannot endure. For State Socialism in practice is the embodiment of the jealousy that the unsuccessful feel towards the successful. Meanwhile, when the cloud of bankruptcy comes up over the horizon, the State (as may be observed in Australia) suddenly relaxes its hold of individuals and begs them to go to work as they will, so they do but consent to save it; in a word, State Socialism falls back on personal liberty and private enterprise as its only hope of salvation. It is noticeable too that in this way, as in others, the State, so far from holding the highest place in men's minds, grows to connote something of inferiority, to become, in fact, somewhat a term of opprobrium. In the public offices of the whole world the delay which the State alone can afford to permit in the transaction of business is so well recognized as to enjoy its own name of 'red-tape.' But this is a small thing compared to certain others. In London, for instance, some of the working class prefer to pay for the education of their children in private establishments rather than suffer them to associate with those that they meet in the State schools. So also in a New Zealand town I saw a private school, which undertook no more, nominally, than the elementary State schools, filled up immediately with children of parents for whom the State standards were not high enough. These parents, almost all of the working class, preferred to educate their children at their own expense rather than make them over to the State to be educated gratis; and this, not from mere vulgar love of ostentation, but from honest preference for what was good though dear over what was cheap and nasty. In plain English, the State standard represented with them the lowest, and was accordingly contemptible to them. So likewise with the Civil Service. While the State lived on borrowed money the Civil Service was overgrown and overmanned. When the State came to live upon its own resources all this was changed and the service became, very naturally and justly, a byword. Thus, not only did the State earn an evil name as an employer, but, worse still, it was badly served. Finally, we come to the crucial instance of State credit. Dr. Pearson's remarks on the superstitious trust reposed in a State guarantee are so admirable that they must not be weakened by paraphrase in these pages. It is sufficient to say that he shows with unerring force that a guarantee by the State, to merit confidence, requires as good testimonial to character as that of any other corporate guarantor. We use the phrase 'as safe as the Bank of England.' There is no corresponding Bank of Australia; but the Government Savings Bank takes its place as the nearest equivalent. Yet the State Savings Banks in Australia, as we have seen, are used by the Australian Governments as milch kine; and the deposits in one case have been swept into the national debt. As to State railways and State works, enough has already been said. State balance sheets seem to be at least as dubious in some European countries, where State Socialism is in the ascendant, as in Australia itself. Latterly, State prosecutions have also fallen into disrepute, as they well might, after the Panama scandals in France, and the minor, but equally unpleasant, 'Davies' scandals in Australia. All these things tend to bring the State into contempt, and, more, into well-deserved contempt—a dangerous and lamentable thing, even in a free community; a fatal calamity in a country governed according to the standards of State Socialism.

But, in spite of the acknowledged and unacknowledged drawbacks of State Socialism, it is likely, so Dr. Pearson warns us, to be forced upon us by circumstances, e.g. by the limits imposed on the higher races by climate, the consequent closing of present outlets for trade and energy, and the turning of every nation inward upon itself. But, admitting as we freely may, the reality and pressure of these dangers— what deliverance is to be expected from the State? Compulsory military service—a people in arms. I am not one of those who lightly dismiss the advantages of compulsory military service, and condemn it as anathema; but surely efficient military service is as much dependent on national character as any other national service. Surely a people which throws itself in despair into the arms of an helpless abstraction; which fears the bare idea of the worst going to the wall; which shrinks from the laws of nature and tries to evade, instead of obeying and so subduing them—surely such a people will never win battles. Destruction of family ties (a consummation which is rapidly accomplishing itself) and decay of individual character—are these the stuff of which conquering armies are made? It must be remembered too that highly civilized communities have generally ended by hiring mercenaries to do their fighting for them; and the same may happen now—nay, is more than likely to happen, if the natural outlets to individual energy are closed—with the usual results. State Socialism, in seeking to lessen competition, is destroying the fighting spirit.

Then once more the question of money crops up—money, the sinews of war. Also there is another consideration to which we are led by Dr. Pearson's vision (amply justified by existing conditions all round us) of future increase of great cities, standing armies and national debts, viz. How are these communities, cramped within their own limits, to be fed? If the town population is for ever to increase at the expense of the country, where is the food to come from? From the inferior races outside those limits? But they may have none to spare, or refuse to spare what they have. State Socialism delights in large towns, for it is in them that the power of the State may be most strikingly exhibited, while the sense of oppression born of confinement within streets helps to render men more docile to its teaching. In the country the State can never obtain the ascendency which it may gain in the towns; and it is in the country accordingly that the men who love liberty and independence are most likely to be found. In Australia, as we have seen, State Socialism, which for a time kept town and country alike in subjection, by pampering both at the expense of the British capitalist, has been compelled to transfer all burdens to the country. Whether the country will stand it remains to be seen; but that it will do so without a struggle to assert its political supremacy I do not believe. Thus there is every indication that State Socialism, so far from promoting peace and contentment within a community, simply tends to embitter the country against the town; and it is in the combat between the two that we may expect to see it fall, both in Australia and elsewhere. For though we have few clues as to the issue of such strife, we have at least one, and that of no ordinary significance, viz. that life in large towns means physical degeneration. In England the country has now lain for some years under the heel of the towns; but the towns must decline with the decline of foreign trade, which townsmen in their wisdom are doing their best to accelerate. When the 'boom' on which the English towns grew and throve for half a century has been finally broken down (the process of destruction is still going on)—then, perhaps, we may expect the English State to remember that there are country districts and country interests even in England. Whether the country districts will feel as kindly towards the State, and help her in her hour of need, is another question.

Altogether, we are forced to accept Dr. Pearson's conclusion, which is (if I understand it aright) that State Socialism is the death-cry of our civilization. It is only reasonable to assume that our civilization will perish just as other civilizations have perished before it—for it seems to be incontestable that the lower races tend to outbreed the higher, just as curs outbreed pure foxhounds. The tendency of the moment (and it may be of more than the moment) is to abandon all effort and to yield place to the inferior races, provided they will but let us alone to enjoy our State Socialistic dreams. Ireland, it is said, stops the way—is the bar to all English legislation. In that case—long may she stop the way, and keep us from the most ignoble form of national suicide!

J. W. FORTESCUE.

V.

THE INFLUENCE OF STATE BORROWING ON COMMERCIAL CRISES.

WYNNARD HOOPER.

V.

THE INFLUENCE OF STATE BORROWING ON COMMERCIAL CRISES.

COMMERCIAL crises are primarily the consequence of the imprudence of bankers, merchants, financiers and other members of the business classes, and also of the credulity of the general public. Crises vary very much in the details of the phenomena composing them, but they all possess certain well-marked characteristics which it is necessary to describe with some minuteness, as otherwise it would not be possible to indicate the important part which the action of governments in regard to finance and commerce have had on the crises of recent years.

A commercial crisis is a state of things resulting from a period of inflation and over-speculation; its characteristics are usually a breakdown, for a short time, of the ordinary machinery of credit, followed by a period of inactivity. The violence and extent of the collapse is proportionate to the strain that has been put upon credit by the previous inflation. For inflation of prices is the concrete expression of over-production and over-speculation, and over-speculation is only possible when a great many people have trusted others too much and have been trusted too much themselves. Sooner or later the more cautious lenders begin to get anxious about the money they have lent and restrict the accommodation they afford to borrowers, who are then obliged to try and obtain what they need from less careful, or worse informed people. The latter, in their turn, eventually become uneasy, and as they are a large class, the bulk, indeed, of the business community, their newly acquired fear of continuing loans soon produces a considerable effect on the money market, necessitates sales of stock and commodities, and causes failures. When once the process we have briefly described has commenced its effects are felt even by manufacturers and traders who have not operated beyond the extent which in ordinary times their means justify. The paralysis of credit eventually becomes acute, and even the most careful and wealthiest people have to be content to abstain from all but the most necessary transactions in which no risk is involved, until by sales of securities and commodities the embarrassed portion of the business world has either paid what it owes or made a composition with its creditors. After a certain lapse of time an approximately 'clean slate' is shown, creditors having taken what they can get and written off the balance of what is due to them from their books as a 'bad debt.'

Of course the condition of affairs is never in practice so simple as this. There are no men who are creditors, or debtors, pure and simple; but there are always men who are, on balance, creditors, that is, have more owing to them than they owe. That is, or ought to be, the position of the bulk of the community, with one important exception, the bankers. A banker is a person who is at all times a debtor, on balance. He owes a great deal more than he could pay if all the people whose money is left with him asked for it at once. But he is in no danger whatever on that account provided he has observed what are known as the rules of sound banking. The normal condition of a careful trader is to be a creditor, on balance, but he can only be in this position if some one else is always a debtor, on balance; and this latter function is fulfilled by the banker.

The safety of a banker depends partly on the character of the liabilities he has assumed, but even more on due proportion being kept between the various classes of those liabilities, and above all on his preserving a proper amount of actual cash constantly in hand, or, under the London system, in the Bank of England. What the 'proper' amount may be each banker must judge for himself, but it is necessary to observe that even a proportion of cash which would rightly be considered large in ordinary times may be insufficient in times of general discredit, when the banker, the universal debtor, is called upon to pay an unusual amount on demand. What he can keep in cash is a small portion, at the best, of what he owes, for cash kept as a reserve, *ex hypothesi*, earns no interest, and as bankers have to pay interest on most of the money left with them, they have to use the bulk of it profitably or become bankrupt. The universal debtor, therefore, must be very careful to whom he lends and even more careful how he lends it. If a banker lends more than a small portion of his resources to even the most wealthy of his customers for a long period, he is courting danger. In technical language he has allowed his money to be 'locked up.' It avails him nought to be able to say, 'So and So is a good man, the interest is fair, and the loan is secure of repayment when it is due.' The banker can be made to pay large sums on demand under pain of commercial death, and his demand creditors will not be put off by being informed of the promise of Messrs. So and So to repay him, for they want cash at once, and must have it, under pain, perhaps, of commercial death themselves. Bankers, therefore, cannot hold a large proportion of long dated securities, no matter how good they may be, unless these securities are what is called marketable, that is, are freely dealt in at all times on the Stock Exchange. Now, the number of such securities is not great, for though under normal conditions readily marketable securities of good quality are fairly numerous, they become few during periods of commercial distrust. In the extreme case of a panic they are, to all intents and purposes, reduced to one, namely, Consols. The rest of the 'readily marketable' class can, indeed, sometimes be sold at such times, but only at a ruinous fall in their price. Consols on the other hand can be sold at a moderate decline, or borrowed on, even in a panic, and this is why bankers always keep a considerable quantity of Consols in spite of the low rate of interest they yield.

If all merchants were careful to remain, on balance, creditors and took care to give credit only to people who could eventually pay, and if all bankers invariably kept the money lent them in proper proportions of cash, short loans, bills and marketable securities, there would never be a commercial crisis, though owing to failures of crops, wars and revolutions, and unavoidable accidents which can only be partly covered by policies of insurance, there would still be occasional times of comparatively dear money. But merchants, bankers, and the general public, are human beings, and are consequently liable to be led from the path of safety, from time to time, by the delusive hope of abnormally large gains. The desires of even the humblest man or woman may be said to be infinite relatively to his or her resources for gratifying them, and though most people learn at an early age that their desires can only be fulfilled to a strictly limited extent, and only by constant hard work, and though, as a rule, they also learn to act on the knowledge they have acquired, the desires never wholly become extinct, and occasionally play strange pranks with the mental equilibrium of usually staid and grave persons. This is the secret of the never-failing attraction of lotteries, and of the periodic outbursts of insane speculation in Stock Exchange securities. The class of people who live by promoting and dealing in loans and public companies have an enormous mass of latent cupidity to work upon, and from time to time this cupidity becomes ungovernable and leads large masses of people to do things which they would not, in their normal state, have dreamed of doing, and which they bitterly regret having done for the rest of their lives.

It must not be assumed that the people who promote and deal in loans and other securities of a speculative character are intentional cheats. If they were they would not be as dangerous as they are. In nineteen cases out of twenty they too are misled by their desires into greatly exaggerating the profits which can be derived from their undertakings. It is true they are usually better informed as to the risks run than they allow the public to be, but they underrate the risks, even to themselves, when under the influence of Desire the mother of Hope. That this is so is plain from history, for there have been occasions when the public even when 'on the feed,' to use an expressive phrase sometimes heard on the Stock Exchange, have shrunk back in fear from some palpably dangerous undertaking which its promoters have nevertheless persisted in going on with, having rashly committed themselves to it. A striking example of this infatuation was afforded by the issue of the Buenos Ayres Drainage and Waterworks in 1888, which was conducted by Messrs. Baring Brothers, and was one of the principal causes of the destruction of that famous firm two years later. Messrs. Baring, who like most other great finance houses were 'registered as bankers,' had allowed themselves, under the guidance of their senior partner, to drift into the position of bankers in fact as well as in name, without at the same time taking the precautions which a banking business demands. Instead of being, on balance, creditors they gradually allowed their necessarily very large liabilities to assume enormous dimensions, by entering into engagements, chiefly in Argentina, which they could only fulfil if everything, political as well as financial, went smoothly in that country. They had undertaken to find five millions of money within a short time and another five millions subsequently for the Buenos Ayres Drainage and Waterworks, thinking that the public would gladly relieve them of a large part of the shares by which this liability was represented. But the public was scared at the magnitude of the scheme, which fairly staggered the wiser heads among them, who began to feel uneasy about other investments which they had acquired from a firm which showed so strange a want of prudence on such a huge scale. There is nothing to show that Messrs. Baring felt any misgiving at that time as to their own safety, to say nothing of other people's, for when, after the collapse of the Comptoir d'Escompte of Paris in the spring of 1889, the Russian Government asked Messrs. Baring to take over a deposit account they had kept with that institution, Messrs. Baring did so with alacrity, thus placing themselves under a fresh liability of a very dangerous kind. It also lent the Argentine Government money, on security, of course; but though fairly good as an investment, the security was not of a kind that could be readily converted into cash in time of financial pressure, and was, as a matter of fact, quite unsaleable for some time after Messrs. Baring's collapse, though it was at length disposed of.

The mistakes of Messrs. Baring have been dwelt on because they afforded the biggest example that was ever seen of the peculiar kind of madness which comes over the public generally at times. The breakdown of Overends in 1866 was equally striking, but it did not occur in the same way. Overends were broken because, being from the nature of their business, debtors, on balance, at any given moment, they lent the money under their control foolishly, so that they could not get enough of it back immediately when they required cash to meet payments due on demand. Barings, who ought never to have been debtors, on balance, at all, slipped into the position of being so without intending it. Now, small capitalists and manufacturers, who also ought not to be in debt, are from time to time seized with a species of madness, and commit themselves to liabilities which they cannot meet, thinking that they will never have to meet them, that 'it is a mere form,' or that their speculations, whether in stocks or commodities, will have turned out well by the time they have to pay calls or take up securities they have 'underwritten,' or to pay for materials consumed. They do this under the influence of various delusions, such as belief in the infallibility of great finance houses, in the indefinitely great riches and prosperity of foreign countries, and in the ability of foreign governments to construct an unending series of 'productive public works,' or works which, though not directly productive, are supposed to add to the 'efficiency of production.' The general public, which does not underwrite new loans or intentionally speculate, buys with its savings securities which it fondly believes to be good investments, and thus frequently becomes committed to speculations of a more or less uncertain character. The end of all this is weeping and gnashing of teeth, furious denunciation of the great finance houses, for it is on them that the 'investing public' relies, and equally furious denunciation of foreign governments, ending with rueful acceptance of the fact that a good deal of capital has been lost and a solemn determination to gather up the wreckage and be content with 'a safe Three Per Cent.' in future. The manufacturer who has risked his capital in a struggle for a new market, and has lost it owing to the general breakdown of credit, suffers in the same way. Many have gone through this experience during the last three years, owing to events in South America, Australia, Portugal, and elsewhere, and until sounder ideas are held as to what a government can wisely do in the direction of 'developing the resources' of a country, similar experiences will probably be the lot of many more unwary persons.

Mistaken speculation there will always be. Railways, steamships, waterworks, gasworks, breweries, mines, and industrial undertakings generally, do not always yield the profits expected of them, and sometimes give no profit at all. These unsuccessful companies, however, are a small minority, as an inspection of that marvellous embodiment of the financial and industrial energy of this country, the *Official List of the London Stock Exchange*, shows. But during the last ten years there has been a steady increase in the number of loans to governments and public bodies, which depend for their revenue in the main upon taxation, frequently excessive taxation relatively to the normal income of the people, which is a more precarious security for the payment of interest than the receipts of a well-planned railway carried out entirely by private enterprise. But governments not only raise loans, the proceeds of which may or may not be used for constructing public works; they also frequently give what are called 'guarantees' to railways, and sometimes to industrial undertakings, by which they undertake to pay an annual subsidy to the companies concerned. When carefully thought out and properly limited, arrangements of this kind may be beneficial. The Government aid given to the early Indian railways was wisely given, but in other countries the principle of granting guarantees has been much abused. In Argentina it was abused to such an extent that payment of the sums promised became impossible, even supposing the revenue of the State had not been unduly pledged in other ways.

The world is at present suffering almost everywhere from

excessive government interference with industry and commerce. It has always suffered in this way, sometimes to a formidable extent, and probably always will in some degree, owing to the exigencies of political parties. As this is not an essay on politics, the ways in which the working of the party system tends in all countries to the establishment of bad financial and economic arrangements intended to place patronage in the hands of party managers can only be touched on incidentally. Politicians will always find suitable excuses for any line of action they may wish to take, and their line of action in regard to finance and commerce is almost always the same, namely, an extension of the sphere of State Action, on pleas which vary much at different times and places. The course of events in the United Kingdom after the great war must be considered as an episode. Owing to a series of fortunate accidents this country got rid, during the fifty years ending with 1870, of an enormous mass of mischievous laws tending to restrict trade and enable the State to control it. We are still enjoying some of the benefit of the supremacy of the philosophic theories which dominated politics during those years, but for some time past legislation has shown a tendency to resume its normal direction, the sphere of State control being extended in several directions. *Laisser faire* is no longer the economic maxim of either of the great parties of the United Kingdom. On the contrary, both of them have of late made tentative advances towards socialism, and seem likely to move still further in the same direction. So far, however, these advances have not taken the form of open encroachment by the State on the sphere of private enterprise; but if the outcry for the management of railways and other public works by the State becomes sufficiently powerful to make it worth attending to, the politicians will not be long in finding pretexts for accepting that policy. Already some progress has been made in this direction in the sphere of Local Government, gasworks, waterworks, and tramways having in many cases become the property of municipalities. Local bodies, however, provided they are controlled by the ratepayers of the area they administer, are less unfitted than the national government to manage undertakings of this kind, though even in their case abuses of patronage and other forms of corruption are sure to become prevalent sooner or later. We must look abroad, to our own colonies and to foreign countries, for full-blown examples of administrative control of public works, and of interference with trade generally. In Australia practically all the railways are owned by the State, with very unsatisfactory results from a financial view alone, and almost equally bad consequences politically. In all the Australasian colonies there are strong parties in favour of extending the principle of State ownership still further, but recent events have checked their influence for the time.

We are not now concerned, however, with the mode in which the extension of State ownership of public works and the general spread of socialistic theories affect the finances and political stability of countries, but with the effect of these tendencies on the markets for money, securities and commodities, throughout the world, more particularly in London, the centre through which a large proportion of the world's transactions are 'cleared,' and where considerable quantities of money are lent to states, municipal and other semi-public corporations, and joint-stock companies. The means whereby these various bodies obtain money to carry out their objects are the issues of loans, bonds and shares, or stock. The issues of governments or municipalities are made through finance houses, but the larger public companies sometimes do the work themselves, or employ a bank merely to receive subscriptions. An issue backed by a house of good repute is sure of success in ordinary times, for 'good repute' means that the firm in question is believed to look carefully into any issue they allow their name to be connected with. Sometimes this belief turns out to have been mistaken, and the repute of the firm becomes less 'good' in consequence.

We will suppose that a foreign or colonial government raises a loan in London to provide for some 'productive public work.' Either it has already begun the process of construction, borrowing the money from a bank or finance house in order to pay the contractor such portion of the contract money as becomes due to him from time to time, or it commences operations after raising the loan. In the former case orders for materials have already been placed by the contractor, or whoever is in charge of the work. In the latter they are still to be placed. Either way, the effect of the government's use of its credit is to create a demand for certain commodities. If the government has entered on an extensive scheme of railway-making, which will require many thousands of tons of rails, chairs, fishing plates, &c., as well as girders and other 'heavy structural ironwork' for bridges and stations, there is a considerable addition to the previously existing demand for all these commodities. If several governments are committed to large operations of this kind at the same time, which is not unlikely to be the case, a perceptible rise in the prices of such commodities is probable, the makers of the articles wanted will extend their works, and new men will put capital into the iron and steel trade, probably raising wages by doing so. So long as the works undertaken by the various governments go on uninterruptedly, the iron and steel trade is prosperous; but eventually one of two things happens—either the works contemplated are all completed and the governments cease for a while from stimulating the iron market or, which is only too likely in the case of the governments of the rash and impulsive peoples of young countries, they find they have undertaken too much, and that they cannot meet the interest on what they have borrowed. Sometimes their creditors come to the same conclusion before the actual breakdown arrives, and refuse to lend them any more. In either case there are no more orders for rails, girders, &c., from this source, and the makers of these articles suffer severely in consequence. When a trade has been stimulated by two or three years of extra demand, which looks as if it would last for as many years more, it is a serious thing when the demand suddenly stops. And the demand artificially created by the government of a young country whose people are full of extravagant ideas of what it needs, and still more extravagant notions of what is necessary to its future development, is liable to stop with great suddenness. The Argentine

Republic was kept well supplied with money up to 1890 by the issue of national and provincial loans for all sorts of purposes, in addition to the considerable sums raised by companies. In that year, although the country's credit was distinctly on the wane, it imported 274,000 tons of iron and steel rails. In the following year, after the complete collapse of Argentine credit, these imports only amounted to 88,000 tons, and in 1892 they were barely 13,000 tons. This enormous falling off in the purchases of rails was only typical of what took place in regard to all our exports to Argentina after the great collapse of 1890, the total of these exports falling from £8,416,000 in that year to £4,241,000 in 1891, and a similar reduction took place in the exports to most countries which depend for the capital required to develop them on the issue of loans here.

Now, it is quite natural that new countries should be indebted to this country for the means of developing their natural resources. Simply stated, and ignoring for the moment the financial and commercial machinery by which the end is accomplished, Great Britain hands over to her Colonies and to foreign countries a certain amount of plant, machinery and materials every year, and takes in return a percentage of the profits they yield. That is the transaction in its essence, though it is obscured somewhat by the form it takes in practice. The question that arises is, Are there not serious drawbacks to the carrying out of this useful and, indeed, necessary transfer through the medium of extensive loans contracted by governments? There unquestionably are. First, public works carried out by governments are sometimes badly done, and are always extravagantly done. Secondly, the power of raising money for productive public works is sure to be employed sooner or later for non-productive works whose usefulness can be plausibly maintained. Thirdly, the public never troubles its head, when it is 'in a buying mood,' about works of any kind, but insists on regarding the loans as the obligations of a 'rich and progressive young country,' New Gerolstein, let us say, vouched for by that 'eminent house' X, Y, Z & Co. There is not much, therefore, to prevent the Government of New Gerolstein, with the aid of Messrs. X, Y, Z & Co., raising loans for any purpose it may think fit, including the reimbursement of Messrs. X for advances previously made, perhaps to provide interest on loans for 'productive public works' which have, quite unaccountably of course, failed to yield profits. To sum up, the process of equipping a new country with the appliances of a modern commercial and industrial community by lending largely to its government, involves waste of money and bad work from the commencement, and bad and, very possibly, corrupt finance eventually. It is almost an infallible way of producing a breakdown of the credit of the country concerned, unless it is conducted with more prudence on all sides than can reasonably be expected of human nature. And, as has been shown, the consequences of the breakdown in the credit of a country which has been a large customer for commodities is a sudden stoppage of demand for them, and a violent fall in their price, followed, of course, by forced restriction of production, loss of capital, eventual reduction of wages, and all that results therefrom.

It may be said that in a new country the only way in which development is possible is through the credit of the government; or, if the absurdity of this contention is demonstrated, it will certainly be alleged that the development will be 'too slow for the modern spirit' unless government loans are raised. As we have shown, however, more haste may be worse speed in this matter. Rapid development attained in this manner is often over-development, involving either a heavy burden to be borne by the taxpayer (or by one set of taxpayers for the benefit of another) or an injury to the State's credit, and possibly actual default. Moreover, talk of this kind about the requirements of 'the modern spirit' is not sincere, being merely part of the stock-in-trade of corrupt politicians and officials leagued with contractors and financiers in want of a *job*, in both senses of the word. There is not the slightest fear of a country which is really worth developing not being developed quite as fast as is good for it by private enterprise, provided it affords reasonable security for life and property.

Of course private enterprise, conducted by independent companies, is not likely to make railways merely to help the election of supporters of the government—a motive for railway construction not wholly unknown either in our Colonies or in foreign countries. But all really useful lines or other works are sure of support in London, except in times when a series of commercial and financial collapses has temporarily destroyed confidence, as has been the case for the last three years.

There is one argument, however, against leaving the making of public works, such as railways, to private enterprise which is advanced frequently in perfect good faith and deserves consideration from the economist. It is the well-known socialistic plea that governments ought, as a matter of principle, to possess control of all instruments of production, and consequently of the means of communication which subserve production. To combat this notion, however, which is based on a profoundly mistaken view of the functions of government, would open up a discussion of greater extent than is contemplated in this essay, in which it is merely intended to show that the construction of public works by means of State loans necessarily aggravates commercial crises. If young countries insist upon disregarding the experience of past ages, and imagine that because they are new they require new principles for their guidance, they will probably involve themselves in considerable trouble, but they will be useful to the rest of the world as 'object lessons,' to use the slang of the New Journalism. The United States, a young and vigorous, but overweening community, has lately performed a series of most interesting experiments on itself—first, by deliberately adopting Protection in its most extreme form; and, second, by converting its Treasury into a Pig Silver Warrant Store, in the mistaken hope of keeping silver at the old American ratio to gold of sixteen to one. Although it is easy to extract amusement from the spectacle thus afforded, the results of this latter freak on the part of our lively cousins are by no means wholly comical, or entirely confined to their affairs; and everybody is heartily glad that this attempt to perform the impossible has been abandoned, for it had caused temporary paralysis in most of the great markets of the world by disturbing confidence in American securities.

The commercial and financial relations between countries are now so close that no country can arouse distrust in its own ability to fulfil its obligations without causing general uneasiness. The principal creditors of the world are capitalists in Great Britain, and if one of the debtor countries gets into difficulties of any kind the capitalists become not only less able to lend money elsewhere, but, for the time, less willing to do so. This is why the breakdown in Argentina produced such serious effects, even in quarters quite unconnected with that country. After the great collapse of November, 1890, there was hardly a country which depends on the London Money Market for aid in developing its resources which did not find its supplies of capital curtailed. All second-rate investments are liable to risks, which are, more or less, recognized by those who engage in them; but, as a rule, the perception of these risks is dormant. Where, however, some one of this class of investments, to which the securities of most new countries belong, ceases to yield interest the whole class becomes temporarily discredited, because it is impossible for even the dullest not to perceive that what has happened in one case may happen in others. All the weak points of securities of this class are suddenly brought home to those who have been in the habit of holding them, and, for a time at any rate, are probably as much exaggerated as they had previously been underrated. As we have shown, government borrowings are much more likely to lead a country into financial trouble than the borrowings of companies conducted by private enterprise—first, because the governments are pretty sure to obtain more money than they can productively employ (which is not so much the case with companies); and, secondly, because even what they employ productively would have gone further in the same direction if managed by companies controlled by private individuals. Moreover, if a private enterprise is found to be hopelessly unremunerative, the company carrying it on will, indeed must, go into liquidation, while a government which can draw on the revenue of its subjects by taxation, is very likely to go on throwing good money after bad, long after an undertaking it has committed itself to is proved a failure. The facilities for borrowing enjoyed by governments have been too great for many years past. There is something dangerously seductive both to lender and borrower in the power possessed by governments of mortgaging the future revenue of the countries they administer. The government of a new country is especially prone to take a sanguine view of its prospects; the people are at least equally certain of their capacity to provide the interest required; the finance houses, which stand as sponsors for the loans, may be credited with a belief that at any rate their particular issues are safe, and the public here too often blindly follow the finance houses. In the majority of cases all the parties concerned are actuated by perfect good faith, and the evils which follow from excessive issues are the results of being oversanguine, and sometimes, as regards the finance houses, of neglect to look sufficiently carefully into all matters connected with such issues, especially the amounts of those already in existence.

Now, this too ready belief on the part of the borrower in his future ability to pay, and the tendency on the part of issuing houses to shirk examining carefully the troublesome details of a loan operation, are examples of ordinary failings of human nature, which must be reckoned with at all times. They are constant elements in the situation, and their effects are certain to make their appearance sooner or later in cases where governments habitually raise loans outside their own country. Of course it is true that any country may without danger have a small foreign debt; but the interpretation of the word *small* must be strict—that is, the debt incurred must be compared with the right quantities, and not with quantities whose relative dimensions have no real bearing on the question at issue. Occasionally, it is to be regretted, figures are introduced into prospectuses of loans which suggest quite irrelevant comparisons, of course tending to show that the proposed issue is 'small' and the resources available for meeting it 'great,' whereas comparison with the proper quantities would have brought out a very different result. These are matters in which finance houses allow themselves to be 'caught napping' more often than is good for their reputations or for the pockets of those who place confidence in their judgement. But it is necessary to emphasize the fact that the investing public, in demanding infallibility from finance houses, as they practically do, are asking for too much. Every investor will admit this obvious truth individually, and yet readily forms one of a drove of similar persons who collectively act as if Messrs. X, Y, Z & Co. were both omniscient and exempt from all human failings, whether moral or mental. Is it surprising under these conditions that the said public sometimes finds that its money is lost, in whole or in part? If all finance houses had taken as much trouble as they ought, the number of foreign government loans would be about half what it is; but the same result would have been attained if the public had not foolishly accepted the belief that the promise of a government is always a good guarantee for payment.

The economic objections to the principle of allowing governments to raise big loans abroad for public works are equally strong as regards similar loans made at home. It is interesting to observe, however, that, except in the case of naval and military expenditure, where it can be defended on other than economic grounds, few countries ever attempt to raise money for public works except abroad. In most countries there is none to be got; and in those where it has been tried the plan has by no means proved to be a success economically. Even in France it broke down. The gigantic railway scheme elaborated by M. de Freycinet in 1879 could not be carried out, the State having, some years later, to beg the great railway companies to take over the lines it had partly constructed and was unable to complete, and to transfer to them most of the remainder of the mileage originally intended to be built as part of the addition to the *réseau d'État*. Whether the possession of the Prussian railway system by the State will eventually turn out well remains to be seen; but it can be plausibly justified by considerations connected with the military safety of the country. It is doubtful if the Belgian railways are as efficient as they would have been if made by private enterprise. The acquisition of the telegraph system of the United Kingdom by the State is defended, even by those who are no friends to State Socialism, as a necessary corollary of the administration of the Post Office by a Government department. It can also be justified, with some plausibility, on political-military grounds. But, although it has long been an accomplished fact, and must be tolerated, it is economically bad—first, because the actual service rendered is less good than would have been furnished by private enterprise; and, secondly, because the ordinary defects of a bureaucracy, namely, morbid hostility to change and dislike of criticism, are formidable obstacles to the adoption of improved methods in a business which depends largely on adequate recognition of the progress of science. The delay in the extension of the telephone system in this country was entirely due to the fact that the Telegraphs are managed by one of the Revenue departments of the United Kingdom, and that the Treasury is an octopus, which insists that there shall be surplus revenues for it to throw its tentacles around—in the interest of economy, no doubt, but in disregard of efficiency.

In conclusion, the opinion of the present writer is that, to employ a well-known formula, the sphere of action of governments in matters affecting trade and commerce 'has increased, is increasing, and ought to be diminished.' The more strongly the current of general opinion, which necessarily means ill-instructed opinion, runs in favour of more government interference, the stronger should be the efforts of those who see the evils it produces to make them plain. And if we cannot easily begin 'at home' in this case, it is comparatively easy to begin abroad. For the evil results of entrusting large amounts of money to foreign governments, ostensibly for the construction of productive works, can be made patent to every one.

WYNNARD HOOPER.

VI.

THE STATE IN RELATION TO RAILWAYS.

W. M. ACWORTH.

VI.

THE STATE IN RELATION TO RAILWAYS.

The writers of this volume I understand to be in agreement on this main principle—that individual initiative, or where that is from the nature of the case impossible, the initiative of bodies spontaneously organized on a voluntary basis to meet each new necessity of civilization as it arises, is, unless in exceptional circumstances, and then for due cause shown, to be preferred to State management. It falls to me to apply this general principle to the particular case of railways.

The relation of the State to the railways in any given country may take one of five forms.

(1) The State may both own and work.
(2) It may own and not work, but lease.
(3) It may work without owning.
(4) It may neither own nor work, but merely control.
(5) It may let the railways alone altogether.

Of these various forms No. 3, working without ownership, practically only arises in countries where the State, already owning and working some lines, agrees for convenience' sake to work certain other lines which it does not care to purchase. No. 5, which may be described as *laisser faire* pure and simple, has practically never existed except in the United States; even there it is now obsolete. In fact, a state of things in which a stockbroker and two of his clerks could register themselves as a company desiring to build a line from New York to Buffalo, and thereupon *ipso facto* obtain powers to take compulsory possession of any house that might happen to be in the way in the course of a 400 miles progress across country, with further powers, if and when they opened the line, to run what trains they pleased, over bridges as shaky as they might see fit to build, charging such rates and fares as they thought proper—such a state of affairs could evidently only exist in a new and unsettled country where the great object was to get railroads—proper railroads, and in a proper manner if possible, but by all means to get railroads.

The second alternative, that the State should own the railways and lease them to operating companies, is out of fashion at the present time in this country, not being a sufficiently root and branch reform for our modern State Socialists. But it enjoyed at one time considerable popularity, and was, indeed, recommended by no less a person than Sir Rowland Hill in his minority report as a member of the Royal Commission of 1865. Moreover, it was the principle adopted after the most exhaustive inquiry by the Italian Government as recently as the year 1885. Still more recently the same policy has been systematized in Holland. Indeed, it might be said to be the French policy also, for French law regards the soil on which the French lines are laid as part of the public domain, and the railway companies as only the occupants on a terminable lease. And France is a type of not a few other continental countries. But we need not concern ourselves with the political problems of our neighbours; we have quite enough to do to solve our own; and may therefore pass by the question of the State owning and leasing. There remain therefore for consideration but two possible methods; and for us the alternative is between Government railways pure and simple, such as those of Prussia or Victoria, and railways as we have them now, owned and worked by private companies and subject to a State control of more or less stringency. We have, therefore, in the first place to consider the arguments for and against Government railways; and if these lead us, as I think they will, to conclude against them, to go on further and discuss the principles on which State control of private lines should be based, the end at which it should aim, and, in broad outline of course and not in detail, the methods which it should adopt.

It is impossible within the strict limits of an essay such as this to do more than touch the fringe of the subject of State ownership. A very recent writer has indeed published a tolerably bulky book on the subject, and yet found no space in it to come to the actual point at all[1]. An adequate treatment of the question would evidently imply, in the first place, an exhaustive consideration of the proper functions of the Executive Government as a general principle, and of such modifications of that principle as the varied forms of the Government (despotic, aristocratic or democratic, as the case might be), and the different genius and quality of the nation concerned might seem naturally to suggest. Secondly, it would imply an equally exhaustive consideration of the nature of railways and railway transportation. Such questions as, for instance, whether railways should compete with or only supplement water carriage; whether the cost of the railroad itself, as distinguished from the expenses of carriage along it, should be charged against the individual users as on the old turnpikes, or paid for out of general taxation, as being public necessities like any other highways; whether rates and fares ought to be fixed on what may be called the postal principle, ignoring distance altogether, or on the opposite principle of charging so much for each mile travelled, or again, on the merely commercial principle of 'charging what the traffic will bear'—in other words, endeavouring to lay on the consumer of each kind of railway service the least possible burden consistent with the raising from the traffic as a whole the revenue necessary to pay working expenses and interest on capital—questions such as these must evidently be faced and solved at the outset, for on the solution arrived at will largely depend whether we finally decide for State or private ownership of railways.

Nor could any treatise on this subject be complete which failed to supplement these two heads of more or less abstract inquiry by a history tracing the experience of the civilized

[1] *National Railways*, by James Hole. London: Cassell & Co., 1893.

world in the last half-century, showing the progress of railway development in the different countries, and indicating which of the failures of the one or of the successes of the other might fairly be ascribed to the management of that system by the State or private enterprise, as the case might be. To write such a book would be the work of a lifetime, and when written its author would probably be the only person to feel bound by its conclusions. For the facts under each of the suggested heads of inquiry are so multifarious and so obscure that no writer, however capable and conscientious, could ever count on getting them all in front of him, still less on appraising each of them at its precise value. We must be satisfied here with presenting the outline of the abstract arguments upon the question, and sketching in as few words as possible the history of State-owned lines in other countries.

It is equally impossible to deal here with the general question of State Socialism. The delegates, for instance, who at the Trade Union Congress of 1893 voted, after five minutes' discussion, for the nationalization of all the means of production at one gulp, will evidently not be deterred by a mere mouthful such as the thousand millions of capital represented by our English railway system. We must confine ourselves here to arguments that apply to railways more particularly. Now there is no reason to praise the existing system too highly. It gives us unquestionably in some instances what it is common to describe as the waste of competition. That waste, however, is by no means so large as is believed by the public unfamiliar with practical railway accounts. To take the stock instance of the London and Dover expresses. Whenever either of the competing trains is carrying as many as four first class passengers—and it is difficult to believe that they often run with less—it is earning a net profit. Further, we cannot ignore the question whether two simultaneous trains, both run under the stimulus of competition, may not carry twice as many passengers as one train run without this stimulus. If X be the gross revenue and Y the cost of earning it, $3X - 2Y$ is greater than $X - Y$, whatever values be assigned to X and Y. Still we must acknowledge after all that the waste of competition has a real existence.

Another argument is to the effect that commercial companies may, in spite of extravagance of management, earn bloated dividends by what is practically a tax upon trade. This too no doubt is theoretically true. I can, however, recall but one instance—that of the Taff Vale Company—in modern English railway history; and here commercial competition has already done its work, and the Barry Company has taught its elder rival to modernize both the rates and the methods of working. Then, again, it may fairly be said that the natural tendency of a company bound to return to its shareholders twice a year a dividend at least not less than that for the preceding half-year, is to fight shy of bold and radical concessions. For instance, it is quite arguable that third class fares at a halfpenny a mile might in the long run pay the company; undoubtedly they would be an enormous benefit to the community; but no railway company dare try such an experiment. Again, the objection is not without weight. Once more, however, it is more theoretical than practical; for, in fact, experience shows that State railways do not venture the reductions which theoretically they might be expected to make. Far and away the most sweeping reductions the world has seen have been those made by the highly competitive railways of the United States. The latest exploit of the commissioners of the State railways in Victoria is a proposal for the universal increase of the rate of charge. Similarly, the tendency of a State railway system ought to be in the direction of regarding the general good, and giving the blessings of adequate communication to all the parts of the country alike. Commercially-minded companies, on the other hand, must surely hesitate to extend their systems into poor and profitless districts; content with the splendid profits of the main trunk lines, they will naturally—so one would reason *a priori*—decline to water their dividends by investing capital in new lines which can never pay more than a very moderate rate of interest. Again, the facts are the other way. That England led the world in railway extension sixty years back is notorious; that the Cape and Australia lag behind even Argentina, much more behind the Western States of America at this moment, is equally obvious now.

Once again. Commercial companies will act from commercial considerations, and every merchant knows that the bigger the buyer the larger discount he will demand as his right. Translated into railway language this means the concession of cheap special rates for wholesale traffic between great centres, and the maintenance of a high standard of charge for the transaction of the general retail business of the country. Of course, the natural tendency of this is to make the great greater, and thereby the small smaller. And it is a common and, I think, a reasonable belief, that this tendency, if not indeed wholly mischievous, is at least of questionable advantage to the community. But once more it may, I think, be answered that the tendency is too strong to be resisted by any Government department. The Prussian State makes special rates just as freely as the North-Western Railway; the English War Office and Admiralty do not venture to place on their list of contractors the names of any except the leading and most powerful firms in their respective branches of industry. Moreover, whether the preference of one trade or trader, of one town or district over another, be justifiable or unjustifiable —be or be not, to adopt the legal phraseology, an undue and unreasonable preference—is a matter involving careful and detailed consideration of all the circumstances of the individual case. As such it is eminently suitable for judicial decision. Now a court of justice can much more easily curb the action of a private corporation, however powerful, than it can that of a department of the Executive Government with a majority of the House of Commons behind it.

One more objection, and perhaps the most serious, has been kept to the last. Where a body of shareholders are so blind to their own interests as to leave the management of their railway in the hands of an incompetent and effete body of directors and officials, the public lacks definite and positively legal right of interference to prevent the service of the line becoming quite disgracefully bad. It is, I think, undeniable that such cases have occurred and do still occur in England; and, further, that a Government department would not dare to treat any large section of the electorate with neglect as gross as that from which some parts of the country suffer at the present moment. But, after all, we must regard the interest of the country as a whole rather than any individual section of it. It would need a great deal of levelling up in services which only concern, perhaps, 5 per cent. of the community to counterbalance even a small amount of levelling down in the services given to the remaining 95 per cent. And experience goes, I believe, to show that the tendency of State management is towards uniformity indeed, but towards uniformity on a lower level than the average of private management. There is another point: 'The price of liberty is eternal vigilance!' and if the inhabitants of A, B and C—there is no need to mention names, they will rise instinctively before the mind of every reader—are suffering—and some of them do suffer grievously—from the badness of their railway service in this free country, where, after all, public opinion is in the long run supreme and irresistible, they have mainly their own supineness to thank for it.

I have endeavoured to sketch the objections commonly made to private railway management, and to outline the answer which can be given to each. Let us now see, in the same general fashion, what are the main arguments advanced as justifying State ownership. It may be noticed in passing that, *pro tanto*, according to the extent and minuteness of the system adopted, some of these arguments apply to State control also. It is said in the first place that railways are a monopoly, and a monopoly of an article of public necessity; but this is a point I should wish to reserve for consideration at a later stage. Again, it is claimed that, if the credit of the State were behind the railways, the portion of the rates and fares which represents interest on capital could be largely reduced. The facts, however, do not bear out the statement. It is true that railway capital at this moment receives on an average within a fraction of 4 per cent., and that the State can borrow money at something like 2¾ per cent. But the great railway companies can borrow practically as much as they please at almost the same rate [1]. It is not a question of the price at which the company could raise the money to-day, but of the price which they had to pay when their lines were built originally. And when we remember that, even as lately as the Crimean War, the State issued consols at about 85, we can hardly admit that through lack of credit the companies have on the whole paid very dear for their money. At 2¾ per cent. the Exchequer must make up any possible deficiency of railway earnings; purchasers of ordinary railway stock can at present prices get in normal times about 3½ per cent. for their money; but then they take the risk of a coal strike at any moment annihilating a half-year's dividend altogether. Economy of interest would then, I think, be something quite trifling.

There is the question also of economy in working expenses. I have already said that the economy secured by the abolition of competitive services would be very much smaller than the public seems commonly to suppose. I may add that the economies resulting from unity of management would also, I believe, be comparatively insignificant. In Ireland, with its fifty or sixty separate companies, each with its own board of directors, they would no doubt be proportionally great; but the whole working expenses of all the Irish railways put together are a mere bagatelle. In Great Britain the undertakings are already big enough to give every man as much as he can do, and for my own part I fail to see how the re-organization of the service would enable a single official to be reduced. On the other hand, everybody who has had experience of methods of business of public departments and private undertakings knows well that the former are more complicated and therefore more expensive. Nor is it generally believed that the State gets more work out of its servants than the private employer. Similarly, I think one might go through all the branches of railway expenditure and show that

---

[1] London and South-Western 3 per cent. debentures have, I believe, been dealt in at 107.

in none of them, except possibly in that much magnified mole-hill, Parliamentary and legal expenses, could any reduction worth speaking of be effected.

Again, it is said that at present our railways are worked in the interests of the shareholders; the State would adopt a different principle, and work them for the benefit of the community at large. This sounds, of course, very nice and pretty. When we ask for particulars, however, of the improvement, we are generally informed that the Government department would improve the revenues by a series of judicious reductions in rates. Stated thus broadly, the claim would appear to be that, because certain reductions in rates, made deliberately by the skilled managers of existing lines, have proved to be profitable, all other reductions of rates, which those same skilled managers have *ex hypothesi* rejected as likely to be unprofitable, would in the future increase the net revenue of the State railways. The fallacy is obvious, and comes back really to the theory of the Irish apple woman who could afford to sell her apples at a loss because she sold so many of them. And it will not be forgotten that, while at the present time the railways shareholder pays the piper for unprofitable experiments, under a State *régime* the cost would fall on the taxpayer at large.

There is another point worth notice. If we can persuade our would-be reformers to descend from the general to the particular, we do not always find them agreed as to the principles on which the reform should be based. Liverpool, for instance, is the nearest port for the manufacturing towns of Lancashire. Accordingly, we find the mayor of Manchester telling a House of Commons' Committee that railways ought not to be permitted to 'deprive a town of the advantage of its geographical situation.' In other words, the distance carried is to be the governing factor in the rate. Other places—say, for example, Southampton and Plymouth—have behind them only thinly-populated agricultural districts. Their representatives, therefore, are equally persuaded that the true principle on which judicious reductions will be based is to be found in an approximation to the postal principle of one uniform rate—that the great duty of a railway is to annihilate distance. Evidently, till all the inhabitants of Liverpool and Plymouth respectively are agreed to the principle on which the judicious reductions which they both equally desiderate are to be based, it will not be very easy for the State officials of the future to set about making them.

But, after all, the question of State purchase of the railways in this country will never be decided on *a priori* considerations. In so complicated a subject practical men will be guided by the sum of practical experience. For railway experience of course we must go outside England itself. But we may fairly call in our own experience of the Government undertakings most nearly comparable—the Post Office and the Telegraphs—to supplement it. A lengthened experience of State railway management, even as railways count length, is only to be found in Belgium and in the smaller states of Germany. As for Würtemberg, Bavaria and Saxony, it may safely be said that, as far as speed goes, their railway services are among the very worst in the world. Those of Baden are distinctly better; but Baden has from the beginning had the benefit of being on an international route, and taking part in keen competition for international traffic. It is true that rates and fares are low in these small German states, but it is difficult to call them low considering the quality of service that is given in return. Moreover, they are not low according to the general money standard of the country. The difference between a Bavarian and an English railway fare is nothing at all so great as the difference between a Bavarian and an English hotel bill, or between the wages of an English and a Bavarian artisan or day labourer. Belgium undoubtedly affords a more favourable instance of the result of State control. Taking into consideration both the rates charged and the service given, the Belgian railways can fairly hold their own with any continental country. But then we must remember that the Belgian State railway system is a small affair; the whole of it not as important as our own Midland Railway. It is very much as though the State here were to buy up the Midland Railway, remaining exposed not only to the competition by water on all sides, but to that of the North-Western on the one side and of the Great Northern on the other.

Further, it cannot be said that Belgium has developed any special principles broadly differentiating State railways from those of private commercial companies. 'In Belgium,' says Professor Hadley, 'State railroads were simply roads owned by the State, but managed on the same principles and with the same abuses as competing private roads.' 'At one time,' the quotation is again from the same authority, 'the Government railroads themselves granted special rates to prevent people from using the Government's own canals ... they abandoned schedule rates, and had recourse to personal discriminations and to special contracts of every kind. It is probable that in these respects the State was a worse offender than the private companies themselves. ... Charges have been made in official form by one of the best authorities in Belgium, Le Hardy de Beaulieu, that the connexion between railroads and politics has produced distinctly bad results; that there has been a multiplication of forms and offices of no use in actual business, and that there has been serious manipulation of accounts to make an unduly favourable showing for the Government.' Still, on the whole, it would I think be fair to admit that there is no evidence that a private company would have managed the Belgian railways better than the State has done. Those who are satisfied to put forward the example of Huddersfield, where the Corporation works the tramways so far at but small cost to the rates, as the main argument to prove that the County Council should work the tramways of London, which carry a number of passengers equal to the entire population of Huddersfield once every two hours, will doubtless be likewise ready to generalize for the railways of England from the experience of Belgium.

If from Belgium they pass to Prussia they will certainly not find much to strengthen their case. Even had the State management of railways in Prussia been proved a triumphant success, it would be inadmissible to argue that England was capable of doing likewise. No one doubts, for instance, that Prussia can organize and administer an army: it would be rash to found on this fact a belief that England can do the same. Says Mr. Charles Francis Adams, with the statesmanlike wisdom hereditary in his family: 'In applying results drawn from the experience of one country to problems which present themselves in another, the difference of social and political habit and education should ever be borne in mind. Because in the countries of Continental Europe the State can and does hold close relations, amounting even to ownership, with the railroads, it does not follow that the same course could be successfully pursued in England or in America. The former nations are by political habit administrative, the latter are parliamentary; in other words, France and Germany are essentially executive in their governmental systems, while England and America are legislative. Now the executive may design, construct, or operate a railroad; the legislative never can. A country, therefore, with a weak or unstable executive, or a crude and imperfect civil service, should accept with caution results achieved under a government of bureaus.'

But in fact there is no need to enter any such *caveat*. The Prussian Government did indeed, when it was urging the purchase of the railways upon the Prussian Parliament, point out that private companies were actuated only by greed of gain and care for their dividend, and steadily opposed to any reduction in rates; that the State alone was in a position to work the railways in the public interest; that the Government ownership would secure more judicious and equitable employment of the railway capital, as well as more rational and economical methods of working; further, that the State, freed from the obligation to consider particular interests, would regard the railways as the instrument of the general prosperity, and would devote itself constantly, as far as financial prudence permitted, to the development of the entire railway system, to improvements of service and reduction of rates.

But the facts have belied these high-flown assertions. The railways have been worked mainly as instruments of taxation. They have been managed on precisely the same commercial principles that were denounced when put in practice by the companies. The development of the system, the improvements of service are not yet visible; when traders cry out for trucks to keep their works going, they are calmly told that they ought to have laid in a supply of coal or raw material during the slack months of the summer; when passengers petition, not of course for English and American speeds, but for expresses at say 35 to 40 miles an hour, they are assured by the official apologists that the physical condition of the lines would render such speeds unsafe. As for reduction of rates, they have been made, of course, here and there, but there has been no general reduction, no simplification in tariffs, nothing but partial concessions, made from time to time to particular interests and particular localities, concessions absolutely insignificant in amount by the side of those granted in the same period by the competitive systems of the United States.

There is, no doubt, in Prussia an elaborate machinery of district and national councils, whereby the public can express opinions as to changes of tariff which they consider desirable. But such expressions of opinion remain opinion only, for the State has carefully retained all actual authority on the subject in the hands of its own employés. It is true that in the years of good trade the State railways have paid over large surpluses in reduction of general taxation; but, now that the good years have come to an end and the lean years have followed, the railway revenues have fallen off in an alarming manner and, spite of new taxation, there is a threatened deficit of four millions in the Prussian Budget. Of course it is easy to produce witnesses on either side to testify for or against the existing system. Professor Cohn, whose authority I should be the last to question, has recently placed it on record that no one outside of the Radical opposition wishes to go back to the former state of things. But certainly the said Radical opposition have recently uttered very caustic criticisms in the Prussian Parliament. I shall not, I think, go beyond the fact if I say that, even without any discount for the undeniably superior efficiency of the executive organization of the Prussian Government, the success of the Prussian State system has not been so striking as to constrain us to imitate it.

The country whose experience of State management should really be of direct example to us is Australia. With the Australian evidence I have recently dealt at some length elsewhere[1], and I need only mention it here in the merest outline. Australia may fairly be compared with the Western States of America. These latter States have of course now a population many-fold that of Australia, but they had none till the railways went there. They would have had but little now, had the railways charged the rates which are apparently found necessary on the Government lines in Australia. This, however, is not the only, hardly even the chief, difficulty. The railways of the different colonies have all passed through a stage of direct management by a minister immediately responsible to Parliament. That such method of management meant jobbery, extravagance, and inefficiency, is admitted on all hands. One after another the colonies found themselves compelled to interpose a buffer, in the shape of a non-political and largely irresponsible Commissioner, between the railways and the political minister. The system is as yet on its trial. Sir Robert Hamilton, ex-Governor of Tasmania, whose competence as an observer can as little be questioned as his democratic sympathies, has publicly expressed the opinion that the experiment cannot permanently succeed[2]. 'I believe,' he writes, 'that any guard upon our parliamentary representatives, in the shape of permanent commissions appointed by them to exercise their powers, must, as experience appears to be already showing, break down.' The Victorian experiment has indeed already broken down. How far, during its short life, it availed to protect the public from jobbery, may be judged from the one fact that the *Melbourne Age* recently published a list, occupying 11½ closely-printed columns, of free passes over the State railways granted to the wives and

---

[1] Government Railways in a Democratic State. *Economic Journal*, December, 1892.

[2] Lending money to Australia. *Nineteenth Century*, August, 1892.

families and dependants of members of Parliament. In New Zealand, too, the non-political Commissioners will probably by the time these pages are published have been reduced to a condition of subserviency to the Ministry of the day. In New South Wales, thanks to the exceptional personality of the Chief Commissioner, they have so far held their own, but after a life and death struggle. In Queensland and South Australia their position has not, as far as I know, been challenged. But in face of the fact that direct State management in Australia has confessedly meant in the past, and would again mean, extravagance and inefficiency, and that no substitute for that system has yet been found which can offer any reasonable pledge of permanency, he would, I think, be a bold man who should claim the experience of Australia as in favour of direct Government management.

Such then is in outline the case against the State management of railways. It cannot be better summarized than it was by the famous Italian Commission of Inquiry, which sat for three years, from 1878 to 1881, collected six quarto volumes of evidence both oral and written, and finally embodied the experience of the civilized world in these conclusions[1]:—

' 1. Most of the pleas for State management are based upon the idea that the State would perform many services much cheaper than they are performed by private companies. This is a mistake. The tendency is decidedly the other way. Private companies can do for their patrons many things which the State cannot; but it is doubtful whether the State would be justified in doing anything of the sort which private companies cannot. The State is much more likely to attempt to tax industry than to foster it. And when it attempts to tax industry, it is more omnipotent and less responsible than a private corporation.

' 2. State management is more costly than private management. Such at least was the conclusion of the commission, on comparing the results of the two systems. The differences which they bring out are quite marked, though it is fairly

[1] The summary of the text I borrow verbatim from Professor Hadley's invaluable *Railroad Transportation*.

open to question just how much they prove. Comparing State and private railroads in different countries, they find that the ratio of operating expenses to gross earnings is always greater on State railroads—averaging eleven per cent. more in all the countries compared. In their more detailed comparisons, the commission take carefully into account the various elements which involve cost of handling; but unfortunately they do not take up the question whether the rates charged on the State railroads considered may not be lower than on the private railroads—a thing which would make the percentage look unfavourable, and yet be rather a credit to the management than otherwise. We cannot, therefore, accept this point without reserve.

'3. The political dangers would be very great. Politics would corrupt the railroad management, and the railroad management would corrupt politics. These effects have already been seen in actual working. Changes of rates are made for the sake of influencing elections. A questionable experiment was recently made in Belgium in the matter of railroad tariffs; it had been adopted by the Government as a means of currying popular favour—a kind of bribery to which there is great temptation. It would not be hard to find similar instances in other countries on both sides of the Atlantic.'

So much for the foreign experience. It is worth while to supplement it with a few words as to our English experience of the nearest analogous business in the hands of our Government—the Post Office. For a century and a half, from the time when 'an enterprizing citizen of London, William Dockwra, set up at great expense a penny post which delivered letters and parcels six or eight times a day, in the busy and crowded streets near the Exchange, and . . . as soon as it became clear that the speculation would be lucrative, the Duke of York complained of it as infraction of his monopoly, and the Courts of Law decided in his favour[1],' the Post Office has been constantly worked as primarily an engine of taxation. 'The State has shown itself much

[1] Macaulay, *History of England*, Chapter III.

more inclined to tax industry than to foster it[1].' The modern history of the Post Office might be given in a sentence. Half a century back an outsider of energy and genius, Rowland Hill, converted the nation to a belief in the possibility of

[1] The following summary of Post Office history from the time when the idea of using the Post Office monopoly as an engine of taxation first took root, down to the time when an outraged public opinion thrust Rowland Hill into the office to prevent State officials doing after their kind, is not mine. It is extracted from Mr. Joyce's excellent *History of the Post Office* (London, Bentley, 1893). As Mr. Joyce is a trusted and high-placed officer of the Department, we may fairly assume that his indictment is at least not overdrawn. 'Let us compare for a moment the beginning of the nineteenth with the end of the seventeenth century. In 1695 the postage from London to Liverpool, or to York, or to Plymouth, was, for a single letter, 3*d.*; in 1813 it was 11*d*. In 1695, wherever letters were being carried clandestinely, the policy was to supplant; in 1813 the policy was to repress. In 1695 the King would not consent to a single prosecution, even for the sake of example; in 1813, when the Post Office revenue had passed from the King to the people, prosecutions were being conducted wholesale. In 1695 a circuitous post would be converted into a direct one, even though the shorter distance carried less postage; in 1813 a direct post, in place of a circuitous one, was being constantly refused on the plea that a loss of postage would result. In 1695 London enjoyed the advantage of a penny post, and this post carried up to one pound in weight; in 1813 the penny post had been replaced by a two-penny and three-penny one, and, except in the case of a packet passing through the general post, the weight was limited to four ounces. In 1813, moreover, the complications were bewildering. In some places there were fifth-clause posts, and in others penny posts; and the charge by these posts was in addition to the charge by the general post. Some towns, over and above all other charges, paid an additional 1*d*. on each letter for the privilege of the mail-coach passing through them. Of two adjoining houses one might receive its letters free of any charge for delivery and not the other. This difference was to be found in towns where building was going on —as, for instance, at Brighton—old houses being considered within, and new houses without, what was called the usage of delivery. In London itself, the complications, if possible, were more bewildering still. The three-penny post began where the two-penny post ended. Thus far the practice was simple enough. But the general post limits did not coincide with the limits of the two-penny post; and the limits of both the two-penny post and the general post differed from those of the foreign post. Indeed, it is probably not too much to say that in 1813 there was not a single town in the kingdom at the Post Office of which absolutely certain information could have been obtained as to the charge to which a letter addressed to any other town would be subject. More than ten years later, Post Office experts, examined before a Committee of the House of Commons, were unable to state what, even on letters delivered in London, would in certain cases be the proper postage.'

penny postage. The State organization fought tooth and nail against the innovation. Public opinion, however, was strong enough to thrust Rowland Hill inside the office; there he carried out his reform; and the Post Office has lived on his reputation ever since. The claims put forward in the annual report of the Postmaster-General, that the Post Office is a progressive and business-like department, are not a little amusing in their stolid self-complacency. For indeed letter-distribution is one of the simplest businesses to manage in the world. It is fenced round by a statutory monopoly; it is transacted exclusively on a cash basis; and no complicated commercial questions are involved. The standing difficulty which confronts a railway company is the question of differential rates. The inexorable laws of supply and demand compel a railway company to sell its services for what they will fetch. But it is only human nature that A should object to a fifty per cent. profit being made out of him while B's business is done on a margin of five per cent. The Post Office is spared the whole of this difficulty by the relative insignificance of the amount of its charge. If the sum were worth fussing about, depend upon it we should soon have a league in existence to protest against the iniquity of charging one man a penny for a sheet of paper from Lombard Street to the Temple and another a halfpenny for two ounces of paper from London to San Francisco.

One might admit therefore to the full that the Post Office does its present work well—and compared with the average English Government Department no doubt this admission ought to be made—and yet be very far indeed from admitting that this proves its capacity for managing the infinitely more difficult business of a railway. But let us examine the Post Office record a little more closely. Let us see first how it has used its statutory monopoly. Take, for example, the telephones. Tens of thousands of pounds were spent in litigation to prove that the wording of an Act of Parliament, passed before telephones were born or thought of, might be strained to include a monopoly of all forms of electric communication. In the result London is ten years behind Stockholm or Rotterdam in telephone communication. Take again the more recent instance of the Boy Messengers Companies. There was no need, thought the Post Office, of an express messenger service, but no sooner does a private company make the attempt at its own risk to afford the public a new convenience, than the Post Office starts a rival service of its own, judiciously handicapping its more nimble rivals with the weight of a heavy royalty for the infringement of a statutory monopoly. Of course, the plea for these royalties is to be found in the alleged interests of the public revenue. It is, however, difficult to understand why a tax on communications becomes economically justifiable because its effect is to spare State officials the exertion of using their brains to cope with the competition of private enterprise.

Not that one would wish to deny for an instant the wisdom of the Post Office from its own point of view in insisting on this taxation. For, where it has no monopoly behind it, it is usually beaten out of the field. Take for example the annuity business, in which the Post Office, with the credit of the Government at its back, does about as much business in a decade as a single private company gets through in a week. How long, one wonders, would the inconceivably clumsy money orders and the scarcely less inconvenient postal orders hold their own, if it were not for the stamp duty of one penny on cheques even of the smallest amount. Or take again the carriage of newspapers. Sixty years back the Post Office had a monopoly, not legal this time but only practical, of the carriage of all the newspapers out of London. To-day the Post Office has retained the unprofitable part only; the single paper carried in a separate parcel to remote country districts. Out of the wholesale business one firm alone of newsagents has built up a fortune of over two millions for its head.

The State, we are told, will operate the railways, not actuated by greed of gain but in the interest of the public as a whole. As a salient example of this spirit, we may point to the Post Office, which runs a wire with alacrity into the betting ring of every gate-money race meeting, while it turns a deaf ear to all demands for the extension of its lines to lighthouses, to fishing harbours, or to agricultural villages. Or again, who can fail to appreciate statesmanlike economy which refuses to recognize the unity of the British Empire by the establishment of a uniform rate of postage when a revenue of no less than £70,000 a year might be jeopardized by the innovation. Take another instance: For forty years past express legislation has made it impossible for private railway companies to contract themselves out of liability for the negligence or misconduct of their own servants. For this interference with freedom of contract public interest was undoubtedly the motive. Yet the Postmaster-General can and does repudiate all legal liability for the deliberate theft or injury by his own servants of property entrusted to him, even in cases where extra fees have been paid as an insurance premium. A union of continental railways led by the commercial companies of Switzerland has recently procured the enactment of international regulations, facilitating the recovery of claims against railway companies. A man whose property is lost on a railway in Holland can settle the matter after his arrival at destination with the railway company in Italy. The State Postal Union, on the other hand, devotes its energy to barring out the claims of individuals altogether. Here is, for example, one regulation. 'Under no circumstances is the charge for an unrepeated telegram which has been inaccurately transmitted refunded.' In other words, if the sender, after having paid five shillings for the despatch of a certain message, declines to pay x shillings[1] additional to discover whether the message which the Post Office has sent is really the message which he handed in, not only will he have no claim for any damage which may result to him from Post Office carelessness, but actually he may find himself compelled to pay for a service which has never been rendered him at all. Conceive a railway company which loses a man's portmanteau and delivers him instead a sack of damaged potatoes. Not only does it refuse to pay compensation for the loss of the

---

[1] I have written x shillings because, after exhausting perambulations through the mazes of the *Post Office Guide*, I am quite unable to understand what the additional charge actually is.

portmanteau, but it insists on being paid for the carriage of the valueless potatoes.

But indeed the comparison between railway and Post Office methods is fruitful of results. Imagine a railway company placarding its station with a notice 'The booking clerk is not required to give change or authorized to demand it,' or with another notice requiring passengers personally to paste the labels on their portmanteaus. Or again, what would the public say, if the railway companies issued notices at Christmas and at Easter calling upon them to travel in the early days of the week, in order to make the work as easy as possible for the companies' servants? And yet an extra passenger needs more accommodation than an extra letter. One instance more. When a railway company puts on a new train or opens a new station it makes up its mind to face an almost certain initial loss. The Post Office refuses to open a new telegraph office, however great its indirect advantages to the locality may be, unless the actual cost is guaranteed from the outset. Heads the department wins, tails the guarantors lose.

And yet, for all its penny wisdom, the Post Office can be at times extravagant enough. The rate, for example, for press telegrams—100 words for one shilling—is, we are officially told, a rate which not only does not pay, but never could pay. But the rate continues, for the Press is powerful, and the profits of a handful of millionnaire newspaper proprietors must not be lightly interfered with. On the whole, it is not too much to say that, before anyone can call the management of the Post Office successful, consciously or unconsciously he must have determined that a private enterprise is to be judged by one standard and a Government department by another and a much lower one.

If then we admit State management of railways to be undesirable, we have next to consider what are to be the objects, the extent, and the methods of State control. Now the control of railways falls under two main heads. There is first what may be called the police control of working in the interest of the public safety, and secondly control from the commercial side of the tariffs and services. The division is for practical purposes a fairly accurate one, though some subjects, as, for instance, new construction and train punctuality, are on the border line. In the early days of railways the police control was much the most important. In those days every town was a centre of demand and supply, and enjoyed, not of right but of necessity, 'the advantage of its geographical situation.' People bought the food grown within a few miles of them. If it did not grow they starved, or, always supposing the roads to be passable, they migrated to another district. The idea, I will not say of New Zealand and Texas, but of Devon and Aberdeen competing in the London Meat Market, had not yet dawned. It was a question not of relative but of absolute tariffs, and railways were—always considering the accommodation they gave—so immeasurably cheaper than any other mode of conveyance that no one grumbled. Nowadays the absolute *quantum* of a rate is unimportant. It is all a question of relation and proportion. The farmers of Devonshire may find themselves competing at a disadvantage in the London Market, in spite of a reduction of five shillings a ton in the railway rate, because a reduction of ten shillings has been made in the rate from Aberdeen. Naturally, therefore, with an ever-widening area of supply, tariff questions have constantly increased in intricacy and importance.

As far as police control is concerned there would seem to be no special principles affecting railroads, nor is it necessary to discuss the theoretic justification for such control. No one, practically speaking, argues against marine inspection, boiler inspection, building act regulations, notification of infectious diseases, and so forth. The practical justification of any or all of these is of course a matter for discussion on the facts of the individual case; but in theory they all seem comprised within the four corners of the old legal maxim, *sic utere tuo ut alienum non laedas*. In more modern phrase the community coerces certain individuals so far as may be necessary to secure that the freedom of all other members of the community shall be at the maximum. So far as our present subject is concerned, it would seem to be absolutely a matter of detail whether certain injuries, to which railway passengers are liable, and from which they are not strong enough individually to protect themselves, shall be dealt with by the co-operative machinery of the State, or by the machinery of a voluntary co-operative Railway Passengers' Protection Association. As for the kind of interference which has been shown by experience to produce the best results, there will be a word or two to be said later on.

Meanwhile let us notice some individual points in which State interference is obviously justifiable. First and foremost comes the construction of new lines. A railway cannot be made unless it has the power compulsorily to take the land required for the purpose. The only justification for the concession of this power is the public interest, and in this the existence of a tribunal to decide whether the public interest is really involved is at once implied. Carrying this a stage further, we may say that a railway can only be useful to those whom it accommodates. A line, for example, made without intermediate stations to serve the express traffic between London and Brighton, is evidently no convenience to the districts it passes through. Control therefore of the construction of the line implies control of the arrangements for dealing with traffic along it. On this point it may well be thought that the State—represented in this case by Parliamentary committees—has with us hitherto interfered too little. Running one's mind, for instance, down the line of a single company, the Great Western, it is evident that the public interest would have been better served had public authority prevented the construction of a second independent station, and insisted on the new company's admission to the old station at Reading, Oxford, and Swindon respectively. These, of course, are only given as examples. Any one who takes an interest in such questions could no doubt supply from his own local knowledge scores of instances in which slight modifications of promoters' plans would have resulted in greatly increased convenience to the public. Of course there is a *per contra* in all such matters. One man may lead a horse to the water, but nine men may not be able to make him drink; and so a public department may lay obligations on a body of promoters, with the result possibly of stopping the construction of the line altogether, or at least, in less extreme instances, of discouraging the promotion of similar schemes. No doubt there is need for a large allowance of common sense and elasticity at the back of such interference; still, given the possibility of finding such qualities in a government department, I am constrained to think that State interference with the construction of new lines might with advantage be carried somewhat further than it has been hitherto.

Again, the State may naturally be expected, before permitting owners and occupiers to be compulsorily dispossessed of their lands, to satisfy itself that the new company will really carry out the undertaking which it projects. Obviously, half-finished embankments and semi-pierced tunnels can afford no convenience to the public at large; they may, however, as was found in practice after the mania of 1847, remain as a standing nuisance to landowners, and an eyesore to every passer-by for many years to come. It is, therefore, only right and proper that security should be taken that the promoters are persons who may be expected really to complete and open the line for which powers are given; and further to be able to work it when opened in a reasonably efficient manner. Parliamentary committees and the authorities of the two Houses have in practice striven for half a century past to attain this end, but the scant measure of success to which they have attained is one more proof of the inherent difficulties of railway control. For in fact the Parliamentary control has protected neither the landowner on the one hand, nor the promoter on the other. Hundreds upon hundreds of Bills have been passed whose powers have subsequently lapsed, either wholly or partially unexercised, for want of funds, while a hundred millions sterling is a moderate estimate of the money that has gone in railway construction without yielding any dividend whatever. Indeed it may be questioned whether on the whole railways, though incorporated under special Acts of Parliament, have been one whit safer investments than banks and insurance and steamship companies incorporated in the ordinary fashion under the Companies Acts. After all, the best security the public can have for the success of a new scheme is the character of the persons associated with it as promoters and directors. And as long as Parliament satisfies itself that the promotion of a new scheme is bona fide and responsible, I am not clear that it can do better than accept this fact as sufficient.

But there is another closely analogous function which can, I think, be exercised by the Government with every prospect of more useful result, namely, the supervision of the accounts and statistics not merely of new but of established companies. So long as companies are considered entitled to obtain, if they can, a dividend at the current rate on the money they have invested, the public has a right to know whether the nominal amount of the capital does or does not correspond to the sum spent on the construction and equipment of the lines. Where payments aggregating nearly a hundred millions per annum, more than five per cent. of the gross national income, are concerned, the public is entitled to have access to figures showing what services the companies render and at what price, and what is to them the out-of-pocket cost of doing the business. But no information on these points is attainable at present. The railway returns published year by year under the authority of our Board of Trade have been for years past a byword among railway economists in every other civilized country. The State would, in my judgement, not only be acting within its undoubted right, but be taking a step of the utmost practical importance, if it called on the companies to submit their accounts to State inspection, and to furnish statistics showing in an adequate manner their general course of business.

In the next place, a public authority will naturally exercise control over the arrangements which involve the safety of the public, level crossings, height of platforms, methods of signalling and interlocking, methods of train-working, and so forth. It seems to me impossible to deny the justification for such control, but equally impossible to doubt that its practical working in England is far from satisfactory. A State department is almost bound to establish rigid codes of rules; it dare not lay itself open to charges of partiality and favouritism by varying its regulations to suit the infinitely various circumstances of practical everyday life. Regulations, therefore, have to be laid down more or less by a method of average; but an average can only be drawn too low for the top and too high for the bottom. We find accordingly, on the one hand, important stations left without safety appliances that in their case might fairly be called necessary, and directors and managers sheltering themselves under the plea that the Board of Trade does not prescribe their use as obligatory; while, on the other hand, petty railways in poor districts may be crushed by the burden laid upon them of providing even the average standard of safety appliances. Further, the Government officials are not responsible for commercial results, and cannot be expected to regard the shareholders' dividends, while they do incur a serious personal responsibility if they permit poor railways to forego the use of safety appliances merely on the ground of cost. Naturally, therefore, the average of demand will be fixed too high rather than too low. Theoretically, the result may be merely to reduce dividends, and what is money, says the common opinion, compared to human life. Practically, however, the result is to prevent the making and working of railways in poor districts altogether; in other words, to deprive the public of the almost perfect safety of even the most primitive railway, and to leave them face to face with the comparatively appalling risk of transit in stage coaches and carriers' carts[1].

[1] I believe I am correct in saying that since the beginning of this year more passengers have been killed and seriously injured in stage coach than in train accidents. This would make the percentage of risk run in these two means of conveyance roughly something like 10,000 to 1. The impotence of statistics to touch the imagination can hardly be better illustrated than by the fact that, while we constantly hear of the dangers of railway travelling, the man who dares to climb the box seat of a coach is seldom acclaimed as a hero.

We come, lastly, to the crucial point in railway administration, the control of tariffs, meaning thereby, be it observed, not only the rates and fares charged, but the services rendered in return therefor. That the State must interfere here may, I think, be taken for granted. Our own Government from the very earliest days of canal legislation has always fixed schedules of maximum tolls. In the United States too the States which began to interfere earliest have been precisely those which have found the question of the measure and methods of interference least insoluble. At the same time, we must recognize also that the problem is one of the most difficult in the whole range of economic legislation. To quote from a report adopted by a Convention of the State Railroad Commissioners held at Washington in April, 1893: 'To fix a standard for reasonable rates is a duty that demands the gravest and most serious consideration and the most thorough independence... The law of the carrier requires him to perform the service for a reasonable rate. The railway freight agent, the shipper (trader), the granger, the politician, and the legislator, all agree that rates should be reasonable. This is all they seek and all they ask. When they attempt to arrive at what is reasonable their views are widely different. Who then shall determine? Usually the party who feels aggrieved calls upon the State that has chartered these corporations to fix a standard. What the standard shall be, or how prescribe some rule, some law, or some formula by which rates may be measured, has been a problem that has puzzled the wisest and most thoughtful minds. Our belief is that this invariable standard cannot be found.'

It is usually admitted that the State can only successfully perform services which are of a routine and non-speculative character. All experience shows that the railways which have had the most flexible and most commercial—one might almost say, most speculative-tariffs, have been those which have done most for the development of the country[1].

[1] The fascination of the theory of an ideal uniformity has indeed induced the Prussian Government to subject the ordinary retail traffic of the country to equal mileage rates, the same for a ton of gray shirtings

Government interference must naturally make for inflexibility and routine; yet Government interference we cannot away with. All we can do is to see that the interference shall go on right lines and approach the subject from the proper point of view. What that point of view should be, it therefore becomes necessary for us to inquire.

Control of railway charges is commonly justified on the ground that railways have a monopoly, or at least a practical monopoly. The argument will not hold water when we come to examine it. For what is a monopoly? It is defined in the dictionaries as 'an exclusive right of selling.' This no English railway ever has had. Not only has competition by water and by road always remained open, but Parliament has never hesitated—at least for a generation past—to sanction competition by a rival railway. To take the most recent instance—the North Western and the Midland and the Great Northern asserted, and with perfect truth, that they were ready and anxious to carry every ton of traffic that presented itself between London on the one hand and Manchester, Sheffield, Nottingham, and Rugby, on the other. Yet, after full consideration, Parliament deliberately sanctioned a new competing route. Where then is the exclusive right of the existing railways? But the monopoly, though not legal, is, we are told, 'practical,' 'virtual.' In this sense there are few undertakings that are not monopolies. 'An apple stand,' says an American writer, 'is a monopoly up to the point when it begins to pay.' The existing railways have undoubtedly secured the best location; they have also the advantage of a long-established connexion. But is this practical monopoly? Have Bond Street shopkeepers a monopoly because the number of Bond Street shops is limited? Have

as for a ton of silk velvet. But when it comes to serious matters, to enabling German agriculturists and millers to hold their own against the competition of Russia and Hungary and the United States, or to diverting the traffic of Westphalia from Antwerp and Amsterdam to the German ports of Hamburg and Bremen, theory and ideals go to the winds, and the German Government frankly puts out special tariffs based wholly on what the traffic will bear; in other words, on the very unideal consideration of commercial competition.

London bankers a monopoly because there is no room for newcomers in the Bankers' Clearing House? Or, again, is a newspaper a virtual monopoly? A newly established journal which should fill twenty columns *per diem* with the proceedings of the House of Commons would bankrupt its proprietor, were he a Rothschild or an Astor, in a twelvemonth. The *Times* can do it because it is the *Times*. Is the *Times*, therefore, a practical monopoly?

Again, it is said that the fact that the Company has been suffered to take land compulsorily is a justification not only for State interference, but for exceptional taxation. This argument will hold water even less than the last. The power to take land by compulsion was not a present made to the railway. It is a function inherent in the State itself, exercised indeed through the agency of the Company, but exercised by the direct action of the State itself, as a consequence of the deliberate decision of the legislature that such compulsory expropriation in the particular case is for the benefit of the public at large. So fully indeed is the fact recognized, that public interest is the only justification for compulsory powers of purchase, that the Standing Orders of the House of Lords in terms provide for striking out compulsory powers from any Bill whose 'direct object is to serve private interests in any lands, mines, manufactories, or other properties.' The privilege conferred on the railway proprietors, so far at least as pecuniary benefit is concerned, may be said to be permission to pay every landowner along the route a sum of at least ten per cent. more than the maximum value of his property. There might be some justification for regarding this as a reason for laying exceptional taxation on the dispossessed landowner, but on the expropriating railway hardly.

Once more, it is said, the special Act of Parliament authorizing the construction of a line should be regarded as a bargain made by Parliament, acting on behalf of the public at large, with the Railway Company. Be it so, but unfortunately the bargain secures for the public nothing worth having. We have had schedules of maximum rates imposed with this object for two generations past. Except in a very few instances and under quite special circumstances they were of no use to anybody. The Companies habitually charged far below them. And, though useless, it cannot be said that they were innocuous, for it is, I think, unquestionable that the tendency of holding up before the railway managers the schedule of rates fixed by Parliament as reasonable for them to charge has been to keep rates higher than they would naturally have been, had each Company been left free to experiment for itself. It is impossible to doubt that in some instances managers, had they been free to charge what they liked, would have established ridiculously prohibitive tariffs. That no doubt, from one point of view, would have been hard on the district, but at least the district would have been no worse off than it was before the railway was made, and the reduction of rates which self-interest must shortly have compelled would not only have afforded a valuable object lesson to neighbouring lines, but would very possibly have gone much further than if, owing to Parliamentary compulsion, a less unreasonable scale of rates had prevailed at the outset.

It will, of course, be understood that I am not arguing against the abstract justice of statutory maximum rates. Theoretically there is nothing to say against them; practically, however, the policy has proved a failure. 'Every careful student of the question,' writes Professor Hadley, 'from Morrison in 1836 down to the Committees of 1872 and 1882 has come to the conclusion that fixed maxima are of next to no use in preventing extortion.' Unfortunately, the British public and the British House of Commons has a sovereign contempt for careful students, and prefers to trust to the rule-of-thumb guidance of the practical man. Its recent experiments in the revision of maxima have, however, now, I hope, finally convinced even that most impractical of mortals, the practical man, that a schedule of maximum rates is a double-edged weapon. The fixing of maximum rates is not likely, perhaps, to come back into fashion as a panacea for railway grievances till a new generation has arisen both of politicians and traders. 'Maximum rates,' said Sir Albert Rollit, in his address as president of the

Associated Chambers of Commerce at Plymouth last September,—'maximum rates are dangerous delusions, and they afford little, if any, practical protection to the trader.' The same may be said of various other forms of control that have from time to time been suggested or attempted. Limitation of dividend, sliding scales, periodic revision of rates,—all may be excellent in theory; only, unfortunately, they are quite unworkable in practice.

But State interference may be based on a different principle altogether. Without regarding railway companies as grantees of a monopoly, and as such subjecting them to exceptional burdens, the State is surely entitled to say that their position is such that real free contract between a railway company and an ordinary private citizen, in reference to each individual passenger journey or consignment of goods, is out of the question. Neither cabmen nor pilots have, in any ordinary sense, a monopoly, nor have they ever been regarded as fit subjects for exceptional taxation[1]; yet the civilized world agrees that cabmen and pilots must be licensed and their charges regulated by outside authority. So too I believe that the State should interfere in order to secure that the charges of railway companies shall be equal and fair to all their customers alike. In other words, the State must abandon the attempt to deal with railway charges as excessive and concern itself, not with their total amount, but only with their relative proportion. The principle is simple enough; the application of it is, it must be confessed, of extraordinary difficulty. To take a well-known instance of Mr. Grierson's, the Great Western rate for coke from South Wales to Wiltshire may give the Westbury Iron Company an undue preference over

---

[1] The hackney carriage license duties in London are historically a survival from the days when locomotion, like everything else, was taxed. And it is mainly owing to the fact that the Chief Commissioner of Police is a subordinate of the Home Office and not a London local official at all that they have not been swept away, or at least largely modified, ere this. But, of course, these duties might quite well be justified on the ground of the excessive user by hackney carriages of the London streets, and in that case would be only another form of the very equitable principle involved in the Highways (Locomotives) Amendment Act, 1878.

its competitors at Coalbrookdale in Shropshire; or, going yet further afield, the rate for American meat from Liverpool to London may be unfair to the cattle dealers in Yorkshire or Norfolk.

We have admitted it to be the duty of the State to prevent undue preference. Before, therefore, going further, it is desirable to see clearly what undue preference is. The phrase is often used to cover two widely different things. *A* and *B* are, let us say, rival tradesmen in London sending goods to Cambridge. If each of them sends a hundredweight of sugar of the same kind, packed in the same way, and the one is charged 1s. and the other 1s. 3d., that is one kind of undue preference. But suppose that they are both charged by the North-Western Company 1s. to Cambridge and 1s. 2d. to Oxford, though the distance carried in the former case is fourteen miles more than in the latter, this may be called undue preference of Cambridge over Oxford[1]. But it is undue preference, if it be undue, of a very different kind. The first case is practically non-existent in England. It happened largely in the early days of railways, and it has been continued, more or less, down to the present time in the United States. It is in conformity with the ordinary principles of business life. *A* is perhaps a large customer whom it is desirable to conciliate; *B*'s custom may not be worth consideration. Or, again, *A* may be a keen man of business who always drives the best bargain he can; *B* a happy-go-lucky individual who pays what is demanded and asks no question. In ordinary commercial life *A* would undoubtedly get better terms than *B*. No merchant sees anything disgraceful in allowing a friend to purchase from him retail quantities at the wholesale rate; no merchant would deny that he shades off his prices sooner than allow his customer to go away without doing business at all.

---

[1] In this case the explanation is, of course, obvious on the face of the map. The North-Western is not the direct line to either town. To Cambridge the rate is fixed by the Great Eastern, with a route only 55½ miles in length; to Oxford by the Great Western, with a distance of 63 miles. For its 78 miles to Oxford the North-Western can charge, therefore, as for 63 miles; while for its 92 miles to Cambridge it can only charge as for 55½.

Prima facie, there is nothing immoral in such transactions. But from very early times it was seen that when one party to the bargain was a railway company, doing business on such a scale that it could afford to forego a profit, or even to incur a loss, on individual transactions, or sets of transactions, for an indefinite time without feeling the consequences, such liberty must lead to serious abuses. A company would be able to wreck the business of any merchant or manufacturer against whom it had a grudge, or even, it might be, out of mere caprice, or in order to favour a rival firm. Such a state of things was obviously intolerable. As long ago, therefore, as 1845, public legislation—Private Acts of a much earlier date contained the same provision—required that all charges should at all times be equal under like circumstances, and that no reduction or advance should be made, either directly or indirectly, in favour of or against any particular company or person using the railway. The Traffic Act of 1854 carried the matter a stage further; and subsequent Acts have laid it down that all rates shall be public, so that every one can see for himself what the company professes to be charging for the carriage of each article. The upshot of this legislation, coupled with the very determined action of the courts of justice under it, has been that for a generation past undue preferences in the first sense—they call them 'personal discriminations' across the Atlantic—have been a thing unheard of. 'It is remarkable,' says the Report of the House of Commons' Committee of 1882, after an exhaustive investigation, 'that no witnesses have appeared to complain of preferences given to individuals by railway companies as acts of private favour or partiality, such as were more or less frequent during the years immediately preceding the Act of 1854.'

The other class of preferences exist by the million, and are given by every government railway in the world; whether they be due or undue is a question of extreme difficulty—a question on which, when the cases get near the dividing line, two equally competent and equally impartial judges may hold diametrically opposed opinions. Preferences of this kind may be roughly classified into preference of one locality, whether of origin or destination, over another, and of one method of consignment (including therein volume, method of packing, responsibility for loss or damage, and so on) over another. Undue preferences, then, in the first sense, 'acts of private favour or partiality,' are, like St. John's famous fox, to be knocked on the head, wherever they are found, with every weapon the State may have at its disposal. It remains for us to consider by what machinery the State shall exercise its control to prevent preferences of the second class, which must of necessity exist, from becoming undue.

In the first place, of course, it can act by legislation; but, practically speaking, such legislation must simply confine itself to generalities. Some American State legislatures have indeed attempted to embody detailed railway rates and regulations in statutes, but their success has not been such as to encourage others to emulate their example. Other States have entrusted a power of fixing rates to the almost unfettered discretion of one or more commissioners appointed for this purpose. This experiment too has practically been abandoned as a conspicuous failure. In some States, however, it lasted long enough to prove that the equitable adjustment of the conflicting claims of rival localities was not made easier by the fact that the person entrusted with the task happened to be a State official. Even where the legislature has confined itself to generalities its incompetence to deal with questions of this character is only too apparent. Take, for example, the twenty-seventh section of our most recent general Act—the Railway and Canal Traffic Act 1888: 'The Court may take into consideration whether such difference in treatment is necessary for the purpose of securing in the interests of the public the traffic.' What public? And who is to represent the interests of this indefinite public before the court? a lawyer asks, in respectful bewilderment. Or, again: 'No railway company shall make, nor shall the court or the commissioners sanction, any difference in the tolls, rates or charges made for or any difference in the treatment of home and foreign merchandise in respect of the same or similar services.' No doubt the noble lord who was responsible for the insertion of this proviso, and the two Houses of Parliament who passed it into law, did so with the best intentions. The railway companies were so determined to 'favour the foreigner'—from whom at best they could only get a mere fraction of their traffic—even at the risk of bleeding to death his English rival, on whom they were bound to rely for ninety-five per cent. of their livelihood, that it was no doubt necessary to stop them at all hazards. But really this proviso does not help much. What are 'similar services'? Is the service of carrying a ton of Texas beef, part of a consignment of a hundred tons, the one-twenty-fifth part of its journey which lies on English soil, the same as the service of carrying the four quarters of an English bullock the whole way from the pastures in Cheshire to the Smithfield Meat Market? Or is it totally dissimilar? The Act of Parliament sounds very patriotic, even though its patriotism seem not wholly in conformity with the teachings of the Cobden Club, but it fails to guide us as to the principles to be kept in view in the solution of the practical question.

If, then, legislative regulation be impossible, the task must be left in the hands either of the Executive or of the courts of justice. The leading example of Executive control is furnished by France. In France no railway rate can be altered either up or down; none of the conditions of carriage can be modified in the slightest degree, without the formal assent and consent of a minister of State. The initiative rests with the companies; but before any alteration suggested by them comes into practical operation it is submitted to a whole hierarchy of State officials for report, and finally to the exhaustive consideration of a council of over fifty persons, one-half of them highly placed Civil servants, and the other half representatives of mercantile, agricultural and manufacturing interests. Having regard to the constant financial support given by the Government to the French railway companies, such a system may be possible in France, and yet not be capable of transplantation here, where the companies have built their lines at their own sole cost and risk.

But even in France its disadvantages are tolerably obvious.

For one thing the cost is enormous. To say that the company must first of all propose a change, and that, secondly, the Government must investigate and decide whether to approve or no, means in plain English that the whole work of management must be done twice over. The French control staff numbers over 1,000 persons. It costs about £160,000 per annum, and the complaints are constant that both staff and salaries are insufficient. Further, a duplicate system, especially when one-half is in Government hands, naturally implies very considerable delay; and such delay, though none too acceptable in France, in the main a self-contained country, would be quite intolerable here, where we have to face the competition of the world at large. Tenders, for instance, are invited for the construction of a bridge over the Danube at Pesth. At Derby there is a famous firm of bridge-builders who would like to put in. Before doing so, however, they must know whether for a consignment of 10,000 tons of steel, the Midland is prepared to give them a special rate to Hull or to Liverpool or to the London Docks. The matter can be settled at present by a call at the goods manager's office, followed by an interchange of telegrams with the North-Western and the Great Northern. An answer is given next morning at the furthest. But it takes an English Government department as a rule ten days to acknowledge the receipt of a letter, and certainly two months to investigate the simplest cases.

But there is yet another objection of principle. It is a fatal blot on any system that it divorces power from responsibility. In France the Government guarantees the railway dividends; having, therefore, the power, it has also the responsibility. But with us? A new special rate might develop trade, and so add, not only to the dividend of the company, but to the wealth of the country at large. But it is certain to rouse the jealousy of a host of neighbours to whom it is not extended. Why should any Government department sanction such a rate and risk the asking of a dozen inconvenient questions in the House of Commons? It is always so easy to utter platitudes about the obligation of preferring the general welfare to the interest of one particular applicant. On the other hand, the general manager of the railway cannot fairly be held responsible if he is not permitted to manage it; and, further, it takes the heart out of a man's work if you keep him in leading strings at every step[1]. The following generalization is not, I believe, too wide. The whole tendency of modern commerce is to concentrate business into great aggregations, and the concession of special railway rates is only one exemplification of this tendency. In its working it undoubtedly inflicts some hardship on individuals, but this is more than counterbalanced by the benefit to society at large. Any interference by an outside authority with the free play of commercial forces may be expected to be in the interest of the tangible individual who complains rather than in that of the public at large, which has no opportunity of making its voice heard, even if, indeed, it were conscious of its interest in the matter. Such interference, therefore, is, in the public interest, to be deprecated and to be kept down to the irreducible minimum.

For that there is such a minimum has been admitted from the outset. The free play of commercial forces is all very well in its way; but when the scales are pulled by the North-Western Railway on the one side and by the local shopkeeper on the other, the interests of the latter are likely to kick the beam. Still, as it seems to me, the shopkeeper should be sufficiently protected by an appeal being given him to a properly constituted court of justice. Such a court, of course, can interfere only after the event; and prevention is usually regarded as better than cure. Still, if prevention is only possible at the price of a bodyguard of physicians in constant attendance, one may buy one's immunity from

---

[1] It is five years since we had any conspicuous improvement in English railway service. Even in passenger service, in which we led the world, without equal or second, a few years back, the Americans are going ahead of us in all directions. This is no accident. The Board of Trade and Parliament and the public have been regulating railway rates, railway methods of working (signals, brakes, block system, mixed trains, &c.), railway servants' hours of labour, employers' liability, &c., &c. The railway chiefs have been occupied, mistakenly perhaps, in endeavouring to minimise that regulation. They have had neither time nor heart to think of improvements.

disease too dear. Moreover, a court of justice, by a series of decisions, gradually builds up a code of law on the subject; and in this way the cure of one case really constitutes the prevention of fresh outbreaks of the same complaint.

Obviously such a court is no patent remedy for all railway diseases; but experience shows it to be the best attainable in this imperfect world. The difficulty is, however, to get it. Such a court must consist of several members, for the bearings of these railway cases are so wide that no one mind can be expected to grasp the whole of them. Then the questions involved are not merely legal. The ideal judge should be not simply a lawyer, but a trained economist, with a practical knowledge of railway management and business methods as well. So far from a judge being thrown away on such matters, as more than one Member of Parliament has stated of late, what we want is something more than an ordinary judge. And we shall only get such men when the public realize that this question of railway control has come to stay, and is not to be settled off-hand by haphazard resolutions of chambers of commerce, or even by the passage of unworkable statutes. There is another point. Having got your court, you must make it possible for a complainant who is not a millionaire to go there. The railway companies have already expressed their readiness to accept the idea that as a general rule each side, whatever be the results, should pay its own costs. I believe that substantial justice would be done by going even further and providing that, while the railway company was left, if successful, to pay, except in extreme instances, its own costs, the commission should be empowered to give, under ordinary circumstances, to a successful applicant costs against the company.

But, even when we have got an ideal court for the decision of these questions, there will still remain important functions to be discharged by the Executive Government. It is as true in the moral as in the material world, that corrupt matter is rapidly oxygenated and rendered harmless by the action of light and air. It should be the business of the Executive to investigate alleged abuses, and, where they are proved to exist, to publish the fact. Abuses brought to light will mainly right themselves. There is nothing more remarkable than the sensitiveness of great corporations to public opinion. Not but that such sensitiveness is natural enough. A great corporation offers so big a mark to shoot at that it is bound to be hit if once it provokes the public to take to their weapons. And the men who manage our great companies are well aware of this. Or, if any one amongst them should be for a moment foolish enough to forget it, his colleagues may be trusted to remind him by the exercise of some such corporate discipline as is exercised, almost as a matter of course, in the old-established professions. Of this sensitiveness to public opinion this very year has furnished a most striking instance. Parliament, after an exhaustive investigation of the subject lasting for over eleven years, solemnly enacted that from the first of January the railway companies should be entitled to make certain charges. Unadvisedly, as their own official representatives have since admitted, and without explanation or apology, the railway companies proceeded to exercise in full the rights which Parliament had most deliberately given them. Public opinion strongly disapproved of their action. An unopposed resolution of the House of Commons condemned it, and within three months the companies had been constrained to abandon the attempt to exercise their unquestionable legal right. In the face of this experience it would seem evident that public opinion does not, at any rate, lack force. The object of the interference of the Executive Government should be to supply it with the facts and, where necessary, with the commentary required for its correct guidance.

It may seem almost an insult to the Executive to propose to confine it to the humble function of purveying information. And yet we cannot be too often reminded that the action of the State—however large be the capitals in which we write the word—means only the action of the handful of fallible, perhaps arbitrary, possibly not wholly disinterested individuals, who on any particular occasion are its instruments. Now we may fairly expect that these individuals will investigate more carefully and weigh their decisions more deliberately when they have to make them prevail by their own inherent rightfulness than when they are empowered to give a peremptory order and let their will avouch the deed. And in matters such as these, where, to borrow from a recent judgement of Mr. Justice Wills, a wrong decision would 'check competition, hamper enterprise, and enhance the price of many articles of primary necessity, . . . ruin many individuals, and amount to an economic revolution in much of the business of the country,' we must be satisfied to move but slowly, so only that we move in the right direction.

Experience of our own railway history, still more of the railway history of the United States, is available to confirm these *a priori* reasonings. For twenty years the inspecting officers of our Board of Trade had practically no powers except to investigate and report. But by the constant employment of these powers, and with the force of public opinion behind them, they made English railway travelling incomparably the safest in the world. In an evil hour Parliament passed the Railway Regulation Act, 1889. The Board of Trade could order where before it could only advise, and rejoicing, one must suppose, in its new-won authority, it proceeded forthwith to strike a general average for the railways of the United Kingdom, and to prescribe for the railways of Caithness and Cardigan requirements well enough adapted for the latitude of London. Last session we heard more than once of public bodies in remote localities imploring in vain that the Board of Trade would suffer passengers to run the risk of travelling in company with goods waggons rather than be deprived of a train service altogether. But the Board was inexorable. It had formed its ideal of what a passenger service ought to be, and the railway companies must be compelled to give that or nothing. So in fact they will give nothing, and the Board of Trade will no doubt be satisfied.

To take another instance, fortunately of a more satisfactory character. In America the control of railways was down to 1887 exclusively, and is still mainly, in the hands of the separate State governments, and the experience of these forty different bodies is a perfect mine of instruction for those who wish to appreciate at once the difficulties and the possibilities of government control[1]. Broadly speaking, the States of the American Union have divided themselves on this question into two opposite camps. Those of the East and North, led by Massachusetts, have acted on one principle; those of the South and West, led by Illinois, have adopted quite another. Both groups of States have appointed commissions to control the railways; but while the Illinois Commission possesses large powers, the powers entrusted to the Massachusetts Commission—so says Mr. C. F. Adams, who for ten years was its chairman—'hardly deserved the name ... The only appeal provided was to publicity ... The Commissioners had to listen, and they might investigate and report—they could do little more.' To quote Mr. Adams again, the Massachusetts type of commission means only publicity, the Illinois type means the constable.

And now to summarize, equally broadly, the results. The commissions of the Illinois type have been in perpetual hot water from the day of their birth. Their powers have been increased and then again diminished, or even withdrawn entirely at a stroke. They have reduced railway companies by the score to bankruptcy. But the more they have oppressed the companies the less the public at large have appeared to be satisfied. Finally, in despair, they have thrown the reins on the neck of the steed, and left the companies to take their own course almost unchecked. At the present time there is hardly one of the State Commissions of the compulsory type which attempts to exercise the powers which are nominally vested in it. Meanwhile, the Massachusetts Commission has constantly increased both its authority over

---

[1] There is no one work with which I am acquainted adequately dealing with this chapter of railway history. Its general tenour may be learnt from Hadley's *Railroad Transportation*, C. T. Adams' *Railway Problem*, and Clark's *State Railroad Commissions*. I have myself attempted, in evidence before the House of Commons Committee of last session on Railway Rates, to make the outlines of the story accessible—if anything in a Blue Book ever is accessible—to English readers.

the railways and its hold over public opinion. Whenever a question arises, the Massachusetts Commission investigates and publishes its conclusions. If it concludes against the view taken by the railways, the company concerned finds itself constrained to submit; if, on the other hand, its report endorses the action of the company, the public acquiesces and the agitation dies down. In a word, the corner-stone on which the Massachusetts railway legislation rests—and it is the true foundation for the legislation of a free people—is, to quote Mr. Adams yet again, 'the one great social feature which distinguishes modern civilization from any other of which we have a record, the eventual supremacy of an enlightened public opinion.'

It might be argued that Massachusetts is not England. 'The men of Massachusetts,' says Lord Macaulay, 'could work any constitution.' Be it so, but we are not without precisely similar experience in this country. The Railway and Canal Traffic Act of 1888, by a clause avowedly based on the Massachusetts precedent, gave to the Board of Trade in the matter of goods rates alleged to be oppressive these very powers of investigation and publication. The clause has only been in operation four years, and during almost the whole of that time the goods rates of the different companies were in the melting pot, and till they finally emerged, in their new shape, it was scarcely worth any one's while to raise fresh issues. Even so the Board of Trade has thrice reported that the effect of the Conciliation Clause, as it is termed, has been markedly beneficial. The railway companies have almost without exception adopted the recommendations of the Board of Trade, and as a rule their differences with their customers have been amicably settled. But four years have not been long enough to eradicate all trace of original sin even from the three hundred and fifty thousand railway officials and servants, still less has a method been found to make any concession satisfactory to claimants who urge simultaneously claims diametrically opposed the one to the other. So we are now told that publicity has failed; that the constable's truncheon must be thrust into the reluctant hand of the Board of Trade. It is not safe to prophesy unless one knows. But no one who has studied these matters can have the smallest doubt that if any government passes an Act giving, either to a Court of Law—the Railway Commission—or to a government department—the Board of Trade—or even to the *tertium quid* suggested by some leading authorities—a 'cheap and expeditious tribunal' composed of gentlemen neither lawyers nor railways experts and with no experience of administration—a power to arbitrate between railway companies and their customers and to force both sides to accept as final its decision whether a rate is reasonable or unreasonable—if any government does pass such an Act as this—and strong pressure in this direction is being brought to bear by traders' associations at the present time—that government will, before many months are out, have bitter reason to regret its action, and may quite possibly find itself in the humiliating position of being forced publicly to avow its mistake and retrace its steps.

But enough. No attempt has been here made, nor is indeed possible within the limits of this paper, to discuss questions of detail. How far railway companies should be free to amalgamate, or to enter into agreements to abandon competition and divide traffic with each other; whether they shall be confined strictly to railway business, or allowed to embark in subsidiary undertakings as dock and steamship owners, or warehousemen, as hotel keepers, or cartage agents—these and a score more questions of a like nature need the most careful and deliberate consideration, but they cannot be touched on here. Again, it is a question of principle of most vital moment, how the railways of a country can best be made subservient to its general prosperity. On the answer to that question, which at any given time commends itself to the minds of the controlling agents, must depend the opinions they express and the judgements they pronounce on the facts of the concrete cases as they are brought before them[1]. But

[1] The United States Interstate Commerce Commission, in its sixth and latest annual report, declares that 'the practice of the Commission is so to administer the law as to protect each locality in the enjoyment

this question, though its importance cannot be overrated, is also foreign to our present scope. We must confine ourselves here strictly to the question of the measure and method of State interference. And on this question we may now formulate our conclusions as follows:—

State ownership is undesirable, but State control is unavoidable. So far as that control has to do with matters of police, with the security of the public, the proper treatment of employés, and so forth, it is on all fours with inspection in numerous other departments of daily life, and will naturally be carried out by officials appointed by the Executive Government. To the control of railways as commercial undertakings, on the other hand, a different set of considerations apply. Here the broad principle seems to be that the private investor, paying the piper, must be allowed to call the tune, subject only to this proviso—that no one customer of the railway shall be allowed to obtain an unfair advantage over the rest. Whether any particular advantage be in a given case fair or unfair is a matter best left to the judicial decision of a technically as well as legally qualified court. Where there is no general agreement even as to the most elementary principles of tarification—I make no apology for importing across the Channel an absolutely necessary word—we are less likely to go wrong if we confine ourselves to *ex post facto* judgements on concrete facts which have arisen in actual practice, and refuse to construct in advance symmetrical

---

of its natural advantages. . . . Each community is entitled to the benefits arising from its location and natural conditions.' With all possible respect for the Commission I venture to assert that *its practice is nothing of the kind*. The only practice that even approaches conformity to this theory would be the enjoinment on the companies of equal mileage rates for like commodities in like quantities. And from such a course the strong common sense of the Commissioners may be trusted to preserve them. Further, had the theory that a locality has a right to be protected in the enjoyment of its natural advantages been suffered to control the railway policy of the past, the problem which the Commission now has to solve of an equitable adjustment of competitive rates over the continent of North America would never have come into existence, for the buffalo must have still shared with the Red Indian the undisturbed occupation of the larger part of the area of the United States.

edifices of theory. But there is also scope for useful action on the part of the Executive Government, whose officers can investigate and report, both generally and when their attention is specifically directed to alleged abuses. In this manner the public will gradually be educated to form an intelligent judgement, and the railway companies will be kept on their good behaviour.

Such is the railway creed which I would put forward as suitable for adoption, not *semper, ubique, ab omnibus*, but by Englishmen in England at the present day. If it be objected that it is mainly negative, that it amounts to little more than dotting the 'i's and crossing the 't's of the existing system, I venture to reply that therein lies its greatest recommendation. In the dark it behoves us to feel our way cautiously; and our legislators, with all respect be it said, are really very much in the dark as to the economics of transportation. To begin to run, as some distinguished persons are urging at this moment, when we are not certain that we have started in the right direction, and have no idea what obstacles there may be across the road, may be human nature, but is certainly not philosophic. Besides, simple publicity is an instrument whose value cannot be exaggerated, and it is a weapon which has hitherto been used, where used at all, only in the most hesitating and half-hearted manner. Given the right men as Government inspectors, with full access to facts and documents, and the power to publish the conclusions which they draw from them, powers of compulsion will be not merely superfluous but actually a hindrance. For, in England as in Massachusetts, 'the eventual supremacy of an enlightened public opinion' is matter of certainty. In our present temper, however, 'eventual supremacy' is not enough for us; we are all for reaching immediate supremacy by the short cut of compulsion. In the words of a distinguished railway authority, Professor H. C. Adams, of the Interstate Commerce Commission, 'there is danger lest the quietness with which the principle of publicity works should deprive it of the confidence which it deserves.' The more reason, therefore, to press home the point that the nearest approach to success in the very difficult task of controlling without fettering the commercial management of railways has been attained by a system which, refusing altogether the assistance of the constable, relies on the support of public opinion for its sole sanction.

W. M. ACWORTH.

VII.

THE INTEREST OF THE WORKING CLASS IN FREE EXCHANGE.

T. MACKAY.

VII.

THE INTEREST OF THE WORKING CLASS IN FREE EXCHANGE.

'THE property which every man has in his own labour, as it is the original foundation of all other property, so it is the most sacred and inviolable.' Such is the axiom in which Adam Smith proclaims the charter of human freedom. It is a pregnant phrase, and the corollaries which follow from it are far-reaching and important. A man's property in himself gives him a right of exclusive use in his own labour, and, as under the present subdivision of labour its principal use will consist in being exchanged for wages, it gives him also a right of Free Exchange. To argue that exchange should be other than free is to countenance slavery. This monopoly, or exclusive power of sale over his own labour, is sacred and inviolable. It can only be exercised by the free will of the seller, that is to say, in Free Exchange. This universal right vested in every seller of labour does not confer on any one man a right to compel others to purchase his labour, for such a forced exchange would be a violation of our axiom, in that it compelled other men to part with their labour, or the results of their labour, against their will. The axiom gives, therefore, no guarantee of employment, no *droit au travail*; it merely affirms each man's exclusive right to take his own labour and services to market. Further, if the greater may be held to include the less, each man has the same right of property over all that he obtains in exchange for his labour. In other words, within the limits set by an enlightened jurisprudence, a man is entitled to dispose of his wages as he thinks fit. In the infinite series of exchanges here foreshadowed, labour is 'the original foundation of all other property.' To complete our view of the organizing influence of exchange, another deduction must be drawn, which seems to follow naturally from the axiom above stated. It is, that if a man has a right of sale he has also a right of gift. Hence the jurisprudence of the civilized world, recognizing that economically as well as physiologically the life of the child is a continuation of the life of the parent, has sanctioned, what it is probably powerless to forbid, the right of inheritance and bequest, as being on the whole the simplest and most equitable method of passing property from one generation to another. Every man, then, has property in his own labour, his own mental efforts, and in the values which neighbours freely give him in exchange for these. Liberty and Property, or, as relatively to an industrial society it may more suggestively be stated, Free Exchange and Property are two inseparable ideas.

It is hardly necessary to depart from the precedent of our axiom, and to complicate the question by considering the case of property held in virtue of alleged acts of illegal appropriation in a prehistoric past. Practically speaking, at the present day all property rests on a title of labour bestowed, or on some legal act of exchange or bequest. The current controversy as to the 'unearned increment,' that is, as to the right of private ownership in an undertaking like the New River Company, or in ground-rents in the city of London, has nothing to do with the validity of the original title. The point raised is whether the State should not retain to itself any increment of value which may arise from a future concentration of demand on a particular water supply or a particular bit of land. Our answer to this will depend on our judgement as to the ability of the State to forecast the course of demand, and as to the wisdom of leaving speculation in land to private persons. If we admit that the State should be a speculator in land values, there is no reason why now or at any other time it should not, with a view of lightening future taxation, purchase at the market rate land which, its advisers think, is likely to rise in value. It is well, however, to remember that if by chance it finds itself in possession of a site of enhanced value, it can only do what the private owner does, namely, let it at a rack rent. To let it under its market value, as fixed by the intensity of the demand for it, is at once jobbery and favouritism, and has further the mischievous consequence of concentrating population where the high price of land, if left to itself, would tend to disperse it. This intense concentration of demand on particular articles is an unavoidable incident so long as men naturally or by fashion continue to desire the same thing. It has, however, this convenience, that the values which it creates are a kind of natural consols. This is appreciated by the poorer classes, as is evidenced by the fact that their own provident institutions invest a large amount of their funds in ground-rents. All this, however, has nothing to do with the question of title, and for the purpose of this discussion it is proposed to accept the proposition that the property which every man has in his own labour is the original foundation of all other property.

One assumption has been made, that a man has a monopoly in his own labour and in the values for which he exchanges his labour. If this be conceded, we have a justification of the principle on which, though there are many lets and hindrances to its full influence, the present basis of society mainly rests; we have also an acknowledgement that these lets and hindrances are contrary to justice; it remains to be shown that we have found a principle, which, if these lets and hindrances could be removed, is capable of 'moralizing' the whole organization of social life.

All things in process of evolution are of necessity imperfect, and if we are analyzing society with a view of discovering the principle of association most conducive to its welfare, we waste our time if we search for one which has attained a paramount ascendency. If there is any principle which at this moment has a complete and undisputed authority, the present imperfect condition of society will be its conclusive condemnation. If we are looking for a principle to which we can without misgiving entrust the progress of the race, it ought to have some of the following characteristics. It ought, in the first place, to be a force already at work. It ought to be a rule of conduct which has already established some authority for good over human nature. It were hopeless to try to reorganize society by a force which in the past mankind has consistently ignored. Further, if we wish to recognize the influence which makes for social progress, we should look for one which has power to transform the lower and purely selfish motive into the higher and social motive. To adopt the epigrammatic phrase of Mr. Huxley's Romanes lecture, we must look for some principle which, in itself, is a 'pedagogue to virtue.'

All these conditions seem to be present in the principle of Free Exchange. Without doubt it has played, and is playing, a great part in the social economy of the civilized world. It has not permeated, it is true, to every corner of society. It has been restricted by the nature of things, and by human artifice. Still, to those who permit themselves to indulge in ideals, it is a principle capable of exorcising from human character the instincts of the 'tiger and the ape,' by making mutual interchange of service the all-pervading motive of our associated life.

Even under our present subdivision of effort, no activity of the economic man is entirely self-regarding. Men labour and exchange their labour, or the products of their labour, for the labour or products of other men. The man, therefore, who wishes to receive much in exchange, must strive to perfect his capacity for the service of his fellows. This influence affects not only manual labour, but every act of capitalization, for the application of capital to production can only bring reward to its author, so long as it ministers to the requirements of the public. Capitalization, as we shall presently see, is essentially a process of exchange. In this blending of the private with the public motive, we may perceive the birth of a new sentiment and a new rule of conduct awakened, as it were, by this elementary lesson of the 'cosmic pedagogue.'

On the other hand, it is acknowledged that this process of evolution is incomplete, that the lower nature of the 'tiger and the ape' is by no means eradicated. Is it not conceivable, however, that the slowness of our progress is due to the inherent difficulty of the subject, to the dullness and obstinacy of the pupil, rather than to any defect in the teaching of the pedagogue?

It is the purpose of the following pages to trace the development of the principle of Free Exchange, more especially as it has affected the property and savings of the working class. How far has it already been the foundation of social welfare? To what further heights of prosperity does it seem to beckon us? To what extent is it a 'pedagogy' creating competent social habits and character in the beings that live within its organizing influence?

To the poor man, his most important, as well as his most sacred, possession must ever be his own labour. His savings are in all probability of small amount, and their rise upon the original foundation of his labour has been of recent date. The labour market, therefore, is to him of the highest importance. To the man who has anything to sell, more especially to the man who deals in a commodity, which, like labour, will not keep, it is an advantage to be brought into contact with the largest possible number of buyers. This is the function of a market or exchange. In a great organized market, prices are fixed in an automatic fashion, into which no personal element can enter. In the general extension of the open market which has been going on for many years under the influence of free trade, some things tend to rise in value, others to fall in value. To which of these classes does labour belong?

A sovereign will exchange for a greater quantity of wheat or for a greater quantity of clothing than fifty years ago. On the other hand, it will purchase a less quantity of labour. The rule would seem to be, that those things which can be produced practically at will, tend to depreciate in value; while those things of which the supply is more or less incapable of being immediately increased, tend to appreciate in value. There would seem to be reason for thinking that in the past, at all events, the value of labour has been enhanced.

We are hearing a good deal nowadays of the alleged appreciation of gold. It is argued that the value of gold has risen because the number of exchanges in which it has to serve as a measure has increased far more rapidly than the production of gold. This, of course, is denied by some who are of opinion that the annual production, and the economies in the use of bullion effected by various expedients of credit, have kept pace with the public requirement for this precious metal. No opinion is here offered on the question, it is cited only to bring out the general admission, that if an article of universal demand is supplied in limited quantities, its value relatively to other exchangeable commodities, which increase less rapidly, must be enhanced. The universal demand for gold consists largely in the right of mintage afforded by the governments of the gold-using countries of the world. By means of the mint, gold bullion is assured of its market, and passed into the currency of the country. It is the object of civilization to organize a similar market for labour.

Let us pursue the comparison a little further. Labour even more than gold is a necessary element in most operations of industry and exchange. Credit can serve as a substitute for gold, but no substitute can be found for labour. Improved machinery does not dispense with labour, on the contrary, it makes a higher demand for skill and trustworthiness and for the higher forms of labour. Labour, moreover, unlike gold, can be applied to an infinite variety of purposes. Every increase of the labour population ought, and to a certain extent does, create a demand for its own employment. Given a number of employable but unemployed labourers, a well-organized market ought to afford them an opportunity for a profitable exchange of services. A glut of gold in the bullion market, owing to fresh discoveries, is a conceivable thing, and indeed has happened before now, bringing with it a depreciation in the value of gold. No operation of the mint could prevent this. On the other hand, with a really effective labour exchange, and a real mintage for labour, an excessive supply of labour is impossible.

I argue that this certain market for labour can be organized, not by a recognition of any *droit au travail*, but by the operation of the principle of Free Exchange, and by that only.

The foregoing comparison between the gold and the labour market establishes a presumption in favour of the view that, in an absolutely free market, the price of labour must tend to rise. The trade unionist, however, will not trust himself to the open market, and seeks to raise the price of his labour by combination and by various restrictions on the right of Free Exchange. Let us consider this opinion somewhat more in detail.

The attitude of the trade unionist would seem to rest on a certain phase of the Malthusian terror. As a general proposition, the doctrine attributed to Malthus has lost its force. If a really effective labour exchange were established, all labour would be passed into currency. Malthus' theory can only be true in markets which are artificially limited. There is unfortunately congestion of population in certain industries, and when relief is sought, as it too often is, by action which results merely in limiting production, it may occasionally be true that population increases more rapidly than subsistence. Still, if there is no absolute mobility of labour, there is certainly no absolute immobility, and Mr. Henry George is, I think, right in arguing, not perhaps that subsistence actually does increase more rapidly than population, but that with a better organization of the labour market it certainly would so increase. The idea of the trade unionist that there is a limited amount of work to be done, is parallel to the Malthusian fallacy that there is a limit to the increase of subsistence. There is no truth in either proposition so long as no artificial impediment is put on those Free Exchanges which at once employ labour and increase subsistence.

To what extent under existing circumstances are labour, and the capital necessary to its employment, distributed in the industries most proper to them by the operation of Free Exchange?

Dr. G. B. Longstaff, in an elaborate paper on Rural Depopulation, read before the Statistical Society on June 20, 1893, sums up the matter as follows. 'Reduced to a sentence, what does this mean? It means that the dream of the free-trader is being fast realized. That we are more and more learning to do in each place that for which each place is most advantageously circumstanced.' As between the town and the country we have already reached a point where it is a somewhat nice calculation to determine whether the higher wages of the town are really preferable to the lower wages, lower rents and allotments of the country. The migration to the town has to some extent levelled up the rate of wages all over the country. An expression of this opinion does not debar one from thinking that a greater freedom of exchange in the matter of land values might turn the tide of migration back again to the country. The phenomenon of labour and capital migrating in search of greater freedom of enterprise is nothing new. It is the motive of the colonization of America and Australia. Hitherto these countries have for the most part taken our unskilled population only. We have preserved our market for skilled labour, because of our international free trade. It is suggested, however, by Mr. Maitland, that in the event of the United States adopting a policy of Free Trade, the greater internal freedom of American industry would attract both skilled labour and capital to a country where a career is open to talent, just as in mediaeval times industry deserted the chartered towns, where it was protected and regulated, for the open villages which grew to be the great manufacturing centres of to-day.

Nor in this connexion should it be forgotten that the worst incidents of our feudal laws of settlement lasted down to the end of the last century, and that up to 1795 no poor man could come into a parish in search of work without being liable to removal to the place of his settlement, not because he was chargeable to the poor rate, but lest he should become so.

Considering the many impediments to its mobility, the wonder rather is that labour has acquired even its present measure of fluidity. When we speak of the mobility of labour as between the town and the country, we do not, of course, mean that each labourer is able to transfer his labour from one market to another. A curious demographer might find in a Dorsetshire village a labourer who had never heard of

Yorkshire, but there is probably not a village in England from which there has not been some migration, some dispersion of the young labour that comes each year to the market, and this is all that is needed to relieve an overstocked market.

Again, it is sometimes argued that the great specialization of employment in modern industry is inimical to the mobility of labour. This, however, seems by no means to be the case. Some interesting information on the subject has been collected by Mr. Llewellyn Smith, in a pamphlet on 'Modern Changes in the Mobility of Labour.' From this it would appear that ability to manage machinery increases rather than diminishes a labourer's power to change his employment. A remarkable instance of this is mentioned, in which, at the close of the American war, a gun factory was turned without change of staff into a sewing machine factory. Although we are still very far from the time when there is one market and one price for all competent and employable labour, those who see no other solution of our social difficulties than that which involves a natural organization of society on a basis of Free Exchange may find some comfort in the progress already made.

Before leaving this aspect of the question, it is worth noticing that there is an alternative to the mobility of labour, it is the mobility of capital. We shall have occasion later on to discuss the question of popular banks. I may, however, so far anticipate, as to suggest that the Dorsetshire labourer who never heard of Yorkshire may be a competent and trustworthy agriculturalist, that if by means of a co-operative bank he could obtain the use of capital, his ignorance of geography would not interfere with the profitable cultivation of his allotment any more than the Lord Chief Justice's indifference to the fame of music hall singers stands in the way of the due discharge of his judicial functions. The Dorsetshire labourer may refuse to move, but the capital may come to him. The thing required is not mere mobility, but a certain character of economic competence. The career opened to the humblest agricultural talent by the system of popular co-operative banks in Germany and Italy is an element in the problem worthy of careful attention.

The following practical instance will illustrate my contention that Free Exchange is the best available distributor of labour, and that it is to the interest of the labourer more than any one else to allow his labour to be directed by its influence.

The wages of domestic service are a familiar but often neglected instance of the rapid rise in the value of labour in an open market. Within the experience of many people still living the wages of domestic servants have at least doubled. This result has come about in a market in which transactions have all been made in detail. No person willing to accept wages has been prevented from so doing by any labour organization. Undoubtedly here and there persons have served for very low wages, but the general result has been a great advance in the average price paid for the various qualities of domestic labour. No harm has come to the interest of labour, because some transactions, rather than not take place at all, have taken place at a very low rate of exchange. The tendency of the market has been upward, and continues to be upward. The balance of advantage is certainly with the servant rather than the housekeeper.

This, I contend, is largely due to the fact that domestic servants have done their bargaining in detail, and in a free market. The free bargain in detail, far from being a cause of low wages, is the only method by which an impersonal market can be organized without at the same time depriving it of its sensitiveness and power of expansion. The wages of a good cook or housemaid are just as well understood, and just as impersonal, as if they had been settled by the arbitration of a chamber of commerce or a long series of strikes. Servants' agencies, the advertisement columns of the papers, the good offices of friends, are sufficient to constitute an open labour exchange in which domestic servants have more than held their own. Any other organization of the market would have deprived it of its sensitiveness, for wages rise not because the whole bulk of the labour in a particular trade can at once command a higher price, but because in virtue of the bargain in detail the better class of labour gets a rise first, and establishes a precedent which others follow. Any other arrangement would have prevented the expansion of the market, and this perhaps is the most important point of all. If, by means of a trade union combination, attempt had been made to force the market in order to give to the servant something over the free market rate, it would of course have prevented many people from employing servants. This actually has occurred in America, where the high wages of labour, and the greater equality of condition, have justly enough enabled domestic servants to set up higher pretensions. As a consequence, hotel life has been adopted by many American households which otherwise would have employed servants. In America this is a natural and legitimate adjustment, for the free market enables those who would otherwise be servants to make a better use of their labour. In this country the conditions are different. To have kept persons willing to enter domestic service out of the market, without providing them with some equally good occupation, would have been most mischievous.

The modern trade unionist is inclined to overlook these advantages of the free market, and to ignore the objections to the organization of the market by forced combination.

Looked at from another point of view, it may be said that the favourable conditions of the domestic service market are due to the fact that the demand has always been in excess of the supply. This, again, is due to the continuous increase of wealth, and to the ever-growing number of persons who can afford to keep servants. This same increase of wealth gives rise to greater demand for all articles of consumption. Under a proper organization, therefore, there should be no break in the continuity of demand, for then the man who 'demands,' makes his demand effective by 'supplying' *something* in exchange. Only a free self-adjusting employment of labour and capital can discover what that 'something' is, and what quantity of it is required. If by coercion of the market a higher price is kept up, say in miners' wages, than employers can for long afford to give, we lose the valuable warning of the free market which says, 'there is too much labour here already, let it be diverted elsewhere.' If, as must, I think, be conceded, wealth, and consequently demand for something, is increasing, what is required is that new population shall be diverted to the making of this something, and not to producing more coal, which in the case considered is not wanted. Even under present restrictions demand does grow, but how much more rapidly would it grow if we really gave ourselves up to the free market, and allowed it to direct both labour and capital to the supplying of the thing that is really required. It is much to be feared that our present policy is rather in another direction. I may be wrong in thinking that labour will find its most profitable market in the entire absence of all combination, but if so, such combination as there is should surely not ignore the fact that all increase of wages must come from increase of supply, and that to restrict the supply of a thing that is not wanted is not as advantageous as to discover the thing that is wanted, and to set to work to create a supply of it.

The strong belief which exists in most quarters as to the efficacy of combination to increase the wages of labour, is based on the indubitable fact that when an industry is unprofitable, single sales of labour at a reduced price will come more rapidly than when labour is combined in one great association which stands and falls together. This is precisely the point on which I am insisting, namely, that the market is more sensitive if left uncombined. It should, however, be observed that what is true of a fall is true also of a rise of wages; both will come more rapidly in a sensitive and free market. I have already given my reasons for thinking that labour will of necessity have an enhanced value in proportion as the productive transactions, in which it forms a part, increase in number and in efficiency. If, then, the tendency of the price of labour in a free market is to rise, it might be argued that it is more important to keep the market sensitive for the sake of the rise that is inevitable, than to restrict the market for fear of the fall which is very unlikely. Further, though the values of gold and ground-rents are subject to fluctuations, it is clear that under a free organization of labour there can be no fluctuation, but only a growing intensity of demand for the *proper* things *produced in their proper quantities and places*. It is only through the organization of an ever-increasing freedom of exchange that we can discover what these things are, and how and where they are to be produced.

India is a country where the enterprise of Free Exchange is not very highly developed, yet during normal times, the staple foods of the country are circulated with unerring precision to the places where they are required. In times of famine it becomes the duty of the executive to provide maintenance for a starving population. The Indian Civil Service consists of a body of the most disinterested, most able, and most highly trained officials that the world has ever seen. Yet how inferior to the free principle of exchange have been their attempts to distribute the food of the people. In some famines they have failed utterly to gauge the requirements of the people, and wholesale starvation has been the result. At another time they have fallen into the opposite extreme, and there are instances on record where the grain has either rotted away, or where dealers have gone up into the famine districts in order to purchase the superfluous supply which the government had carried up at vast expense. So it is with the labour supply; no human ingenuity can devise a system so likely to distribute it to advantage as that of an absolutely Free Exchange.

While, therefore, I argue that a fall in wages is an event under a free system not likely to occur, there is something to be said for allowing the labour barometer to be extremely sensitive of the causes that tend to a fall of wages. Far from being matter of regret, it is on every account most desirable that labourers should have timely warning that too much enterprise of capital and labour is being applied to some particular industry. This indication they receive when wages show a tendency to fall, and the sooner this tendency makes itself felt the better. In each instance in which by a warning of this kind labour is diverted from one industry to another, a step is taken towards the perfecting of the market. Nothing but congestion of industry can follow from a neglect of these signs; in one market a glut of supply which no one will purchase; and elsewhere capital lying idle, and labour starving, because we have broken the machinery which would have attracted them to a point where they could have co-operated with profit.

To those to whom the matter presents itself in this light, the wisdom of putting down coercively exchanges of labour which do not conform to Trade Union pattern will appear very doubtful.

It will, for instance, appear to them manifestly unjust and by no means conducive to the object in view, to prevent an old man taking service at the best wages he can command, because those wages do not happen to be trade union wages. I have been informed that, as a consequence of obtaining a contract with the London County Council, which has fallen in with the views of trade unionists in this matter, a certain firm had to choose between dismissing a number of old workmen whose ability was failing, and employing them at a rate of wages which they were unable to earn. This crusade against the aged has without doubt thrown many very worthy persons out of employment, and in some places has increased the rate of pauperism. A similar policy is pursued with regard to the young and the less competent. Young men just out of their apprenticeship, and those who have not established a reputation for competence, are occasionally dismissed or rejected because the employer does not see his way to employ them at the wages of a fully competent man. This denial of a right of market prevents them from ever becoming competent, and they are left to deteriorate in the ranks of the unemployable. Society is then left face to face with the insoluble problem of how to employ an aggregation of the least competent labourers collected from all points of our industrial system. This difficulty of the unemployed is of our own creation. Collectively, the unemployed are the unemployable. Remove these restrictions, and in small numbers, here a few, and there a few, this residuum will be distributed throughout our national industries by the ordinary action of Free Exchange. All will not exchange at the same price, for there are different qualities of labour, but all will exchange at a price which at the moment is an advantage to all concerned, and that price must always be an upward tending price.

The trade unions have a difficult and responsible task to perform, and for their main objects they have the sympathy of all fair-minded men. The question at issue, of course, is whether this restrictive policy is really conducive to the end desired. Even if the wages-regulating policy of the unions could be proved a mistake, they could still render great service to their constituents. They could enlarge, unify and give publicity to the labour exchange; they could increase the sensitiveness with which labour allows itself to be distributed by Free Exchange. They could advise as to the best methods of dealing with savings, and take part in breaking down the imaginary line which separates the labourer and capitalist. They could make the labourer's life cease to be purely proletariate, purely dependent on the daily hand-to-mouth sale of his labour; they could do much to hasten the time when every labourer shall also be a capitalist.

The trade union, however, is not the only impediment to Free Exchange. The absurd jealousy of Parliament has, as Mr. Acworth has shown, brought railway construction to a stand-still. In a letter to the *Standard* of June 20, 1893, Miss Octavia Hill points out that the action of the London County Council in threatening to use the ratepayers' money to build eleemosynary dwellings is restricting private enterprise. Earlier restrictions on our system of land transfer have in recent years brought things to such a pass that we are now vainly trying to correct the results of former error, by using public money to enforce sales and leases of land which earlier legislation had rendered impossible. He is a sanguine man who looks for anything but confusion worse confounded as the result of this empirical homoeopathy.

Looking at the situation generally, it is not too much to say that the larger forms of enterprise have been practically closed to the present generation by reason of the confiscatory threats of the well-meaning but half-educated controllers of votes who now contrive to call the tune from all political parties. The extension of the larger forms of enterprise under an enlightened acceptance of the principle of Free Exchange would be practically endless. As it is, unless they can be undertaken by a municipality drawing its supplies from reluctant ratepayers, they are left unattempted, and as a further result there is a congestion of labour and capital seeking employment, and battened down in those smaller enterprises where already competition is far too keen.

The terms 'competent' and 'employable' have been used more than once in the foregoing argument, and a word may here be said as to the important qualification thereby introduced. Labour becomes competent by practice; if it is denied a market it is bereft of an indispensable element of technical education. It is not, perhaps, irrelevant to point out that in the domestic service market, the freest portion of the labour exchange, the employer has practically to provide for the technical training of the employed. Servants enter on their calling untrained. How far our present compulsory and uniform system of popular education is a bar to a voluntary but real system of technical education it is beyond the purpose of this paper to discuss. Certain it is that we have not, and probably never can have, a general system of technical education other than that which is to be gained in the workshop. This fact, together with the right claimed by some, if not by all, trade unions to limit by various expedients the number of workmen in various trades, must have an appreciable effect on the distribution of labour. One result is that an undue proportion of the young labour becoming available each year in the towns is driven into the ranks of clerks and unskilled labourers. The limited application of free trade principles under which we live is not able to work miracles. It cannot organize industry with an excessive supply of clerks and unskilled labourers; it looks for some assistance from the intelligent and responsible human beings, whose operations it seeks to direct to the best advantage.

There is no subject more keenly debated at the fireside of the labourer than the question 'What are we to do with our boys?'

Parents are extremely anxious to direct their children to the career open to talent; but the restrictive policy of the time obscures the signs of the market and obstructs elementary arrangements for technical education. Much of the competence of labour must always depend on this exercise of parental responsibility. In the interest therefore of a better distribution of labour, artificial monopolies of the right to labour, as claimed by a certain section of Trade Unionists, ought to be strenuously resisted.

Again, when a man passes from parental control he still must study his market and seek to offer the quality of labour most in request. He must not simply deposit himself as a lump of unskilled labour, or think that society is disordered because permanent and profitable employment does not come to him unsought. He will be wrong to assume that the world has use for nothing but his mere labour, that it is not prepared to give additional reward to intelligence, sobriety, trustworthiness and skill. One of the few points on which all economists seem to agree is that effective and highly paid labour is the cheapest to the employer. The practical man has never doubted the fact. The testimony of the elder Brassey has long been on record. Even in the matter of agricultural labour, often erroneously described as unskilled, superior quality is appreciated and sought after. Very recently I was assured by a skilful agriculturist that there were labourers whose labour he could not profitably employ, even if he got it for nothing. He preferred, he said, looking merely to his own interest, to hire the very best men and to secure them by paying as much as 25 per cent. or 30 per cent. over the market rate. It is these transactions which pioneer the way to higher conditions for all. The attempt to restrict competition, with the object of obtaining for the less competent labour the same wage as for the more competent, is a policy likely to defeat itself. It prevents the pioneer movement of the best, and in the long run is by no means a benefit to the inferior workman. Competition makes war on the person of no man, it acts rather as a friendly pedagogue for the repression of unprofitable habits and for the inculcation of serviceable social character. To withdraw a class from the educative influence of this force is to leave it at the mercy of those ever-present lower motives of self-indulgence which in the interest of progress should be controlled if not eradicated.

Important as these considerations are, the coping stone cannot be set on the edifice of industrial competence till the labourer learns something of the art of capitalization. Under certain conditions responsible character, even such as is attainable in the humblest ranks of labour, is capital. Under the popular banking system already mentioned the German and Italian peasant is enabled to exchange his mere promise to pay for the most material form of capital, paid in the currency of the country. This is an effort of industrial enterprise, a triumph of social organization, to be distinguished from thrift and saving. The development of working-class credit is still in its infancy; but it is obvious that, if a reputation for character and skill can give a man a command of capital, the property which every man has in his own labour has received a vast addition to its value.

A sound system of commercial business, based on the willingness of a successful banking association to give cash on equitable terms in exchange for the poor man's mere promise to pay, is, perhaps, the most highly developed harmony of a system of Free Exchange.

The ordinary thrift of the working class is, however, distinct from this. In depositing in a savings bank it is the poor man who makes what the Roman lawyers called an *emptio spei*, the purchase of a hope; and to complete our survey of the causes that affect the value of labour something must be said of the advantages which accrue to labour from the responsible temperament gained by the practice of frugality and thrift and from the stronger position in the labour market which savings give to their possessor. The point is best illustrated by the following comparison.

It has been contended (and there cannot really be much doubt about the matter) that outdoor relief, more especially as paid in former times to the able-bodied man and now to the able-bodied widow with children and to persons only partially disabled from work, has a tendency to lower the wages of unskilled labour. Some keen but not very wise controversialists have argued that this is excusable, on the ground that the same result is brought about by the work of those in possession of a small amount of savings, and of married women and others not wholly dependent on earnings for their support. Even if this were true it would be no justification for supplementing wages out of the poor rate; but, of course, it is the very reverse of true. In nine cases out of ten, application to the poor rate comes from a class accustomed to live a purely proletariate life, from hand to mouth. Those who have had anything to do with the pauper class know that the whole problem of pauperism is one of character and not of income. When the expectation of a class has for long been fixed on the rates as a source of income, it is extremely difficult to detach it and to indoctrinate it with any appreciation of the advantages to be derived from saving and self-control. To have nothing is the well-advertised qualification precedent to receiving something from the rates. To the class, therefore, which has not detached itself from the influence of the Poor Law there is an artificial impetus given to the natural tendency to consider the present rather than the future. An addition, from whatever source, to the income of this class is, unfortunately, no occasion for rising to a higher level, for it is used merely to allow the hand-to-mouth life to be for the time a little more lavish.

When, however, the imagination is detached from reliance on poor law relief, and is exercised in the accumulation and management of savings, an entirely different tone is created. The possession of savings as a possible source of income is a cause of firmness rather than of weakness in the labour market. The possession of savings makes men, as it is termed, 'very independent.' I have argued that it is to the interest of labour to preserve a sensitive market by allowing transactions both at higher and lower prices to take place freely. The use of a *common* strike fund, a perfectly legitimate weapon, is apt to destroy this sensitiveness. What is required is something of the nature of a universal *private* strike fund at the disposal of every man. This is supplied potentially by the savings bank account. The personal independence of the units of which labour is made up, is a securer basis to build upon than any conceivable form of combination imposed from without.

Leaving, then, the question of the property which every man has in his own labour and the various influences which affect its value, let us now turn to a consideration of the other property in which the working class is interested and see how far in this matter also it is to their interest to rely on a policy of Free Exchange. Labour, though the most important of a man's possessions, is not coextensive with his life. There are times when he is sick and old and unable to work. Labour, moreover, is an expenditure of force more or less painful; and he therefore desires leisure and rest. These are legitimate motives urging him to action. To satisfy them he has again made use of the principle of exchange. He has long outgrown the stage when, to provide for periods of sickness, old age and leisure, he has hoarded provisions. He now makes use of a pure form of exchange. To take the simplest instance: he goes to a savings bank and exchanges a portion of his wages for a credit. His property in the coin deposited ceases, and he accepts as an equivalent the bank's promise to pay. He goes to a friendly society or to an insurance company and he exchanges a series of premiums paid and to be paid by him for the promise of the association to pay him an allowance in sickness or a round sum on his attaining a certain age or at death, as the case may be. The purchase of a share in a railway company or in a co-operative store is of essentially the same nature.

It is most important to realize that all this creation of saving is effected by a series of exchanges. The only new feature in the transaction is the willingness of the wage-earner to exchange the material of his wages for some immaterial instrument of credit. The motive which impels men to this form of activity (which is just as much a phase of human energy as manual labour) is common to all the race. It is a desire to purchase the power of deferred consumption or to economize the painfulness of labour.

This juncture is important, for it is at this point that the Socialist raises his revolt against the principle of Free Exchange. It has not been possible to deny a man's right of exchange over his own wages when used to buy articles for immediate consumption. The attack is on what, with invidious intent, is called 'Capitalism.'

Obviously two men cannot eat the same portion of food or occupy the same cubic space of shelter. In the act of consumption complete private property is *ipso facto* established. In the act of consumption a common enjoyment of property is an unthinkable condition. No one, as far as I am aware, has been bold enough to deny a man a right of exclusive use in his own dinner and in his own clothes. The contention of the Socialist is, however, that private property in capital is something different and for a variety of reasons a thing to be prohibited.

A man may exchange his wages for his day's dinner; may he, one is tempted to ask, exchange them for to-morrow's dinner? If so, at what point does it become wrong for him to exchange his wages for a promise of another man to pay the wherewithal to purchase dinners twenty years hence? Or again, it is permissible to purchase and use exclusively a suit of clothes. Is it permissible to buy a diving dress or a spade, to make or cause to be made a bit of labour-saving machinery or an irrigation work, and to retain the exclusive use and benefit of such action? If not, at what point between the suit of clothes and the erection of a factory does the illegality come in?

In truth there is no logical distinction to be drawn between the simpler and the more complicated forms of exchange. The Socialist, seeing what we all admit, that the beneficent action of Free Exchange is not perfected, rejects its assistance altogether, and seeks for some different, and, as he thinks, more equitable principle. He proposes, therefore, the socialization of capital. He ignores the socialization which is being brought about by the slow and certain organization of society on the absolutely democratic basis of Free Exchange.

Let us see what it is that he is really proposing. At present the advantage gained by successful capitalization is enjoyed in right of an inheritance or in right of thrift and saving. This, says the Socialist, can be improved upon. The work of capitalization should be carried out by public bodies, whose duty it would be to put some men among the overseers and many others among the overseen. For every one man who under this system was obliged, ninety-nine would be disobliged. The causes which at present give success in life are in part, it is true, beyond our control; we think them unjust and we grumble at the partiality of fortune; but should we be better pleased (we, that is, who are set to do hodman's work and to belong to the ranks of the overseen) if our fate was entirely decided in the lobby of the bureaucracy set to rule over us?

The duties of life are not all alike pleasant. If the rewards of life are arbitrarily made equal, the work of the poet—even if he is confined to dithyrambs on municipal sewers—will still be esteemed a pleasanter occupation than that of the scavenger. In every conceivable form of government each man must be guaranteed the exclusive use of the benefits due to him in the performance of his office. We have not, therefore, got rid of inequality or of the fact that one man draws more than another out of capitalization. All we have succeeded in doing is to distribute these inequalities at the fiat of a corruptible bureaucracy instead of on the principle of Free Exchange. When a large proposal of this nature is made, we are entitled to look round to see what are the effects of any existing experiment on the principle suggested. Our present poor law system allows guardians the power to give to one pauper a preferential form of relief, viz. outdoor relief, and to confine another to the workhouse. This is exactly analogous to the power of making some men overseers and others overseen. The poor law is most unpopular, and precisely for this reason—that it passes the wit of man to minister justice indifferently under such conditions.

Be the arguments in favour of a prohibition of private 'capitalism' what they may, in practice they have been disregarded, and the working man has exercised his liberty to acquire a right of deferred consumption in a great many ways. The following table, taken from the last *Statistical Abstract*, shows that the total of working class savings amount to a considerable sum, and that during the fifteen years included in the *Abstract* that sum had as nearly as possible doubled. The fact emphasizes a point which people are sometimes apt to forget, namely, that the hope of those of us who have no property must be in the creation of *new* wealth and not in the redistribution of wealth which is already in existence.

Present Time, say 1891.

	£	£
*Post Office Savings Bank, 1891	71,608,000	
*Trustee Savings Bank, 1891	42,875,000	
*Government stock standing in name of depositors at Post Office, 1891	5,087,000	
*Government stock standing in name of depositors at Trustee Banks, 1891	1,282,000	120,852,000
*Building Societies, 1890		52,482,000
*Industrial and Provident (Co-operative) Societies, 1890		15,261,000
*Industrial Insurance Companies, 1890	8,873,000	
†Friendly Societies	20,167,000	
‡Collecting Friendly Societies, 1889	2,565,000	31,605,000
		220,200,000

In order that some idea may be given of the rate at which these investments are growing, I have made out a second list, showing the state of affairs fifteen years earlier.

	£	£
*Post Office Savings Bank, 1877	28,740,000	
*Trustee Savings Bank, 1877	44,238,000	
*Government stock standing in name of depositors at Post Office, 1881 (no earlier figures given)	738,000	
*Government stock standing in name of depositors at Trustee Banks, 1881 (no earlier dates given)	124,000	73,840,000
*Building Societies, 1876		20,854,000
*Industrial and Provident (Co-operative) Societies, 1876		6,224,000
*Industrial Insurance Companies, 1880 (no earlier figures given)		1,476,000
Friendly Societies, 1876 (as estimated by Mr. Ludlow, Chief Registrar's Report, 1890, Part A, p. 9)		9,336,000
		111,730,000

* *Statistical Abstract*, 1877 to 1891, No. 39.
† Rev. T. Frome Wilkinson, *Mutual Thrift*, estimated p. 191.
‡ Ibid., p. 194.

In following the history of popular savings we shall find that the material as well as the educational advantages of these provident institutions is for the most part proportionate to the liberty of action which they enjoy.

No more remarkable illustration of this truth is to be found than in the history of the savings bank.

The labourer takes his surplus earnings to the bank, and exchanges them for a credit. With a laudable desire to make this credit a safe security to the poor man, it is laid down by Act of Parliament that these sums shall be placed by the Post Office and Trustee Banks in the hands of the Commissioners for the reduction of the National Debt for investment in consols, Treasury bills and other Government securities. All the petty savings of the provinces are in this way carried up to London, a small portion is placed in Local Loan Stock three per cent., and in a sense a percentage of this finds its way back to the country. It has been held, no doubt rightly, that a Government department cannot undertake the whole function of a banker. Our savings banks, therefore, are merely the reservoirs in which petty savings may collect. They make no pretence to be dealers in credit; and if a full exercise of the function of a banker is an advantage to the community society has to that extent been a loser.

An interesting description of the advantage of banking and of the exchange of credits in which it consists will be found in the following passage from Mr. Mac Leod's *Elements of Economics*. He describes how it is part of the Scotch banking system 'to open or create credits to certain amounts in favour of respectable and trustworthy persons. A cash credit, therefore, is a drawing account created in favour of a customer upon which he may operate in precisely the same manner as on a common drawing account; the only difference being that, instead of receiving interest on the daily balance at his credit, as is very common in Scotland, he pays interest on the daily balance at his debit..... Almost every young man commencing business in Scotland does so by means of a cash credit..... These credits are granted to all classes of society, to the poor as well as to the rich. Everything depends upon character. Young men of steadiness and judgement get their friends to become sureties for them on a cash credit—this is as good to them as money; and then they have the means placed within their reach of rising to any extent that their abilities and industry permit them.... Not only has Scotch agriculture been raised to its present tate entirely by these cash credits, but also public works of all sorts—roads, canals, railroads, docks—in fact everything has been created by the same means. It was stated that the Forth and Clyde Canal was executed by means of a cash credit of £40,000 granted by the Royal Bank.... All these marvellous results, which have raised Scotland from the lowest state of barbarism up to her present proud position in the space of 150 years are the children of pure credit.... The express purpose of these banks was to create credit, incorporeal entities created out of nothing, for a transitory existence; and then, having performed their function, vanishing again into the nothing from whence they sprang. And has not this CREDIT been CAPITAL?... But their solid results have by no means faded like "the baseless fabric of a vision."... On the contrary, their solid results have been her far-famed agriculture; the manufactures of Paisley, Glasgow and Dundee; the unrivalled steamships of the Clyde; great public works of all sorts—canals, roads, bridges, docks, railroads; and poor young men converted into princely merchants. What the Nile is to Egypt, that has her banking system been to Scotland....' Mr. Mac Leod is here defending the note issue system of Scotch banks, but his panegyric covers the whole system of legitimate banking.

Compare this picture to the restricted operation of the savings bank. It will be said at once that our commercial banking system already affords the necessary facilities for credit to those persons who are entitled to it, and that the poor man is not a person entitled to credit. If there is any justification for this view it consists in the fact that the character of the poor man is not such as to warrant a banker in making a loan to him. The Scotch banking system has done much to popularize credit; but it has not succeeded in reaching the humblest class. Is, then, the thing impossible?

The experience of the People's Banks of Germany and Italy has shown that the poor man can, under certain conditions, convert his promise to pay into an article of exchangeable value. The main condition is simply that the exchanges must be effected on the mutual or co-operative basis, which is able to solve a difficulty otherwise insoluble. The reason for this is at once obvious and extremely instructive, and, as we shall have occasion to point out, it has its analogy in insurance business and possibly elsewhere. A Scotch farmer or a Scotch tradesman is a person who has had some experience of the mechanism of business; he has learnt that character is capital, or at least can give its owner the command of capital. To such a responsible person a bank, knowing that the risk is not great and that the enterprise in which he is engaged is a reasonable one, can afford to lend at a moderate rate. When we go a little lower in the social scale the character of the people is less trained in this particular form of trustworthiness. They are less familiar with the principles of business. They have a greater disposition to evade their liabilities, and individually their transactions are very small and are supposed to be unworthy of the attention of the high finance. The risk of lending money to them is therefore great, and money lending has degenerated into usury. The inherent disability of a poor man's loan institution, not based on the mutual principle, is aptly summed up in a little story told by Mr. Wolff, to whose interesting volume on People's Banks the reader is referred for much valuable information on the subject. Speaking of a small English experiment in Peoples' Banks, he remarks: 'Nothing seems more striking in the experience of this society than the conscientious honesty and punctuality with which the poor people make a point of repaying loans, once they are constituted trustees of their own interests—even those who would otherwise make no bones of keeping back rich men's money. One man, who sent in his instalments with most praiseworthy regularity, had previously borrowed £2 from the vicar. "How is it that you pay the society, and never offer to pay me?" "Ah, you're the vicar; you don't want it," was the reply.' This puts the case of self-help *versus* patronage in a nutshell. Responsibility is not a natural but an acquired virtue, and the want of it brings its own punishment. The operations of the 'vicar' or other charitable person to whom no one repays are naturally limited; and if a tradesman undertakes the task, he can only do so by charging a rate of interest proportionate to the risk. Hence the 'Gombeen' man and the village usurer. This last was, and I suppose still is, a familiar feature in every German village; but an instrument has been invented by which the peasant is educated in responsible character and set free from the grinding extortion of the usurer.

The history of the People's Banks of Germany as developed by Schulze-Delitsch, and in an even more successful form by Raiffeisen, has been written in an interesting volume by Mr. H. W. Wolff. The element which has made these banks a success has been the mutual or co-operative element. Some of them, particularly the Schulze-Delitsch banks, have shareholders in whose interest a profit is earned. This fact has a tendency to convert an institution originally co-operative into a purely commercial undertaking. The commercial undertaking, to our view, is a simpler and less cumbersome and more fully perfected method of transacting exchanges than the co-operative institution; and when, as between the Scotch banks and their customers, the parties to the exchanges are trustworthy and therefore competent persons, it has, without doubt, a higher efficiency and an equal degree of equity. In dealings with the very poor, however, this condition does not exist, and for this reason Mr. Wolff gives a preference to the Raiffeisen form of bank, where the shareholder element is carefully repressed, and the whole responsibility of making and collecting the loans is put on the members. Under this system in Germany and Italy the savings of the poor form a banking capital which, aided by the credit enjoyed by these banks, is educating the people in one of the most essential of human activities and spreading the advantages of capital among the very humblest classes.

'If,' asks Mr. Wolff, 'Germany can, by the aid of her People's Banks, raise annually somewhere about £150,000,000, circulating in commerce, of which not a shilling remains idle, of which every penny takes effect—stimulating trade, developing agriculture, feeding home industries—what could not we accomplish with our proportionately larger population, our ampler wealth and our more abundant facilities?'

It is said, and said truly, that an increase of capital is one of the necessary conditions for an improvement in the status of the labourer. Here, under this system of People's Banks, is a means of increasing capital, not in the hands of the rich, but in the hands of the poor, to whom a career is thus opened to talent. The development here foreshadowed, discloses an endless vista of progress both material and moral.

Surely this justifies the assertion that the advantage to be derived from our banking system is proportionate to the freedom of the exchanges on which it is based; further, that the principle of Free Exchange is the true solvent of social congestion and incapacity.

Compared with this our present savings bank system, with all its security and other advantages, is a sterile system. Those who have made themselves acquainted with the extraordinary ingenuity and extraordinary success with which English working men have dealt with the much more difficult and complicated problem of sick insurance cannot for a moment suppose that they will fail where German and Italian peasants have succeeded. Compared to sick insurance banking is a simple matter, but it is capable of being made a much more important matter—for it may bring within the reach of the humblest a stream of capital which, as Mr. Mac Leod has put it, may fitly be compared to the fertilizing waters of the Nile.

An analogous experience has arisen with regard to sick insurance. It is a humiliating but also an encouraging fact that the mutual supervision of interested members is the only power which can preserve an association insuring against sickness from speedy insolvency. Commercial companies have undertaken, but have all abandoned, the business of sick insurance. The limited scheme of the German Government is, without doubt, on its way to break up over this difficulty. Even Canon Blackley seems to have given up the idea that a Government sick club could escape ruin from excessive sick claims. The patronized county societies find the difficulty very pressing. The excellent Hampshire society, at its last meeting, had to adopt some stringent new regulations to check this leakage. Centralized and admirably managed societies, like the Hearts of Oak, do not altogether escape. It has been stated with regard to this society that if a number of concentric circles were drawn round the office of the society, in Charlotte Street, it would be found that the percentage of sickness increased in each zone in proportion to the distance from the centre. It is by the locally constituted and locally managed lodges of the affiliated orders, such as the Manchester Unity of Odd Fellows and the Ancient Order of Foresters, that malingering is most successfully controlled. As M. Léon Say has remarked, 'L'usure ne peut être combattue que de près.' Usury—and, to complete the saying, we may add malingering—can only be overcome at close quarters.

The history of life insurance and endowment insurance for making a provision for old age, among the working class, is also very instructive. Here the mutual principle has not to any great extent been called in to assist. The increased intelligence of the workman and the pure competition of business men competing for his custom is bringing about a great improvement.

The gigantic system of industrial insurance has been very hotly condemned on the score of its costliness. It has in the past been a choice of evils. Without the collector —as witness the experience of the Post Office—no insurance would have been done. With him a vast business has sprung up, undoubtedly of a very costly nature to the insured. The cost of collection has of late years somewhat decreased. It is still very high relatively to the amounts collected. Roughly speaking, it costs on an average about a halfpenny to collect the weekly penny. According to the best information I can obtain on the subject, it does not appear to me to be possible to reduce the cost of management and collection much below 40 per cent. of the premium revenue; and it is only one large company that has succeeded in doing this. This, however, is not all. Intelligent working men are very well aware of the costliness of this collecting system, and they have with avidity availed themselves of cheaper and perfectly unexceptionable terms of insurance, *without weekly collection*, offered by the same associations which also transact the collecting business. The expensive collecting system still, it is true, continues to increase; but what is very remarkable, and also very satisfactory, is, that ordinary insurance on exactly the same terms as can be obtained by the middle and upper classes, is spreading much more rapidly among the working class.

To take the figures of one well-known Insurance Company, which does about three-quarters of the *industrial* life insurance of the whole country. The premium revenue for the year 1892, in the Ordinary (i.e. non-weekly collection) Branch, shows an increase of £222,865 over that of 1891; while the increase in the Industrial (i.e. weekly collecting) Branch was £160,819. The total premium revenue of the Ordinary was £1,665,611, as against £3,849,157, in the Industrial Branch; and is only a question of time for the Ordinary business to overtake the Industrial business.

It is worth noticing that while this very enterprising company had succeeded, on December 31, 1891, in placing through its Ordinary Branch something over 170,000[1] endowment policies—a majority of them, without doubt, for the purpose of making provision for old age—it had only succeeded in inducing twenty-three persons to subscribe for a deferred annuity. This fact, combined with the failure of the Post Office to popularize this form of investment, seems to me to be a conclusive comment on the fatuous proposals for compelling

[1] I have, by the courtesy of the manager of the company, been allowed to satisfy myself by personal inspection that a very large proportion of these Ordinary insurances are taken out by members of the working class.

or bribing people to provide for their old age by means of deferred annuities.

I have dwelt on the satisfactory development of insurance business under the natural competition of a free market, in order to show that, even without the aid of the mutual principle, the tendency of Free Exchange is towards a maximum rather than towards a minimum advantage to all concerned.

There is a controversy at the present time within the co-operative movement which has some bearing on the attitude taken up by the working class toward capital. The most successful part of co-operative enterprise has been what is known as distributive co-operation. All over the country there are small co-operative stores, their capital subscribed by shares, on which, as a rule, a fixed interest is payable. Any profit made is paid back to the purchasers in proportion to their dealings with the store, and is known as dividend on purchase. These local stores purchase most of their supplies from Wholesale Co-operative Associations in London, Manchester and elsewhere. The capital of the Wholesale is subscribed by the retail stores, and any profit made by the Wholesale over and above interest on capital is returned to the retail stores as dividend on purchase. The Scottish Wholesale Society pays a part of its profits to its workpeople, but as a rule no share in the profits is in the English societies paid to the employé. This, in the opinion of a section of the co-operators, is a falling away from true co-operative orthodoxy. Resolutions have from time to time been passed at the Co-operative Congress in favour of giving to every workman a share in profits. These resolutions have never been generally acted on, and it seems clear that, in the executive at all events, the dividend-on-purchase party has the majority.

To some of us, the expedient of having a deferred element in every exchange will appear an unnecessary complication. At the same time there is no reason why persons selling their labour or buying their groceries should not stipulate for a percentage of profit; and under certain conditions of society there is a considerable advantage in this plan.

The advocates of the two systems raise several practical considerations. The dividend-on-purchase party point out that the system makes an unbroken phalanx of co-operative purchasers. They stick to the stores, and the stores stick to the Wholesale, and the Wholesale has been able to enter largely into manufacture, and, as a constant and calculable demand is assured, with considerable success. The enthusiasts of the party contemplate a system under which all production shall be carried on by this affiliation of co-operative enterprise. The rate of interest allowed in the English Wholesale Society is 5 per cent. on share capital and 4 per cent. on loan capital. The obvious comment on this is, that if co-operative enterprise can convert all capital into a 4 per cent. preference and a 5 per cent. ordinary stock, perfectly safe, the capitalist will regard its spread as a great boon, and even in its present development it is an immense advantage to the working class to have a safe investment always open in which they have to act as their own trustees. At the same time the more venturesome form of enterprise, involving costly experiment and culminating, perhaps, in something which may be either a Panama or a Suez Canal, is not to be carried on by the necessarily centralized and cautious policy of a Wholesale Co-operative. It is, however, from this class of enterprise that mankind derives the largest benefit; but it is also in this class of enterprise that more fortunes are lost than won.

The dividend-on-purchase advocate, when pressed by the school which wishes to pay a dividend on wages, says, and says truly, that the labourer has an advantage as consumer in the good quality of the store goods and in the cheapness brought about by the dividend on purchase. This, however, is not the advantage which the orthodox co-operator wants. He objects, and, I think, naturally objects, to seeing the system which his enthusiasm has helped to raise turned, as he thinks, into a species of Frankenstein. What he looked for from the co-operative movement was emancipation from the duress under which, as he conceives, the labourer is forced to sell his labour. He wishes to direct and manage his own industry, and he has no wish to be absorbed into one vast and all-pervading association, governed by a 'Vehmgericht' in whose election he has, perhaps, one millionth share. With these feelings it is impossible not to sympathize. At the same time the difficulties which have to be overcome before his ideal can be realized are not to be overlooked. It is made a point against him by his opponents that the difficulties of conducting manufacture under co-operative management have almost invariably proved insuperable unless the manufacturing association is affiliated in the way described with the Wholesale Societies, and through them with the consumer. There seems to be some truth in this criticism. Many attempts at co-operative manufacture have failed, and the successful manufacturing businesses owned by workmen are constituted for the most part on the joint stock principle; and, as Mr. Hardern informed the Royal Commission on Labour, the workmen in those Oldham spinning mills which are owned by the working class, are not as a rule shareholders in the mill where they work. There is an obvious practical difficulty in putting management into commission; it has been overcome in some instances, and it is to be hoped that as business intelligence grows among working people the difficulty may grow less. This solution of the labour problem is a legitimate and honourable one; but in all this controversy there is a neglected element, which both parties appear to overlook.

The fullest and most perfect co-operation is to be found, not in the clumsy expedient of a deferred payment, either to consumers or workmen, but in an equitable and complete exchange in an open market. The educative value of the mutual principle is cordially acknowledged. Just as in the banking and friendly society problem, so here this narrower and more elementary form of co-operation is training the labourer in experience and competence, fitting him to take his place without fear in the open market. There are some forms of enterprise which possibly will always be better done under the mutual form of co-operation than under the automatic co-operation of independent units in an open market. There is, however, no antagonism between the two systems. In the co-operative movement the labourer is gaining experience and property, either in the form of share capital paying 5 per cent., with or without a bonus on wages and purchase, or, passing outside the co-operative movement as in the so-called Oldham Limiteds, he is becoming a holder of shares in a joint stock company, and learning to deal with his property in exactly the same way as a Peabody or a Rothschild. He is, in fact, breaking down the imaginary barrier which divides labour from capital and entering on the true path to emancipation. If he can enter the labour market fortified by a modicum of these two conditions, personal competence and private property held on the tenures recognized by the civilized world, the 'duress' of the market is at an end, his independence and his liberty will not suffer because he sells his labour to an employer and does not direct it himself.

Accident or some, to me at all events, incomprehensible reason has made a certain section of the Socialists throw their influence into the side of the dividend-on-purchase party. This admirable device for accumulating capital in private hands, with comparative safety and at 5 per cent. interest, seems to them to realize some of the conditions of Socialism.

If they would extend their view a little further they would see that a complete organization of society on a basis of Free Exchange would probably reduce the normal interest on capital employed in safe industries to something under 5 per cent., that ample capital would still be forthcoming to experiment in more venturesome enterprises, and that the demand for, and consequently the value of, labour would constantly be increased. In its comparatively restricted sphere, the co-operative movement has not suffered by being confined to enterprises in which a safe 5 per cent. can be looked for; but the useful, cautious financier who organizes safe investments suitable for trustees and widow ladies is not the sort of man who has built up the civilization of the world. The originators of our railway system were venturesome speculators (I use the term in no invidious sense), and until they broke the ground, and had made and lost fortunes over it, the modern railway director with his debentures and preferred stock was an impossibility. So it is surely absurd to suppose that the great industrial revolutions of the future are to be carried out as safely for the capitalist as an investment in consols. As an attractive incitement to the thrift of poor people, a promise of a safe 5 per cent. in a domestic industry is admirable; but it is childish to talk of it as anything else than a very ingenious phase of 'capitalism,' or to argue that there is anything revolutionary in its principle. Another ground of this temporary alliance between the Socialist and the dividend-on-purchase co-operator is the objection which the Socialist seems to entertain against labour-profit-sharing in any form whatsoever. It is conceivable, he argues, that a man may as a trade unionist find himself at issue with himself as a profit sharer or capitalist. A mere statement of this terrible contingency seems to him sufficient to condemn profit sharing and the ownership by workmen of industrial property.

The argument, which I do not think I state unfairly, reminds one of the *sophisme économique*—that it is to the interest of glaziers that the windows of the community should be broken every week. Even glaziers, however, have windows; and the working class is rapidly acquiring capital. It is not to their real interest to prevent the accumulation of capital in the hands of capitalists, much less is it their interest to prevent its accumulation in the hands of their own class. To insure that there shall be plenty of employment for us to-morrow by destroying or hindering the work we have to do to-day is surely topseyturveydom *in excelsis*. The co-operator is a man of a very practical turn of mind; and this, like many another fallacy, is being exposed *ambulando*. It is not for a moment to be supposed that the co-operator will be deterred from applying his savings to such honest investments as come in his way, or that, having done so, he will be induced by the rhetoric of the new trade unionism or Socialism to destroy his own hard-earned savings.

The honest indignation which rails at the imperfections of society may at times stir men up to justifiable and salutary rebellion; but mere revolt can never be constructive. In a recent work M. Rostand, one of the most energetic advocates for the introduction of People's Banks into France, has drawn a comparison between the life of one of the worthies of our English co-operative movement and that of the 'tragicomedian' Lassalle: 'Quelle différence même dans leur influence posthume. L'un continuant l'action féconde par l'exemple contagieux, par l'imitation de types créés, par les nobles semences répandues un peu partout; l'autre propageant de sa tombe l'antagonisme stérile, poussant des milliers et des milliers d'êtres à demi éclairés dans le trouble mental et moral, les faux emplois d'énergies, les gênes accrues, l'envie qui assombrit et fait souffrir, la colère qui n'enfante rien.' The revolutionist knows, he tells us, some road to progress other than through the development of personal responsibility, cheerfully undertaken and successfully discharged—but to what single achievement can he point? Theirs is a record, as M. Rostand puts it, of sterile antagonism. They ignore the remedies within reach; they do nothing to help in their organization; but continue to harp on the barren theme that thrift is a crime, a mere rushing into new privations. Compare with this the silent life-work of a man like Raiffeisen or the quiet unostentatious action of the now happily numerous band of labouring men who devote themselves to the honest and successful management of friendly societies and co-operative stores. It is these influences, and not the arts of declamation, which combat and conquer poverty at close quarters.

T. MACKAY.

VIII.

THE PRINCIPLE OF PROGRESSION IN TAXATION.

BERNARD MALLET.

VIII.

THE PRINCIPLE OF PROGRESSION IN TAXATION.

MR. DAVID A. WELLS, the well-known free-trader, has recently published a vigorous protest against the growing abuse of the power of taxation in the United States[1]. To make the occasion for the exercise of this power other than necessity, and the object anything else than the raising of money for meeting the expenditure of a government economically administered, is, he considers, 'to strike a blow, not only at good government, but also at free government,' and he finds in the policy of protection, which has long ceased in the United States to be other than a 'pretence and a cover for the promotion of private interests,' an all-sufficient instance of the abuses to which such conceptions of the function of taxation are liable. In countries where the public wealth is less enormous, and where what is called the social problem is more pressing than in the United States, a wider and more menacing extension is being given to the purpose and function of taxation—an extension of which the significance has hardly been grasped in this country, although its effects are obvious enough in the rapidly growing demands upon the public purse. It is held by the school of German economists, led by Adolf Wagner, that taxation is to be valued chiefly for the effect it can be made to produce on the distribution of wealth. Social objects are to prevail over purely fiscal objects, and taxation

[1] *A Tariff for Revenue: What it really Means.* Forum, September, 1892.

is to be used as the principal and most powerful means of hastening the supersession of private property by collective ownership. That these ideas are shared by the preachers of the new social gospel in England it would be easy to show; it is perhaps sufficient to quote a passage from a recent work by a writer of this school[1]. '... We can adjust taxation as we please. If we take the view of rent interests and profits advanced in this chapter, we shall regard them as the natural reservoir from which wealth is to be drawn for all public purposes. That is, we should adjust taxation to fall exclusively on the surplus of industry, and not at all on "wages" in their broadest sense. Leaving the smaller incomes as free as possible, we should graduate the income tax so as to fall most heavily on those who are getting the largest share of rent interest and profits, we should find another point for the application of our principles in the death duties and (if we do not deal more drastically with the unearned increment) in the taxation of ground-rents. In this way we should make rent and interest pay for their own extinction. We should inflict no overwhelming loss on any individuals or any class of living persons, as would happen if we pitched on any one particular form of property—say, land and railways—and took them without compensation. There would be no spoliation, but readjustment of taxation on a new principle. And the ground landlord has no more right to complain when the tax-collector comes his way than I have to cry out when the Chancellor of the Exchequer puts an extra penny on my income tax.'

If such a theory were to become widely prevalent, its first result would be seen in a vastly increased public expenditure. Two significant signs of its growth may, indeed, already be noticed in the almost complete disappearance of the old desire for economy and, in the efforts which are being made to discover new sources of taxation, to tap to a greater extent than has so far been done the realized wealth of the community by means of taxes on capital and income. Of the various proposals

---

[1] *The Labour Movement*, p. 78. L. T. Hobhouse, 1893.

now being put forward, that for the systematic incorporation into systems of taxation of the principle of progression or graduation is pre-eminently one as to which hopes and fears, both perhaps exaggerated, seem to be entertained. At the outset it is necessary to emphasize the truth that the importance of the adoption of such a principle as this depends largely on the view which is taken of the legitimate purposes of taxation. If these are held to be confined to what have hitherto been considered the practical necessities of a State economically administered, the questions covered by the euphemistic phrase, 'readjustment of public burdens,' become of comparatively little moment, for no class need then suffer from the pressure of taxation, and progression will be adopted only as a fairer and more scientific means of distributing such pressure as exists; but if the conception of the state which has given rise to what we may call the Wagnerian theory of taxation is to prevail in legislation, the insufficiency of its resources will at once become apparent, the methods indicated by Mr. Hobhouse will inevitably be resorted to, and progressive taxation, adopted in a very different spirit, will take its place as one of the most effective and formidable weapons of the new school. This serious controversy lies at the root of any discussion of taxation, its paramount importance cannot be overlooked; but it lies outside the scope of the present paper, as do the questions of the distribution of wealth and the incidence of taxation direct and indirect, the consideration of which is an essential preliminary to the application of our principle to the case of any particular society. The subject of the following observations is admittedly more abstract and more limited than these; but it may nevertheless be thought useful, with a view to the formation of public opinion on a proposal often mooted, but less often discussed, to endeavour to arrive at some conclusion—first, as to whether the principle of progression rests on any scientific basis; and, secondly, whether, in practice no less than in theory, there is ground for believing that its application for revenue purposes can, under the social conditions which have so far obtained, be successfully confined within safe limits. An affirmative answer may probably be given to both questions; but we must first revert for a moment to the theory of taxation upon which the principle of progression is based.

The chaos of speculation and of practice in which the art of taxation remains is not a little remarkable when it is remembered that the raising of money has been in all ages the first care and the most essential function of government; but two rival theories clearly emerge from the discussion which has of late years been almost entirely abandoned to foreign economists—the one being that the citizen should be taxed according to the benefits or protection he enjoys from the State, the other that he should be taxed according to his ability to pay. It is the last-named which modern economists agree in considering, in respect of imperial as opposed to local taxation, the most applicable to present conditions; and it was stated by Mill in the following terms:

'The subjects of a State ought to contribute as nearly as possible in proportion to their respective abilities, i.e. in proportion to the resources which they respectively enjoy under the protection of the State. In other words, equality of taxation means equality of sacrifice. It means apportioning the contribution of each person towards the expenses of government, so that he shall feel neither more nor less inconvenience from his share of the payment than every other person does from his.'

It will be noticed at once that this seemingly clear statement of the ideal to be aimed at leaves us completely in the dark as to how it is to be attained. Every man will place his own interpretation on the formula 'equality of sacrifice.' It rests, in fact, rather on sentiment than on reason, on the prevailing idea of justice than on any abstract economical principle. The standard varies with every generation. In this country, for instance, at the time when Adam Smith wrote, the labouring classes, owing to the system of indirect taxation, undoubtedly paid a far larger proportion of the revenue than they do now. It has been gradually recognized that what has been described as 'the old idea of taxation according to ability contained for centuries in laws and constitutions,' was not realized under a system which taxed the necessaries of life. The total exemption of these, and the taxation of articles of luxury, although to a certain extent a recognition of the principle of progression, was soon found inadequate to the needs of a modern State; and a system of property and income taxes was accordingly devised to bring under contribution the different sources of wealth.

The convenient principle of equality of sacrifice was next invoked to give sanction to proposals for a system of progressive taxation, proposals to which several circumstances have combined for the first time to give importance in this country.

It is characteristic of English methods that the principle of graduation should have found its way into legislation before it has been accepted by theory. It is hardly necessary to state that the actual fiscal system of this country contains in every part an indirect recognition of the idea of progression, which, however, though often quoted by the socialistic press as a direct sanction, has hitherto been defended on quite other grounds as being merely one of the devices to remedy the obvious unfairness of the pressure of indirect taxation on the poorer classes. Students of politics will not need to be reminded that we are probably destined to witness further experiments in the same direction.

But more important than any possible official patronage of the idea is its prevalence and popularity for other than purely fiscal reasons among the masses of the people, in whom political power is now so largely vested, and who are naturally desirous of placing still further upon the wealthier but less powerful classes the chief burden of taxation. Besides the fiscal, political or social reasons in favour of the proposal, there is a widespread feeling that it is only in accordance with justice that wealth should contribute more largely to the common needs than it has done in the past. The question how much the individual should be asked to contribute to the collective wants of society is indeed a complex one, and no one would deny that the existing hand-to-mouth systems are far from reaching any ideal standard. We need not endorse a recent dictum, studiously indefinite as it is, 'that society should take of the realized riches of those who benefit by the advantages of civilization such a share as the best of the wealthy classes already give of their own accord for the benefit of the victims of our social system;' but there can be little question that the public opinion of a generation, sensitively alive to the evils of poverty and to the inequalities in the distribution of wealth, is favourable to the idea that wealth has obligations towards society which it is well able to fulfil without imposing upon itself an undue burden, and that something more than the exact proportion may be demanded from its possessors, without imposing a penalty on people for having worked harder and saved more than their neighbours. How far such a sentiment is based upon reason, and how far it may be just and politic to meet it, are questions which must be faced by practical men, and the following observations upon one proposed method of doing so may at least serve to bring out a few of the points which will have to be kept in view in further controversies.

Mill, whose position as a philosopher and economist has of late years been so fiercely, and in some respects so successfully, assailed, has yet had so great a practical influence in shaping ideas and legislation in this country that his remarks on the question we are considering are worth quoting, especially as they clearly state the issue.

He begins by inquiring whether an equal sacrifice is demanded from all by making each contribute the *same percentage* on his pecuniary means. 'Many persons,' he says, 'maintain the negative, saying that a tenth part taken from a small income is a heavier burden than the same fraction deducted from one much larger; and on this is grounded the very popular scheme of what is called a graduated property tax, in which the percentage rises with the amount of the income.'

His answer is in the following words: 'On the best consideration that I am able to give to this question, it appears to me that the portion of truth which the doctrine contains arises principally from the difference between a tax which can be saved from luxuries and one which trenches, in ever so small a degree, upon the necessaries of life.' He therefore proceeds to advocate the method of adjusting these inequalities of pressure recommended by Bentham and adopted in our income tax, viz. of leaving a certain minimum of income sufficient to provide the necessaries of life untaxed. I shall return to this subject in a later part of this paper.

Mill further combats the idea of mitigating the inequalities of wealth by means of graduation by saying: 'To tax the larger incomes at a higher percentage than the smaller is to lay a tax on industry and economy, to impose a penalty on people for having worked harder and saved more than their neighbours. It is not the fortunes which are earned, but those which are unearned, that it is for the public good to place under limitation.'

It may be at once observed that a scientific view of the case will not support either the distinction between luxuries and necessaries, or the unearned increment theory, Mill's advocacy of which has probably given a more powerful impulse to socialistic ideas than an advocacy even of a 'penal' income tax which he so emphatically condemns, certainly more than a well grounded and carefully argued defence of the principle of the 'impôt progressif' would have done.

But Mill does not attempt seriously to argue the question in the foregoing passages; and it is impossible not to feel that his objection to taxing the larger incomes at a higher percentage than the smaller ones does not go to the root of the matter. We may therefore proceed to a more fruitful manner of approaching the problem, and inquire how far a justification of the principle of progression may be found in Jevons' theory of value. For the sake of clearness it will be necessary to give the argument at some length, quoting as far as possible the economist's own language[1].

[1] It is perhaps unnecessary to say that the following application of Jevons' final utility theory to the doctrine of progression has no pretension to novelty, but it was noticed by the present writer before he had the advantage of knowing that he had been anticipated in his con-

(i) The foundation of this theory lies in the distinction between utility and value—Adam Smith's 'value in use' and 'value in exchange,' or, as we shall see, Jevons with greater clearness describes it, 'total utility' and 'final utility.'

(ii) 'Utility for the purpose of economics must be considered,' he says, 'as measured by, or even as actually identified with, the addition made to a person's happiness.' 'It is a convenient term for the aggregate of the favourable balance of feeling produced—the sum of the pleasure created, and the pain prevented[1].'

(iii) 'Utility is not proportioned to commodity. A quart of water per day has the high utility of saving a person from dying in a most distressing manner. Several gallons a day may possess much utility for such purposes as cooking and washing; but after an adequate supply is secured for these uses, every additional quantity is, or may in fact become, negative; further supplies may even become inconvenient and hurtful (e.g. in case of a flood)[2].'

(iv) Jevons endeavours to show[3], by dividing into ten parts a quantity of food consumed by a person in twenty-four hours, that each of the one-tenth parts or increments is less and less necessary or possesses less utility than the preceding one. He then distinguishes between the '*total utility* of any commodity and the *degree of utility* of the commodity at any point.' ... 'For the purposes of the theory, it is not necessary to consider the *degree* of utility except as regards the last increment which has been consumed, or, what comes to the same thing, the next increment which is about to be consumed[4].' He therefore adopts the expression '*final degree of utility*' as meaning 'the degree of utility of the last addition or the next possible addition of a very small or infinitely small quantity to the existing stock.'

clusion by the very elaborate investigations of certain Dutch economists. Professor Seligman, in his learned and exhaustive article in the *Political Science Quarterly* for June, 1893, summarizes their results and covers the whole ground of the discussion.

[1] Jevons' *Theory of Political Economy*, 2nd edition, p. 49.
[2] Ibid. p. 43.
[3] Ibid. p. 49.
[4] Ibid. p. 55.

VIII.] *The Principle of Progression in Taxation.* 259

(v) The variation of the function expressing the final degree of utility is the all-important point in economic problems. 'We may,' he says, '*state as a general law that the degree of utility varies with the quantity of commodity, and ultimately decreases as that quantity increases*[1].' We cannot live without water, and yet in ordinary times we set no value upon it—why is this? Simply because we usually have so much of it that its final degree of utility is reduced to nearly zero. Let the supply run short by drought and we begin to feel the higher degrees of utility, of which we think but little at other times. 'No commodity can be named, which we continue to desire with the same force, whatever be the quantity already in use or possession.'

(vi) It is with the final degree of utility that exchange is concerned.

'The value of a divisible commodity is measured, not indeed by its total utility, but by its final degree of utility, i.e. by the intensity of the need we have for more of it[2].' But the power of exchanging one commodity for another greatly extends the range of utility. We are no longer limited to considering the degree of utility of a commodity as regards the wants of its immediate possessor, for it may have a higher usefulness to some other person, and can be transferred to that person in exchange for some commodity of a higher degree of utility to the purchaser.

(vii) We have now arrived at the definition of *value as a ratio of exchange*. Jevons sets out mathematically the condition of exchange in the form of equations, and shows how the laws of supply and demand are the result of the true theory of value or exchange. It is not necessary for our purpose to enter into this. It remains to apply these considerations, especially those stated in (v), to the case of income and money.

'The final degree of utility of money, or that supply of commodity which governs a man's income, is measured by that of any of the other commodities which he consumes. What,

[1] Jevons' *Theory of Political Economy*, 2nd edition, p. 57.
[2] Ibid. p. 148.

for instance, is the utility of one penny to a family earning £50 a year? As a penny is an inconsiderable part of their income, it may represent one of infinitely small increments, and its utility is equal to the utility of the quantity of bread, tea, sugar, or other articles which they could purchase with it, *this utility depending on the extent to which they were already provided with these articles.* To a family possessing £1,000 a year the utility of a penny may be measured in an exactly similar manner; but it will be much less, because their want of any given commodity will be satiated or satisfied to a much greater extent, so that the urgency or need for a pennyworth more of any article is much reduced[1].'

Again, 'The degree of utility to a very rich man will be governed by its degree of utility in that branch of expenditure in which he *continues to feel the need of further possession.*'

A question whether this rule would apply to the higher satisfactions as well as to the purely physical needs appears to be raised in one sentence. After stating the law that the degree of utility varies with the quantity of the commodity and ultimately decreases as that quantity increases, he says: 'All our appetites are capable of satisfaction sooner or later[2].' 'It does not follow, indeed, that the degree of utility will always sink to zero. This may be the case with some things, especially the simple animal requirements, such as food, air, water, &c. *But the more refined and intellectual our needs become, the less are they capable of satiety.* To the desire for articles of taste, science or curiosity, when once excited, there is hardly a limit.'

We thus arrive at what appears to be a justification of the principle of progression up to a certain point. The Dutch economists, says Professor Seligman, 'admit that the number of wants increases as their intensity diminishes. After a certain point the differences between the intensity (and final utility) of wants diminishes with the increase of their number and area, until, finally, when we come to the very large

---

[1] Jevons' *Theory of Political Economy*, 2nd edition, p. 152.   [2] Ibid. p. 5.

VIII.] *The Principle of Progression in Taxation.* 261

incomes, the possibility of satisfying almost all wants becomes equal. Hence, while taxation should be progressive, the rate of progression should itself diminish till the tax becomes proportional.'

A variety of considerations, however, partly theoretical and partly practical, must be mentioned before we are in a position to see how far the admission of the principle, if it be admitted [1], carries us, and within what limits the application of it may be attempted. And, in the first place, it will be necessary to lay stress upon the part which human wants and their satisfaction play in the social economy. Bastiat has well summed up the theory of consumption in the following words: 'Besoins, Efforts, Satisfactions, voilà l'homme au point de vue économique.' Even the meanest necessities, like those of eating and clothing, are subject to the influence of circumstances and habits, age and sex. No one would pretend that a man accustomed to the physical luxuries of an English artisan would be able to support existence on the diet of an Indian ryot or a Russian peasant. One man in a certain state of life would find life intolerable without books and newspapers, while another in a different situation would not be able to read. 'For some men the privation of certain enjoyments is intolerable whose loss is not even felt by others. Some, again, sacrifice all that others hold dear for the gratification of longings and aspirations that are incomprehensible to their neighbours [2].' The luxuries of one age become the necessaries of another; a man would have been thought a madman who, in the sixteenth century, expected to be able to travel at forty miles an hour, or send a message from Paris to London in half an hour.

It is unnecessary to multiply instances to prove the truth of this assertion, which is, indeed, a commonplace of economic science. It is no less clear that the satisfaction of a primary want creates or intensifies the sense of more than one

[1] Mr. Charles Devas (*Political Economy*, p. 197) has some very pertinent criticisms on this law, directed, however, rather against the possibility of its application than against its abstract truth.

[2] Banfield; quoted by Jevons, p. 45.

secondary privation; and the maxim that the '*satisfaction of every lower want in the scale creates a desire of a higher character*' is self-evident.'

Further, it is the action of this fundamental law which causes and determines what we know as progress and civilization. It is this which stimulates the invention of labour-saving apparatus and of machinery, and necessitates the application of human intellect to the arts of life. By the natural operation of supply and demand, it is daily placing within the reach of millions what was formerly the privilege of the great ones of the earth. By the action of free competition it is bringing about the real millennium, the ideal of the Socialists, and removing necessary after necessary and luxury after luxury from the region of 'value' to that of 'utility,' from the domain of exchange and political economy to that of common property[1]. For no less clearly established than the rise in the rate of wages under this system is the fall certainly now in progress in the rate of interest on capital, which the increase of security in business, the increase of capital by accumulation, and the lessened productivity of freshly accumulated capital in old-established societies have all contributed to bring about. The competition for employment of capital with capital is a fact which, if it could only be recognized, would be seen to overshadow the competition of labour with labour or the strife between labour and capital. The rate of interest declines because the stored-

---

[1] As Bastiat, a writer who is not answered when he is taunted with economic optimism, expresses it (*Harmonies Économiques*, p. 291):—

'Toute propriété est une valeur, toute valeur est une propriété;
Ce qui n'a pas de valeur est gratuit, ce qui est gratuit est commun;
Baisse de valeur, c'est approximation vers la gratuité;
Approximation vers la gratuité, c'est réalisation partielle de communauté.'

But although the domain of things common or gratuitous to all, the aggregate of utilities, is constantly increasing, that of things having exchange value, of property, does not decrease, for the horizon of human desires and possible satisfactions is always expanding and with it the field of human labour and service, production and exchanges, without which those desires cannot be satisfied. 'La propriété' is a pioneer which accomplishes its work in one sphere and then passes to another.

up wealth of the world is increasing, and this wealth, as a necessary consequence, is being diffused throughout the community in the shape of higher wages and lower prices. This process tends towards the equalization of conditions in this further way, that a decline in the rate of interest is equivalent to a gradual loss by the class of capitalists and 'rentiers' of part of their advantage over the rest of the community. If this is the case—and facts as well as theory confirm it—what sense, it will be asked, can there be in endeavouring to bring about by clumsy and unjust legislative expedients the conditions of the stationary state of society towards which economic causes may appear to be leading us? A stationary state reached by the gradual process above described might conceivably be one of material comfort, for it could only be so reached when human labour and effort in the satisfaction of desires was reduced to a minimum; reached by socialistic attacks on wealth, if, indeed, such attacks succeeded in doing anything beyond checking accumulation and its beneficent effects, it could only be one of general misery.

This fascinating subject, however, must not detain us, for one instance of the function of capital such as that given by Mr. Atkinson[1] is worth much speculation. 'The late Cornelius Vanderbilt may be taken as an example of a communist in the true sense. He was the greatest communist of his age. He consolidated and perfected the railroad service in such a way that a year's supply of bread and meat can be moved one thousand miles from the Western prairies to the Eastern workshops at the measure of cost of a single day's wages of a mechanic or artisan in Massachusetts.... The work is not that of the labourer in the sense in which that word is used by so-called labour reformers ... yet it is an effort of the human mind of such a quality, that except capital had then come under the control of these men, all the efforts of labourers would have utterly failed to promote the general welfare. The farmers of the West would have smothered in their own grease, and would have continued to

[1] *Distribution of Products*, p. 38.

burn their Indian corn for fuel, while the workmen of the East might have starved.'

'The true function of capital and of the capitalists is of the utmost beneficence. It cannot be exerted in the present condition of the world, except by way of ownership of land and capital, subject to the limitation and to the duties which are implied by existing laws[1].' The able American statist goes on to say, in words which must have caused a shock of surprise to 'social reformers,' that the fortunes which the great directors of industry have made for themselves bear but the proportion of a small fraction to the labour which they have saved their fellow-men.

The bearing of the above observations upon the immediate question before us is easily indicated. Those who look to freedom and equal rights as the only means of ensuring the supreme object of the largest possible production, an increasingly larger share of which goes under such a system to labour, will be unable to regard taxation as anything but a drag on the wheels of the social machine, and they will seek to confine it within the narrowest limits. They will endeavour to meet any unfair incidence of indirect taxation upon the poor by abolishing or reducing such taxation, and they will be inclined to put up with rough-and-ready methods so long as no class can complain of actual oppression, rather than have recourse to expedients like graduation. They are not however on principle justified in condemning an attempt to equalize the burden upon individuals and classes of such taxation as exists, and it is impossible for them to shut their eyes to the deplorable fact that in European states, with their debts and armaments, not to speak of social demands, the pressure of taxation is severely and increasingly felt, and that finance ministers cannot afford to neglect any promising sources of revenue. They may, therefore, without abandoning their view of the economic organization of society as it now exists (and, it may be added, will continue to exist until collectivism can supply a different motive for labour than those which now animate mankind),

---

[1] *Distribution of Products*, p. 41.

perhaps admit that the argument tells, not indeed against a moderate application of the principle for revenue purposes, but against a progression, which would end, as progression logically must on the socialistic theory of rent interest and profits, in the confiscation of all income above a certain point. If human wants were a limited and stationary quantity, any surplus income (if one may for a moment assume that in these circumstances such a surplus could come into being) beyond the amount necessary to satisfy those wants, would obviously be superfluous, and might be confiscated without hurting the owner. Above a certain ascertainable limit, he would not feel the abstraction by the state of all his wealth, for he would have no use for it. But when we bear in mind the progressive character of human desires, which is the keystone of civilization, we shall at once see the doubtfulness of any such assumption. The larger the individual income, the larger will be the accumulations of capital, with all their beneficent effects upon the general level of social well-being. Further, on the supposition on which this argument proceeds—that a system of private property, with its necessary accompaniment of free exchange, is favourable and indeed essential to human progress—we find at once a necessary limit to the application of the principle at the point at which it begins to check accumulation, and thus hinder production[1]. Where that point lies in any particular community is a question which can only be solved by inquiry, discussion and experiment.

If, then, by adopting a plan of degressive taxation (i.e. a uniform rate being fixed for large incomes, but gradually lessened for the smaller, and a minimum being wholly exempted), the danger thus indicated may be met, is it possible to meet the further difficulty of fixing an equitable rate of graduation? The first step, the exemption of a minimum income, finds an easy defence on the

[1] It has been calculated that there is no country where the entire accumulated property would sell for enough to maintain its population on the most economical terms for more than three years, and that the world, as a whole, is always within a single year of starvation.

economic ground above sketched out. It is obvious that all wants or sets of wants are not equally imperious. May it not, therefore, be possible and defensible to mark off a certain limit of desires of the elementary kind, such as those for food, shelter and clothing, which are common to all men, the satisfaction of which is necessary to keep human beings alive, and to supply a lever for the creation of higher wants? Humanity forbids us to allow our fellow-creatures to perish; and society may legitimately, in its own interest, do what it safely can to give a lift up to an indigent class by affording it the chance of conceiving aspirations after a higher level of comfort. This is, indeed, the only real basis and justification from the 'free exchange' point of view for the so-called socialistic legislation of the present day. For this purpose, then, and to some such extent, human wants may be treated as a fixed quantity, and incomes above the amount necessary to satisfy these wants may be held to be alone, or in larger proportion, liable to taxation.

If we desire to apply the same argument to justify graduation above this point, we are met by the practical difficulty of deciding whether, beyond a certain point, one set of desires is more imperious than another. We may assume that a man will make a greater effort to earn the £50 a year which saves him from starvation than another man to earn £1,000 a year. But who can say whether one man will make a greater effort to earn £1,000 than another £2,000 or another £10,000? It may be, indeed, found possible to cut the knot by some such rough-and-ready scheme as that proposed by Professor Ely, who would have three rates of taxation—one for incomes, sufficient to furnish necessities; one for those sufficient to provide the useful; and one for those large enough to warrant luxuries. In these three words, however—*necessities, the useful*, and *luxuries*—what material for dispute and conflict does there not lie? Here, then, we find ourselves face to face with the great practical difficulty in the case, the arbitrary character of all such schemes. Proportional taxation

VIII.] *The Principle of Progression in Taxation.* 267

carries in its very name a permanent and definite rate of assessment, yet even under this system practical financiers tell us that the difficulty of arriving at a fair distribution of the burden of taxation is well-nigh insuperable [1]. How greatly is this difficulty increased with a scale of progression depending on the moderation or caprice of legislators! If however, on the other hand, proportional taxation is in itself unjust, it is clear that its greater definiteness should not save it from condemnation as an ideal to be aimed at in systems of taxation.

Finally, the question may be taken from another side—that of facts and experience. In this part of his remarks M. Leroy-Beaulieu (in his *Science des Finances*) is brilliant and suggestive, some will think conclusive. He gives exhaustively the grounds which lead him to the opinion that a light and uniform tax will produce as much, with less friction and less danger, than the most rigorously graduated tax. Those who advocate this latter expedient cannot, he thinks, have studied (as he himself has done in another admirable work, *La Répartition des Richesses*) the distribution of wealth among the different classes of modern societies. Few better illustrations of what this distribution means from a revenue point of view can be given than the following

---

[1] It has been impossible in this paper to touch on a question, which yet lies at the root of all speculation on the subject of taxation, viz. its incidence on individuals and classes. The following words show the importance of the question in connexion with our present subject: 'Without going so far as some economists in thinking that wherever taxes are first imposed they are so diffused and distributed in the process of exchange as to render all elaborate attempts at a nice adjustment of them a matter of comparative unimportance, it is undeniable that under no system of taxation can any class escape a share of the burden, and, least of all, the most helpless and improvident class. It is conceivable that if a direct tax were imposed on the working classes, they might be unable to recover the whole of it by a rise in the rate of wages. It is not easily conceivable that a tax on capital would not be gradually diffused throughout the community, and ultimately affect wages, and be borne in a large proportion by the working classes.' Again, 'There can be no greater mistake than to suppose that an immense and increasing burden of taxation can be raised by any "adjustments" on what is called the property of about five million persons without a disastrous recoil on the interests of the working classes.'—Sir Louis Mallet, *Free Exchange*, p. 194.

remarks of the late Chancellor of the Exchequer in one of his budget speeches :

'The Committee scarcely realizes, I think, the extent to which both the income tax and the inhabited house duty are paid by men of comparatively humble means. I thought at one time it might be reasonable to allow every income tax payer to deduct £400 from his income before paying income tax, but I was staggered to find that this would involve a loss of £4,700,000 out of a total receipt of £13,000,000. To allow every income tax payer to deduct £200 would involve a loss of £2,500,000. This shows to what an enormous extent the revenue is contributed to by people of small incomes.'

The same fact, which is one of vital importance, is well shown by the table on the opposite page, taken from M. Leroy-Beaulieu's work.

From this table it appears that in a highly civilized and industrial canton, out of a total income of 31 million francs five-sixths (25,628,000 fr.) was in the hands of persons with a no larger income than 3,000 fr., and that one-thirtieth only belonged to persons with incomes of over 10,000 fr. Further, that a uniform tax of 1 per cent. produces 310,020 fr.; while the progressive tax proposed produces 334,266 fr. or only 24,000 fr. or 8 per cent. more; a gain which might easily be counterbalanced by the frauds for which there would obviously be so great a temptation.

The progression here sketched out is considerably less than that which actually exists in many cantons, especially in the Canton de Vaud, where a very interesting experiment is in progress. In this Canton in 1890 the tax on real property yielded £43,956, and that on personal property £52,902; the population being 247,605; the increase of revenue accruing from progression being about £6,000. Its opponents, however, declare that this gain is more than counterbalanced by injury to local trade, and especially by the great depreciation (stated at 50 per cent.) in the value of landed property which it has caused. It seems probable, indeed, that the principle in this instance has been pushed too far. There are five cantons,

PROPOSAL FOR A PROGRESSIVE TAX ON THE INCOMES OF THE CANTON OF NEUCHÂTEL.

Classification of Taxpayers from the Register in 1874.

Incomes.			No. of taxpayers.	Average income in each class.	Totals of taxable incomes.	Rate of tax per 100 Frs.	Estimated product of tax.
	Fr.	Fr.		Fr.	Fr.		Fr.
From	0 to	3,000	42,714	600	25,628,000	1	256,284
,,	3,001 ,,	4,000	410	3,500	1,435,600	$1\frac{1}{10}$	15,785
,,	4,001 ,,	5,000	196	4,550	891,800	$1\frac{2}{10}$	10,700
,,	5,001 ,,	6,000	106	5,500	583,000	$1\frac{3}{10}$	7,579
,,	6,001 ,,	7,000	53	6,500	344,500	$1\frac{4}{10}$	4,821
,,	7,001 ,,	8,000	60	7,500	450,000	$1\frac{5}{10}$	6,750
,,	8,001 ,,	9,000	24	8,500	204,000	$1\frac{6}{10}$	3,264
,,	9,001 ,,	10,000	35	9,500	332,500	$1\frac{7}{10}$	5,649
,,	10,001 ,,	12,000	19	11,000	209,000	$1\frac{8}{10}$	3,762
,,	12,001 ,,	15,000	15	13,500	202,500	$1\frac{9}{10}$	3,847
,,	15,001 ,,	20,000	10	17,500	175,000	2	3,500
,,	20,001 ,,	30,000	14	25,000	350,000	$2\frac{1}{10}$	7,350
,,	30,001 ,,	40,000	2	35,000	70,000	$2\frac{2}{10}$	1,540
,,	40,001 ,,	50,000	1	45,000	45,000	$2\frac{3}{10}$	1,035
,,	50,001 and above		2	50,000	100,000	$2\frac{4}{10}$	2,400
			43,661		31,020,700		334,266

Zurich, Vaud, Geneva, Uri and the Grisons, in which complete systems of these taxes exist, and many others in which a partial use of the principle is made; and these systems are remarkable for the care with which they have been adapted to the circumstances of the people. The insufficiency, however, of this fiscal method in the Swiss Confederation generally is shown by the marked tendency towards increased indirect taxation, which already, in 1881, amounted to 57·9 per 100[1].

[1] A fairly full account of these taxes, whether on income or capital, real or personal estate, is given in a report by Mr. Buchanan (Foreign Office, 1892; Miscellaneous Series, No. 267).

The returns of the new Prussian income tax for 1892-3, the first financial year since its introduction, do not prove much as to the efficacy of progression. There is an increase of £2,264,201, in spite of the amount levied from smaller incomes having been decreased by £350,000; but 440,218 new taxpayers have been laid under requisition, including, for the first time, joint stock companies and trading associations. The moderate graduation adopted appears to meet the sense of justice in the community, and has not had the effect of causing any withdrawal of capital from the country. An agitation, of course, exists for increasing the tax on the higher incomes. It is interesting to observe that of incomes of £4,800 and over there are 1,780, while 35 are over £45,000, 4 over £150,000, 2 over £250,000, and 1 of £350,000. The large figures are accounted for by the fact that the income of the mediatized princes have now, for the first time, been rendered amenable to taxation[1].

The example of the Australian Colonies is so often quoted by democratic reformers that it is well worth while to see what, in regard to graduated taxation, that example really amounts to.

The total revenue of the colony of Victoria[2] in 1887 was £7,607,598, of which nearly 60 per cent. was raised from sources other than taxation, viz.:

Crown Lands	£656,627
Railways	2,741,488
Post and Telegraphs	485,533
Other Sources	653,307
	£4,536,955

Whatever advantages such sources of revenue may possess, they cannot be defended from the point of view of taxation as being charges on wealth. The railway revenue, for instance (36 per cent. of the whole revenue), is a tax on locomotion and on transport, not on 'realized riches.'

---

[1] Foreign Office, 1892; Misc. Series, No. 268.

[2] These figures are taken from Hayter's *Victorian Year Book*; and a year has been chosen before the recent check to the Colony's prosperity; since which panegyrics of Victorian State Socialism have notably diminished.

There remains 40 per cent. of the revenue which is drawn from taxation (as compared with 39·99 per cent. in Switzerland and 84·25 in the United Kingdom in the same year) of this revenue 75 per cent. (or 30 per cent. of the whole) was drawn from Customs and Excise, and therefore pressed unduly on the poor. The remaining taxation, out of which alone can come any application of the principle of graduation, amounted to under 9 per cent. of the whole, and includes excise licences, stamps, succession and probate duties, property and income taxes, amounting to under £700,000. Under this head would fall the new forms of taxation directed against great estates, (1) the land tax and (2) the succession duty. The first of these is not graduated but is 'a tax with considerable exemptions, the classes of exemptions being so constructed that the tax is clearly intended to bring land into the market[1].' The whole tax fell upon under 900 persons and brought in about £124,000 a year. The succession duty which brought in a slightly larger amount was graduated on a scale varying from 2 per cent. on small estates up to 10 per cent. on estates of over £100,000.

We have said enough to show that, although the principle may be recognized and applied in most countries, the practice is certainly not to tax property in any undue proportion, if indeed sufficiently. It is not too much to say that in no stable civilized state has progressive taxation ever amounted to anything like confiscation of the larger incomes, such as is demanded by theoretic Socialism. Further, it does not appear by any means certain, from the experience of countries where it has been tried, that much is to be gained from a revenue point of view by a progressive income tax. Taken by itself as a fiscal instrument, it has even been said that it must either amount to confiscation or it will be useless, that it must either aim at the destruction of private capital, in which case, to quote Proudhon's picturesque phrase, 'Il aurait pour effet de refouler la richesse et de faire que le travail, comme un homme attaché à un cadavre, embrasserait

---

[1] Sir C. Dilke, *Problems of Greater Britain*, vol. i. p. 192.

la misère dans un accouplement sans fin;' or that it will be moderate, and in this case will be little more productive than uniform or proportional taxation. The dilemma, however, is probably less conclusive than it looks. It is rash to imagine that in a matter in which the habits of a people, the distribution of their wealth and the character of their government are all important factors, the example of one country can be of very great assistance to another. The same taxes, or similar methods of levying them, will not be suitable alike to tax-dodging America, frugal Switzerland and bureaucratic Prussia. But the question whether the circumstances of any particular country make it possible or desirable to adopt or develop a progressive system of taxation is one of practical finance upon which it has been no part of my design to touch, having had chiefly in view the greater question, namely, What ideal of justice should taxation endeavour to attain? Even if the comparative inutility of all existing systems of progressive taxation were established, this question would remain for solution; and, since a system of taxation will never be in its highest degree productive which does not conform to some standard of rightfulness in the heart of the taxpayer, it cannot well be neglected. The argument from Jevons' theory, if it is economically sound, has also the advantage of harmonizing with what we may take to be the rough-and-ready sense of justice of the ordinary man. It cannot, of course, be pushed too far; and if it may be held to demonstrate in a general way that, in order to equalize the burden of taxation upon individuals and classes, a higher proportion should fall upon the larger than upon the smaller incomes, it does not help us to a practical scheme of progressive rates, which has sometimes been deduced from it, and which can only be arrived at as the result of carefully guarded experiment.

Taxation indeed belongs essentially to the domain of practical administration, and a conclusion based on considerations of theory, such as those discussed in this paper, must therefore of necessity be incomplete. The judgement of the Economists appears to deprive the principle, in its practical application, of much of the importance which has been claimed for it, but it entitles us at any rate to assume that progressive taxation, in its theoretical aspect, need neither be considered in the light of a socialistic bugbear, nor ridiculed as a mere 'joujou démocratique,' and that, if it be confined within bounds, some of which have been pointed out as essential to its safe and advantageous use, and if the object of equalizing taxation be clearly kept in view and the object of equalizing incomes be as clearly repudiated, it may be found a useful adjunct to a well-balanced fiscal system.

BERNARD MALLET.

IX.

THE LAW OF TRADE COMBINATIONS.

HON. ALFRED LYTTELTON.

IX.

THE LAW OF TRADE COMBINATIONS.

THE proximity into which men are now brought, and the almost bewildering ease with which they can communicate with one another, have given a strong impulse in business to the principle of combination. Combination is the motto of modern commerce. More and more is it apparent that industry will in the future be mainly in the hands of associated bodies. On the one side vast companies and amalgamations of companies quarter out the field in which capital circulates; on the other Trade Unions numbering members in thousands and tens of thousands organize and regulate labour. Already companies have practically absorbed the great operations of Land Transport and Fire and Life Insurance; soon Banking will pass also under their sway. The Salt Union, the United Alkali Company, and the proposed Coal Trust mark the advance in this country alone of ideas of even vaster enterprise. Yet outside the serried ranks of these great associations there yet exist a large though perhaps a diminishing number of individual capitalists and a still larger and probably not diminishing number of individual workmen. Combined capital, guided by salaried managers, measures its long purse and its long arms against the individual proprietor operating in a narrower area, but with more concentrated energy. Combined labour, strong in the discipline of the trade union, confronts the single craftsman, and brings irresistible pressure to bear on him, if he ventures to resist its authority. The interests of labour and capital, to those most nearly concerned, appear only too often to be divergent and furnish ample material for misunderstanding. It will be at once seen that there are here the conditions of conflict. This conflict has none of the decorative aspects of war and is waged for no trophy of chivalry. The prizes striven for are common material things, but the struggle for commercial supremacy is a bitter one, and it is easy for the combatants to overstep the limits of order and the boundaries of the peace. To keep the peace is obviously the primary function of law, and law has thus been always concerned in restraining industrial combatants from any semblance of physical violence. But English law has not confined itself to this modest task. Combinations, especially combinations of labour, inspired such terror among our forefathers that, from the middle of the fourteenth century to the reign of George IV, we find statute after statute prescribing penalties upon all alliances and covines of workmen to alter wages, while the laws against forestalling, regrating, engrossing, and monopolies, coupled with the developed law of conspiracy, confined combinations of capitalists within rigid limits [1]. These statutes which are out of harmony with modern ideas were deemed by their authors to be in accordance with sound principle, and with the well-known doctrine of English Common Law, that every person has individually and the public collectively a right to require that trade shall be kept free from unreasonable obstruction. But it is obvious that the word 'unreasonable' gives an elasticity to this legal doctrine of which the changing opinion of successive generations has taken full advantage, and indeed a full description of its fortunes would illustrate a very curious and interesting chapter in the history of economic opinion in this country. For it is natural that legal theories as to restraint of trade should fare very differently at the hands of mediaeval lawyers keenly alive to the necessity of securing supply in times when

---

[1] A learned writer has recently given good reason for asserting that Christianity was persecuted not as a religion but as an association, and that the Roman Empire was opposed to all associations whatever with the sole exception of Benefit Clubs. *The Church in the Roman Empire*, pp. 354-360. Ramsay.

'stores were small, transit difficult and famine near if supply were delayed,' and at those of a modern judge born in the atmosphere of free trade and steeped from his youth up in the doctrines of the Ricardian economists. The scope of this paper does not permit any historical discussion of this topic. Some recent decisions of the Courts have, however, defined the present law affecting trade combinations in certain difficult and obscure regions, and it may be of use, in view of the great importance of the subject, to ascertain if possible the positions definitely established by their authority. The decisions relate both to the Criminal and the Civil Law, to Statute and to Common Law. In this paper I propose to discuss in the first place the Criminal and then the Civil Law in the light of those decisions. The Criminal Law will fall conveniently into two divisions: (*a*) The Conspiracy and Protection of Property Act, 1875; (*b*) The Common Law Crime of Conspiracy.

I. (*a*) The Conspiracy and Protection of Property Act, 1875.

This Act of Parliament, which hereafter will be referred to as the Statute of 1875, exempts from the operation of the Common Law of Conspiracy all agreements to do any act in contemplation or furtherance of trade disputes between combined employers or combined workmen, which, if committed by individuals, would not be indictable under the common law. So far the Statute gives special privileges to trade disputants which are not enjoyed by any other class;—on the other hand, as it were to redress the balance, it imposes special burdens upon them by making criminal certain acts which may be committed by any citizen but which are in fact peculiarly characteristic of trade combinations. It will be observed that while all subjects of the Queen are affected by the new penalties, trade disputants alone are affected by the new exemptions. I append the actual words of the two sections whose effect I have summarized above.

'3. An agreement or combination by two or more persons to do or procure to be done any act in *contemplation or furtherance of a trade dispute between employers and workmen* shall not be indictable as a conspiracy if such act committed by one person would not be punishable as a crime.

'Nothing in this section shall exempt from punishment any persons guilty of a conspiracy for which a punishment is awarded by any Act of Parliament.

'Nothing in this section shall affect the law relating to riot, unlawful assembly, breach of the peace, or sedition, or any offence against the State or the Sovereign.

'A crime for the purposes of this section means an offence punishable on indictment, or an offence which is punishable on summary conviction, and for the commission of which the offender is liable under the statute making the offence punishable to be imprisoned either absolutely or at the discretion of the court as an alternative for some other punishment.'

'7. Every person who, with a view to compel any other person to abstain from doing or to do any act which such other person has a legal right to do or abstain from doing, wrongfully and without legal authority,—

'(1) Uses violence to or intimidates such other person or his wife or children, or injures his property; or,

'(2) Persistently follows such other person about from place to place; or,

'(3) Hides any tools, clothes, or other property owned or used by such other person, or deprives him of or hinders him in the use thereof; or,

'(4) Watches or besets the house or other place where such other person resides, or works, or carries on business, or happens to be, or the approach to such house or place; or,

'(5) Follows such other person with two or more other persons in a disorderly manner in or through any street or road,

shall, on conviction thereof by a court of summary jurisdiction, or on indictment as hereinafter mentioned, be liable either to pay a penalty not exceeding twenty pounds, or to be imprisoned for a term not exceeding three months, with or without hard labour.

'Attending at or near the house or place where a person

resides, or works, or carries on business, or happens to be, or the approach to such house or place, in order merely to obtain or communicate information, shall not be deemed a watching or besetting within the meaning of this section.'

Section 7, it will be seen, enumerates the various methods of coercion which from time to time have been employed by trade organizations, and may perhaps be said to comprehend the totality of such methods by the word 'intimidate.' It has been objected to this word that it is too vague, and if it be true, as many wise men think, that the criminal law should in all cases be rigidly precise in its definitions, it is a charge which we think is made out; but there is more perhaps to be said in favour of a criminal statute that leaves something to the intelligence of the tribunal which administers its decrees than would at first be supposed. When for instance the word 'intimidate' was limited as in a previous statute to actions which would justify a magistrate in binding over the intimidator to keep the peace, it was only human nature for men to ascertain precisely those actions which would cause the maximum of fear, without giving a magistrate such a jurisdiction.

One of the most effectual penal statutes of modern times is the Corrupt Practices Act, 1883, which imposes fine and imprisonment on persons doing certain acts 'in and about the conduct and management of the election.' Now there is no definition in the statute of the time when an election commences, and during ten years no judge has laid down with precision this fatal hour. The result is that numerous offences subject to severe penalty are left vague. But the objectors to this vagueness are not purists in legal codification but old election hacks, who if the election period had been rigidly ascertained would only have ceased corrupt expenditure at midnight of the day before.

A long stride in the clear definition of the word 'intimidation' has now been made, so that the vice of vagueness, if it be a vice, is largely mitigated. As early as 1880 Mr. Justice Cave ruled that to constitute intimidation within the meaning of the section under consideration personal violence must be threatened; and in 1891 the scope of the section, and in particular the meaning of the word 'intimidation,' were considered and determined by five judges in two cases the importance of which justify a somewhat detailed reference.

GIBSON v. LAWSON.

In this case, in Dec. 1890, a workman named Gibson, a member of a trade union called the National Society of Engineers, was employed as a fitter by Messrs. Palmer & Co. shipbuilders in Northumberland. Another workman, by name Lawson, a shop delegate and a member of another trade union, the Amalgamated Society of Engineers, was employed in a like capacity at Messrs. Palmers. On Dec. 3 the Amalgamated Society of Engineers met and resolved not to work at Messrs. Palmer's after Dec. 6 unless Gibson joined their union. Lawson communicated this resolution to Messrs. Palmer's foreman, who repeated it to Gibson. Gibson thereupon refused to leave his trade union or to join the other, and in consequence, and in order to avoid the threatened strike, Messrs. Palmer's foreman dismissed Gibson from his employment. No violence or threats of violence either to person or to property were used to Gibson, but he swore that he was afraid, in consequence of what Lawson said, that he would lose his work and get no more at any place where the Amalgamated Society predominated numerically over his own society.

Lawson was afterwards prosecuted for having wrongfully and without legal authority intimidated Gibson, under section 7, sub-section (1) of the Statute of 1875. On these facts it was held by a court consisting of five judges that the action of Lawson implied no threat whatever of personal violence, and was not 'intimidation.' It was also observed that the Statute of 1875 expressly legalized strikes, and that a conspiracy, by means of a strike thus legalized, to coerce another's will, notwithstanding certain decisions of Lord Bramwell and Lord Esher, could not be indictable.

Regarding this decision from a purely legal point of view,

it is to be observed that in the repealed Act of 1871, which dealt with the same subject as the Statute of 1875, the word 'intimidation' was limited to such intimidation as would justify a magistrate in binding over the intimidator to keep the peace towards the person intimidated. In the Statute of 1875 Parliament enacted the seventh section containing the word 'intimidation' without any such limitation. It has been a matter of surprise to many lawyers that the word 'intimidation' was construed in face of this contrast as if the limitation of the Act of 1871 were still in force. Two reasons only are given in the report for this decision: (1) The changing temper of the times on the subject; (2) That the Statute of 1875 was preceded by a Royal Commission which recommended a relaxation of the law in favour of trade unions. As to (1), it is submitted that though it is quite sound to permit 'the changing opinion of the times' to modify a common law rule, for such a rule is founded on custom, it is quite unsound to extend such reasoning to a statute. For a statute is to be construed according to the intention of those who passed it, and to construe it, not according to that intention as gathered from its tenor, but according to the fluctuating opinions of its readers, seems obviously to introduce confusion and uncertainty.

As to (2), it is not legally permissible to read or even refer in argument to the debates preceding the passage of an Act, still less to the report of a Royal Commission on which it is supposed to be based. It is moreover inaccurate to say that the Royal Commissioners recommended a relaxation of the law as regards intimidation, on the contrary, they advised that no relaxation should here be made.

CURRAN v. TRELEAVEN.

In this case the Secretaries of certain trade unions had been convicted before the Recorder of Plymouth of wrongful intimidation under the section above referred to. The Recorder stated the following case for the consideration of the Court of Queen's Bench before giving effect to the conviction.

The appellant and two other secretaries of trade unions, in order to prevent the respondent employing non-union men, informed him that if he did not cease to do so, they would call off from their employment by him all the members of their respective unions. After a meeting of the unions, at which it was resolved that this course should be adopted, the appellant and the other secretaries, in the presence of the respondent, whom they asked to attend, made the following statement to the respondent's workmen and others who were assembled:—'Inasmuch as Mr. T. (i.e. the respondent) still insists on employing non-union men, we, your officials, call upon all union men to leave their work. Use no violence, use no immoderate language, but quietly cease to work, and go home.' The union men in consequence ceased to work.

Held, that there was no evidence of intimidation by the appellant within the meaning of the section, and that the conviction must be quashed.

The reasons for this decision may be presumed to be the same as those given in the first case, as no others germane to the subject are given in the report.

Whatever legal criticism may be suggested on the reasons given for these decisions, the law, as laid down in them, has at least the merit of being clear, and I venture to predict the result that no prosecutions will be undertaken under section 7, sub-section (1) of the Statute of 1875 unless proof can be given that physical force has been used or threatened. The other offences aimed at by the second, third, fourth, and fifth sub-sections are defined with great clearness, and require no comment here.

It seems then that if in such cases as the above, the only resort to the criminal law against trade combinations left open to employers and workmen be the Statute of 1875, the conclusion follows that subjects of the Queen, owing allegiance only to the law of the land, can, against their will, be brought under the dominion of a power which they detest, and to which in a free country they owe no obedience, and that too, in matters so vital to them, as on the one hand the employment of their capital, and the hiring of their workmen, and on the other the expenditure of their income, the hours, methods, nay even the disposal of their labour. For it is idle to say that a power is not absolute which, though bound to abstain from physical violence, is yet at liberty to bring upon a fellow-subject industrial ruin. Such a conclusion is startling, for every one knows that the remedies of the *civil* law, for workmen at any rate, against trade unions are practically beyond their means or opportunities.

(*b*) The common law crime of conspiracy.

It has been too readily assumed, probably owing to some dicta in the cases above mentioned which were unnecessary for their decision, that outside the provisions of the Statute of 1875, the criminal law is powerless against combinations of capitalists and workmen. I propose to consider two doctrines of the common law relating to conspiracy which appear to be available against such combinations. There is authority that the following agreements are criminal.

1. Agreements between more persons than one to do acts which are injurious to the public, or as Sir James Stephen puts it, 'Agreements between more persons than one to carry out purposes which the judges regarded as injurious to the public.'

2. Agreements where, with malicious design to do an injury, the purpose is to effect a wrong though not such a wrong as when perpetrated by a single individual would amount to an offence under the criminal law.

1. The statement of this rule appears and is extraordinarily vague. Convictions have in the past been obtained against persons conspiring to impoverish the farmers of excise, so as to make them incapable of rendering the king his revenue, against combinations of officers to throw up their commissions in times of danger, and against persons combining to disturb the price of the funds by false rumours. But the principle has never been applied, in England at any rate, against rings of capitalists or unions of workmen, and though it is possible to conceive cases in which the national importance of the industries affected might justify its use, no judge would venture to enforce it in cases such as those we have considered.

2. The second principle has the authority of the Final Report of the Royal Commission on the Labour Laws in 1875 (a Commission which contained, among others, Lord Chief Justice Cockburn, Sir M. Smith, Mr. Russell Gurney, Mr. Roebuck, and Mr. Thomas Hughes), has been supported by dicta of the Court of Appeal, and its reasoning adopted in cases of high authority in America. If the principle be applied to the facts of the case of Gibson *v.* Lawson I do not think it can be doubted that in the absence of the exempting section of the Statute of 1875, Lawson and those who acted with him would have been found guilty legally of a criminal conspiracy. Their immediate intention was to induce Gibson's employers to break their contract with him. Such an intention is malicious in law, even though there be no personal ill-will. Their remote object was to force Gibson to leave his trade union and join another, i.e. to infringe his legal right to belong to any union he thought fit. Then does the third section of the Statute of 1875 exempt such a combination from the law of criminal conspiracy? That section, it will be remembered, enacts that 'An agreement or combination by two or more persons to do or procure to be done any act in contemplation or furtherance of a trade dispute between employers and workmen shall not be indictable as a conspiracy if such act committed by one person would not be indictable as a crime.' This section has been judicially declared to have expressly legalized strikes. But if it is closely scrutinized it will be found to exempt strikes from the operation of the Criminal Law of Conspiracy only when the agreements at their root are 'in furtherance or contemplation of a trade dispute between employers and workmen.' The whole history of this legislation shows that the object of Parliament in granting this exemption was to remove all fetters from Labour which might seem to cramp it unfairly in the struggle with Capital. The capitalist, it was argued, is a combination in himself. The labourer should then be free also to combine. The intention of Parliament was not to give a dominance which might easily become a tyranny either to rings of capitalists or unions of workmen, but to place

workmen so far as possible on terms of equality in competition with capitalists. The exemption of section 3 accordingly only operates to make agreements otherwise criminal not criminal when they are made in the course or genuine contemplation of a trade dispute between employers and workmen. The belligerents must not be employers and employers or workmen and workmen, but employers and workmen, and there is no sanction in the statute for the notion, now widely prevalent, that a ring of capitalists can combine to ruin rival capitalists, or that a trade union can combine to ruin non-unionists, by wrongfully injuring them. The mere cover of a strike is not of itself to render not criminal all agreements attendant on its inception. It will be seen, therefore, that had Lawson and his friends, for example, been indicted for a common law conspiracy, and had their action been brought within the terms of the definition under consideration, they would not (it is submitted) have been entitled to an acquittal by virtue of section 3 of the Statute of 1875, unless the jury found as a fact that the agreement to procure the dismissal of Gibson had been in bona fide contemplation or furtherance of a trade dispute between the defendants and their employers.

II. As already indicated, it is not intended to discuss the civil remedies of those aggrieved by the actions of trade combinations, beyond adverting in detail to two recent decisions of the Courts in which these remedies have been elaborately discussed, and which illustrate in a very salient manner the bearing of the modern law in this connexion. The first of these cases is called The Mogul S. S. Company *v.* McGregor, Gow & Co. (1889), and will be hereafter referred to as 'the Mogul case.' In that case the defendants were a number of ship-owners who formed themselves into a league or conference for the purpose of ultimately keeping in their own hands the control of the tea-carriage from certain Chinese ports, and for the purpose of driving the plaintiffs and other competitors from the field. In order to succeed in this object, and to discourage the plaintiffs' vessels from resorting to those ports, the defendants during the 'tea harvest' of 1885 combined to offer to the local shippers very low freights, with a view of generally reducing or 'smashing' rates, and thus rendering it unprofitable for the plaintiffs to send their ships thither. They offered, moreover, a rebate of five per cent. to all local shippers and agents who would deal exclusively with vessels belonging to the conference, and any agent who broke the condition was to forfeit the entire rebate on all shipments made on behalf of any and every one of his principals during the whole year—a forfeiture of rebate or allowance which was denominated as 'penal' by the plaintiffs' counsel. It must, however, be taken as established that the rebate was one which the defendants need never have allowed at all to their customers. It must also be taken that the defendants had no personal ill-will to the plaintiffs, nor any desire to harm them except such as was involved in the wish and intention to discourage by such measures the plaintiffs from sending rival vessels to such ports.

In a judgement, which is a monument of legal learning and literary form, Lord Justice Bowen, supported by Lord Justice Fry and afterwards by the House of Lords, Lord Esher dissenting, held that this transaction was only the 'lawful pursuit to the bitter end of a war of competition waged by the defendants in the interest of their own trade,' and that, although a damage to the plaintiffs, intentional in the sense of being necessarily consequential on the defendants' action, had been proved, the defendants had just cause or excuse for inflicting such damage in the instinct of self-advancement and self-protection which is the incentive of all trade. 'To say that a man is to trade freely but that he is to stop short at any act which is calculated to harm other tradesmen and which is designed to attract business to himself, would be a strange and impossible counsel of perfection.' The fundamental ground for this decision is that it is good for the community that competition should be unfettered and that the exercise of a trader's right to trade freely necessarily implies the right intentionally to injure other traders. To ruin a man's trade because you want to ruin him is unlawful, but to do so because you want it for yourself is in obedience to a natural and legitimate instinct.

Since the decision in the Mogul case was given, the action of certain trade unions combining to ruin a person who refused to fall into a scheme for imposing generally, throughout a trade, trade-union regulations, has been discussed in the Court of Appeal. In the case of Temperton *v.* Russell and others (1893), 'the defendants were members of a joint committee of three trade unions connected with the building trade in Hull. A firm of builders there having refused to obey certain rules laid down by the unions with regard to building operations, the unions sought to compel them to do so, by preventing the supply of building materials to them. In pursuance of this object, they requested the plaintiff, a master mason and builder in Hull, who supplied building materials to the firm, to cease to supply them with such materials, but the plaintiff refused to do so. Thereupon, with the object of injuring the plaintiff in his business, in order to compel him to comply with their request, the defendants induced persons who, to the knowledge of the defendants, had entered into contracts with the plaintiff for the supply of materials, to break their contracts, and not to enter into further contracts with the plaintiff, by threatening that workmen would be withdrawn from their employ. The plaintiff sustained damage in consequence of such breaches of contract and of the refusal of such persons to enter into contracts with him:—*Held*, That an action was maintainable by the plaintiff against the defendants for maliciously procuring such breaches of contract, and also for maliciously conspiring together to injure him by preventing persons from entering into contracts with him.'

So far as this decision relates to the maliciously procuring persons to break contracts actually entered into, it merely declares well-settled law and is altogether beyond criticism. On the other hand, so far as it relates to a conspiracy to induce persons not to enter into contracts with others in the future, the decision has no precedent, and appears to be at least questionable. For, if it be sound, it would appear that in all cases the most effective weapon, and in most cases the only weapon, of a trade union, one which has been used for many years—viz., the power to refuse the service of their members to employers, except upon stated terms—would be struck from their hands.

In the Mogul case, for the purpose of establishing a monopoly, the conference of shipowners undoubtedly used means which involved the intentional and injurious coercion of a dissentient fellow-trader. In Temperton v. Russell, for the purpose 'of improving the condition of labour' and in furtherance of a labour dispute, the trade unionists undoubtedly took certain active measures highly oppressive to the person against whom they were directed.

It would be presumptuous to suggest that there are not weighty reasons to be given in support of a judgement of the Court of Appeal, but it is obvious that these two decisions do not make the state of the law clear.

On one side, it will be argued that the cases are distinguishable; that in the Mogul case the defendants only did what any trader is entitled to do, viz., offer exceptional terms for continuous and exclusive custom, and use the power of combination, peacefully and without personal ill-will, to drive all competitors from the field. In the second case, the defendants, it might be argued, went beyond the legitimate furtherance of a trade dispute when they brought injurious pressure to bear on the affairs of one who was no party to that dispute.

On the other side it will be maintained that the two cases ought to be governed by the same rule. The trade unionist will naturally insist that the object in both cases, viz., the improvement of their own market, was identical, and that the steps taken to secure this legitimate end were in both cases the same. If coercion by combination is legitimate in one case it ought to be legitimate in the other. A combination to prevent persons entering into future contracts was held legal in one case and it ought to be held legal in the other. Why is the capitalist's combination merely an incident in a war of competition, waged in the interest of their own trade, and the trade-union combination a malicious and illegal conspiracy?

It is impossible to deny the force of this reasoning, but it would require another paper to discuss the possible developments of legal decisions or statute law whereby the uncertainty of the situation can be removed.

If these two cases are distinguishable, the exact ground of distinction will, no doubt, be made clearer in future decisions of the Courts; if, on the other hand (and to this opinion I am disposed to incline) they are not distinguishable, there can be no doubt that the balance will be righted by the strict and unquestioned impartiality of the judicial bench.

The object of this paper has been to consider the law affecting trade combinations as determined by recent decisions, and we are now in a position to sum up the result of our inquiry.

So far as the law of crimes is concerned, we have seen that Parliament, assisted by the judges, has laboured in the main since 1875 to secure absolute equality of conditions to combatants in the war between labour and capital. The opinion has been hazarded that, so long as every form of physical force is avoided, trade disputants in combination have no interference to fear and trade dissentients no protection to expect from the law of conspiracy; but that if, on the other hand, coercion is used, which, without the excuse of a war between labour and capital, would be otherwise unlawful, the power of the law may successfully be called in.

So far as the civil law is concerned it has been submitted that the principle of acknowledging every man's right to trade freely has been applied by the Courts in a sense which has accorded to combined capitalists a privilege not granted to the trade union.

Further, it has been suggested that, while more use might have been made of the criminal law for the protection of dissentients against trade unions which may act oppressively, on the other hand the power of the civil law has been unduly strained against labour combinations.

Whatever may be the justice of these conclusions, the

discussion has revealed the great complexity of the subject. The law is being called on to deal with a new and very difficult set of circumstances. The power of combinations, such as we have been considering, is always very great and sometimes very oppressive. It is not too much to say that individuals are at times made subject not only to the law of the Queen, but also to the law of the Combination. The possibility of oppression and the difficulty of dealing with it are equally obvious, and it seems a dismal view of the future to say that the law can do no more than keep the ring on equal terms for the combatants in these disastrous and often ferocious contests. But we are here considering only the legal aspects of the question; whether in the future it may be thought desirable to legislate for the protection of private citizens against the tyranny of combinations, the future only can decide.

In conclusion, some hope may be gleaned from the advance of conciliatory principles. In the controversies of nations, for instance, although the law of force is still predominant, the greatest and most civilized races are beginning, timidly and fitfully, it is true, to look to arbitration. In industrial disputes, such as those which have been considered, the element of race animosity is absent, and the interests of the opponents are often not really conflicting. Is it Utopian to hope that the great waste and suffering of war between Labour and Capital may gradually give place to more civilized and more rational methods?

ALFRED LYTTELTON.

LargePrintLiberty.com

Dedicated to offering books on libertarian thought and economics in Large Print paperback.

Titles include:

For a New Liberty, by Murray N. Rothbard (Philosophy)
"A classic that for over two decades has been hailed as the best general work on libertarianism available. Rothbard begins with a quick overview of its historical roots, and then goes on to define libertarianism as resting 'upon one single axiom: that no man or group of men shall aggress upon the person or property of anyone else.' He writes a withering critique of the chief violator of liberty: the State. Rothbard then provides penetrating libertarian solutions for many of today's most pressing problems, including poverty, war, threats to civil liberties, the education crisis, and more."

Principles of Economics, by Carl Menger (Economics)
"In the beginning, there was Menger. It was this book that reformulated, and really rescued, economic science. It kicked off the Marginalist Revolution, which corrected theoretical errors of the old classical school. These errors concerned value theory, and they had sown enough confusion to make the dangerous ideology of Marxism seem more plausible than it really was. Menger set out to elucidate the precise nature of economic value, and root economics firmly in the real-world actions of individual human beings."

Great Wars and Great Leaders, by Ralph Raico (History)
"In the backdrop of this blistering and deeply insightful and scholarly history is the whitewashing of 'great leaders' like Woodrow Wilson, Winston Churchill, FDR, Truman, Stalin, Trotsky, and other collectivists. They are highly regarded because they were on the 'right side' of the rise of the state. But do they deserve adulation? Raico says no: these great leaders were main agents in the decline of civilization in the 20th century, all of them anti-liberals who used their power to celebrate and enhance state power."